MISSIONARIES, INDIGENOUS PEOPLES AND CULTURAL EXCHANGE

FIRST NATIONS and the colonial encounter

Series Editor: David Cahill, Professorial Fellow, School of History, University of New South Wales

Series titles in order of publication

Missionaries, Indigenous Peoples and Cultural Exchange
Edited by Patricia Grimshaw and Andrew May

The Conquest All Over Again: Nahuas and Zapotecs Thinking, Writing, and Painting Spanish Colonialism
Edited by Susan Schroeder

First World, First Nations: Internal Colonialism and Indigenous Self-Determination in Northern Europe and Australia
Edited by Günter Minnerup and Pia Solberg

Colonialism on the Prairies: Blackfoot Settlement and Cultural Transformation, 1870–1920
Blanca Tovías

Aboriginal Dreaming Paths and Trading Ways: The Colonisation of the Australian Economic Landscape
Dale Kerwin

MISSIONARIES, INDIGENOUS PEOPLES AND CULTURAL EXCHANGE

EDITED BY

PATRICIA GRIMSHAW AND ANDREW MAY

sussex
ACADEMIC
PRESS
Brighton • Portland • Toronto

2 4 6 8 10 9 7 5 3 1

First published 2010 in Great Britain by
SUSSEX ACADEMIC PRESS
PO Box 139
Eastbourne BN24 9BP

and in the United States of America by
SUSSEX ACADEMIC PRESS
920 NE 58th Ave   Suite 300
Portland, Oregon 97213-3786

British Library Cataloguing in Publication Data
A CIP catalogue record for this book is available from the British Library.

Library of Congress Cataloging-in-Publication Data
Missionaries, indigenous peoples, and cultural exchange / edited by Patricia
    Grimshaw and Andrew May.
    p. cm.
    Includes bibliographical references and index.
    ISBN 978-1-84519-308-9 (hc : alk. paper)
    1. Missions—Great Britain—Colonies—History. 2. Christianity and culture—
Great Britain—Colonies—History. 3. Great Britain—Colonies—Religion.
I. Grimshaw, Patricia. II. May, Andrew.
    BV2895.M57 2010
    266′.023410171241—dc22

                                                            2009017507

Mixed Sources
Product group from well-managed
forests and other controlled sources
www.fsc.org Cert no. SGS-COC-2482
© 1996 Forest Stewardship Council
FSC

Typeset and designed by SAP, Brighton & Eastbourne.
Printed by TJ International, Padstow, Cornwall.
This book is printed on acid-free paper.

Contents

Contents

Acknowledgements

We acknowledge Australian Research Council assistance with this book through funding support to the editors for the project "Faith, Gender and Cultural Exchange: Australian Missions in Comparative Perspective, 1800 to 1930". We are grateful to Professor David Cahill, General Editor for this series, for first proposing an edition on missions, to Fiona Davis for work on the index, and to Fiona, Claire McLisky and Joanna Cruickshank (collaborators in the ARC project) for their assistance in the book's conceptual planning and editing. We thank also participants in three workshops that problematized the relationship between missionaries, colonialism and indigenous culture and agency, at the Comité International des Sciences Historiques (CISH) conference in Sydney in 2005, and two meetings at the University of Melbourne focused on missions and colonialism, a conference in September 2007 and a panel at the Australian Historical Association Conference in July 2008.

PATRICIA GRIMSHAW AND ANDREW MAY

Series Editor's Preface

Recent decades have witnessed a rise in self-awareness and self-assertiveness of First Nations peoples across the globe. This has brought indigenous histories, cultures, identities and politics into the mainstream of public and intellectual life, often in controversial manner. First Nations peoples across the world are beginning to receive the attention their welfare, cultures, and histories merit. For many of these peoples, this has come after five centuries of contact with European powers and nation states. First Nations have varied histories that are partly the result of their autochthonous cultures, their particular colonial experiences, and increasing integration into the world economy. Notwithstanding this wide variation, however, many of the generic colonial processes they have undergone are similar in character: aspects such as land rights, labour systems, miscegenation, evangelization, and the undermining of traditional laws by introduced legal systems. Similarly, First Nations have been transformed by profit-based economic systems with different values, by new gender and social roles, and new forms of education to wean indigenous children away from traditional values. In effect, new lifeways, a loss of autonomy, new judicial and fiscal systems, and bewildering multiple levels of government, have all posed immense obstacles to the social reproduction of indigenous communities and nations across the world.

First Nations peoples underwent conquest that involved both violence and negotiation. Their responses were many and varied. First, there was resistance, most manifest in all types of rebellion as well as passive resistance. Second, there were processes of accommodation by which they sought to realign traditional beliefs, values, and authority systems with those imposed upon them, forcefully or persuasively, by the colonial powers. Third, there was also considerable opportunism and initiative, by which indigenous communities turned colonialism back on itself by appropriating colonial institutions and legal processes so as to optimize their own colonial condition. Fourth, there were positive outcomes stemming from the initiative of First Nations, notably in the development of native literatures in which chirographic representations were often replaced by, or supplemented with writing systems; in the same way native artistic expressions were often reinterpreted through an indigenous lens. That conquest and colonialism brought many deleterious consequences in its train is evident, but the 'fatal impact' approach to the impact of colonialism upon colonised peoples has always been far too simplistic, skimming over, as it does, the many positive and creative adaptations of indigenous peoples to new and daunting challenges.

Most regions of the world were inhabited by indigenous peoples at the beginning of European conquest and colonization, from the late fifteenth century onwards. The Americas, both north and south, included urban civilizations as well as nomadic peoples, and even today indigenous peoples are not always fully incorporated into the modern world, e.g. Amazonian peoples, who nevertheless manage to make their voice heard, sometimes to great effect, as for example in the 2009 victory of Native Peoples from the tropical Peruvian eastern lowlands over governmental and private development interests. In Oceania, including Australasia, conquests were often seaborne and sometimes took longer to grip, such that even today in New Zealand and especially Australia the condition of indigenous communities is often parlous. Varied processes of conquest, colonization, and colonial control have taken place across Asia with a range of responses that often included major revitalization movements, as for example in Burma, Indonesia and the Philippines. Indigenous peoples of Africa experienced, even into the twentieth century, different types of colonial oppression. Still other, diverse experiences of colonial and nation state control have been experienced by peoples in the Central Asian republics and Mongolia, while even Europe has its own indigenous group in the Sami of Scandinavia.

Some indigenous peoples have largely disappeared either wholly, or at least as cohesive social groups, for example the Guanches of the Canary Islands, who had largely died out by the late sixteenth century. However, many descendants of supposedly native peoples who had supposedly died out vigorously oppose the very idea that their culture and identity were obliterated by colonial rule. The rise of DNA analysis as a mainstream medical diagnostic tool has sometimes given them reason to do so. Though widespread public perception that Tasmanian aborigines disappeared in the nineteenth century has been proven wrong, no serious scholar ever believed it. DNA analysis has similarly disproved the theory of the disappearance of the native peoples of California, long believed by academics and non-academics to have died out, also in the nineteenth century. Rather, it has been shown that some among them escaped a state-backed genocide, based on bounty hunting, by adopting western dress and passing themselves off as Mexicans. Now, thanks to the wonder of DNA, their story can be told (and compensation claims can be lodged). For many erstwhile colonies with large indigenous populations, the attainment of post-colonial independence — from the eighteenth century to even the present day — merely resulted in a substitution of European colonialism by internal colonialism, i.e., the continued (and sometimes worsened) exploitation of native by non-native peoples, exploitation that often had, and has, the explicit or tacit support of nation states. Colonialism didn't die away in post-colonial societies, it merely metamorphosed — same horse, different rider.

Scholars, politicians, journalists and activists of all kinds have interpreted First Nations' cultures, histories, and present-day social conditions in many different ways, sometimes notable for malice borne towards indigenous peoples. This is highly contested ground, with indigenous claim-making posing challenges to conventional interpretations of indigenous histories, especially in the treatment of the early colonial encounter itself. Indigenous groups have made demands for formal apologies by the State for the felt abuses of colonial rule, sometimes accompanied by a recasting of the indigenous past as a kind of Golden Age in which humankind lived in harmony with the natural environment. Not infrequently, this has restored an indigenous storyline to national histories from which they had been largely excluded. Simultaneously, indigenous stakeholders have pressed their case for compensation for their colonial suffering, sometimes viewed as an unbroken continuum to the present. This recompense has been sought in the form of financial payments to groups and individuals, as social and educational programs designed especially for indigenous claimants, and — most controversially — the return of lands alienated during the twin processes of conquest and colonization. Indigenous land claims have provoked sometimes fierce resistance among stakeholders, especially from those present-day, non-native owners of lands alleged to be "tribal" homelands, many of whom dispute indigenous titles or entitlements. Beyond the question of land tenure and right of access to ancestral hunting and even spiritual territories, opponents of such historical rights exhibit a wider resistance, explicitly denying that colonialism was deleterious for indigenous peoples, and alleging that perceived post-colonial conditions among indigenous peoples were and are due to their own inability to take advantage of the civilising possibilities ushered in by colonial rule and later post-colonial, sovereign governments. Put another way, their problems are entirely their own fault.

This denialism is the bane of productive debate. It embraces a wide range of opinions, ranging from journalistic contrariness to, in its worst manifestations, a crude racism, but is not necessarily unsophisticated for all that. Of more moment are contested questions of national, collective and even individual identity. Such debates and conflicts also represent a battle over History, of who should control normative versions of national history, national memory, and essentialised national myths. For example, in Australia, those who deny indigenous sufferings accuse their opponents of creating a "black armband" version of history. The latter respond that their critics, and especially denialists of whatever ilk, seek to "whitewash" national history, editing out shameful episodes of deleterious white policies and actions from national history and nationalistic myth. Whether explicitly or implicitly, each camp accuses the other of falsification of the national history. This standoff is reminiscent of an earlier debate over Spanish conquest and colonization in the Americas, in which partisans of the "Black Legend" were pitched against those of a "White Legend". This historiographical debate, which commenced in the sixteenth century, only petered out in the 1960s. It was resolved after a fashion, but only after a plethora of monographic, empirical studies settled many of the issues involved, such that proponents of both "Legends" were forced to resile from their more extreme assertions. Quite clearly, resolution of heated debates over First Nations histories will depend, in the final analysis, on the harvesting of a significant weight of empirical studies as well as public debates entered into in good faith. A further avenue of progress through these questions lies in a comparative, cross-cultural treatment of the histories of First Nations peoples: debates over indigenous claim-making are usually restricted to national writings, such that an awareness of the historiography on indigenous peoples in other "culture areas" is usually absent from each national debate. The context for understanding First Nations everywhere is not just local and national, but international and global.

However, there is an abundant and rich empirical historiography, ethnologically informed, on indigenous peoples, above all those of Canada, the USA, and Latin America. In the Asia-Pacific region, there are many New Zealand studies of Maori-

Pakeha colonial relations that are variable in quality, but among which are superb analyses of warfare, religion and land tenure. There are also numerous studies of the colonial encounter elsewhere in Polynesia and Melanesia. The historiography on indigenous Australians is even more variable in quality, ranging from ill-informed journalism, through poorly researched essays, to a small cluster of first-rate empirical studies. In order to respond to the lack of comparative studies, there is an urgent need for a general series that would compare the indigenous histories across national boundaries. It is envisaged that each volume in this Sussex Academic Press series will be informed by rich first order research on First Nations peoples. The series will focus especially on native peoples of Canada and the USA, Mesoamerica and the Andes, Oceania and Asia.

The mission was the classic institution of the frontier encounter between indigenous peoples and self-proclaimed 'civilizers'. The present volume by Patricia Grimshaw and Andrew May takes a fresh look at the mission and the interaction between missionaries and the indigenous peoples of Africa, Canada, India, New Zealand, Australia as well as Oceania. It eschews both an institutional approach and an older triumphalist account of missionary evangelisation, aiming rather at the deconstruction of missions, mission activities and outcomes in the British Empire of the nineteenth and early twentieth centuries. It represents newer trends in religious history that focus on how the mission functioned, and missionaries acted, "on the ground", emphasizing acts and outcomes as well as discourse, rather than missionaries' and governments' expressed good intentions. There was often a wide gulf that separated intent and outcomes, and, as the several essays attest, such differences were parsed further by regional and cultural diversity. These original essays provide yet another reminder that the frontier encounter was characterized above all by diversity, of peoples, relationships, cultures, and outcomes.

DAVID CAHILL
University of New South Wales

CHAPTER ONE

Reappraisals of Mission History
An Introduction

PATRICIA GRIMSHAW AND ANDREW MAY

Religious history, once the province of the faithful, has now diversified, as people from various backgrounds have pursued the subject in a range of scholarly ways. In recent decades, Christian missionaries in particular have attracted the attention of numbers of historians who have subjected their varying experiences to serious scholarly reappraisal. Missions and missionaries naturally figure centrally in the history of the spread of Christianity and of the new indigenous-led churches that emerged across the world. They also serve as entry points for understanding the histories of the many peoples, societies and cultures caught up in imperial outreach from the eighteenth century and the histories of the new nations that emerged at the collapse of empires; and for the understanding of settler colonialism where Europeans captured an ongoing political dominance. Mission activities entailed close encounters of peoples from a wide variety of ethnic and racial backgrounds, well ahead of the globalisation and multiculturalism of the later twentieth century. At the interface between cultures and religions, missionaries from the Christian west spearheaded the proliferation of the practices of modernity: capitalist economic systems, social institutions, ideas of gender, class and progress. While missionaries' very particular perspectives on the human condition skewed their accounts of mission affairs, their voluminous writings nevertheless made available knowledge of the workings of empire, the actions of settlers, and details about the many peoples they encountered, making them crucial for recording indigenous pasts.[1]

The central aim of *Missionaries, Indigenous Peoples and Cultural Exchanges* is the deconstruction of missions, mission activities and outcomes in the British Empire in the nineteenth century and the first decades of the twentieth. It does this through a number of focused studies, located in a range of sites of Christian missions supported by various denominations, in which the writers respond to fresh appraisals of the field of mission history. Missionaries, the authors suggest, were ordinary people, struggling to bring the Good News to strangers, while they sustained a fragile presence as exiles on foreign grounds, subject to continually changing political and cultural pressures. For the most part armed with only a smattering of theological training, little of it practical or linguistic, male and female missionaries from Britain, Continental Europe and the

I

United States of America confronted situations for which they had not the remotest preparation, as they stumbled through exhausting, health-threatening, occasionally uplifting but as often demoralizing cultural exchanges. None of this should detract, however, from the necessary task of historians to engage with the very real impact of missionaries' unusual life choices on the people who were the subjects of their evangelistic drive.[2]

The emphases that have emerged in the new scholarship on missions are varied. Postcolonial scholars have been central to proposing meta-narratives of western oppression in the imperial and colonial projects, a powerful perspective that has demanded a response from academic historians. Assessed globally there can surely be no question that missionaries in the nineteenth- and early twentieth-century British Empire, our focus in this volume, clearly sailed for foreign fields in the wake of the exploratory work of precursors of Britain's subsequent exercise of power. Explorers, adventurers, sealers and whalers, and traders, as well as British colonial officials of varying stature, identified peoples outside of Christian influence and brokered the contacts with them that paved the way for missionary ventures. For the British mission-minded, imperial rule was justified because missionaries would save millions of souls from an eternity in the flames of hell. The House of Commons' Select Committee on native peoples in the Empire in 1837 expressed the wish that missionaries would point non-Christian peoples to a superior life of honest toil and thrift, monogamy and familial love, and spiritual comforts.[3]

Further, scholars alert to the interpretative value of whiteness studies have more recently pointed to the missionaries' unassuming acceptance of their right to exert power over others. For a large period in many sites of empire, pale skin appeared the marker of a normative authority, of unreflective convictions of righteousness.[4] Only later in the twentieth century would missionaries become more tolerant of others' cultural practices and less authoritarian in their own. Missionaries of whatever nationality in the British Empire seldom, unambiguously or persistently, opposed imperialism per se, or at any fundamental level the resulting appropriation of the lands, labour or resources of non-western peoples. Mission stations, especially in their early years, most often relied on the protection afforded by their citizenship and the defence capability of the British army, no matter the distance from the location of regiments. Despite their many misgivings, in settler colonies most missionaries found themselves in collusion with white agendas about the control of indigenous people. This arose in their dependence on a degree of government financial support, including the land for missions, and material help with educational and mechanical training activities; missionaries might also comply because on some issues they might more or less agree that white governments' policies were for the good of local peoples.[5]

Such narratives contain within themselves, however, the potential to over-determine the findings of historical research. While they have persuasive impact at a globalizing level, postcolonial frameworks can serve to obscure the varieties of interactions that surrounded missionary ventures. Missionaries differed in some fundamental ways from other colonizers; they cannot be treated as a uniform category, and colonized peoples' reception of missionaries' messages varied even more. A close attention to encounters of missionaries and the peoples they influenced render meaningful the differing outcomes of missions in multiple sites of the British Empire, including the trajectories of new Christian churches within the period of decolonization after World War Two.[6] The writers of this volume observe with insight the layered meanings of interactions within and around missions, and within imperial or colonial power structures. They probe the complexities of missionaries' relationships with British colonial officials and settler colonial regimes, recording how missionaries complicated lines of power and authority. The authors are similar, also, in their attention to the agency of indigenous Christians in the spread of the faith, to the task of indigenous Christian leaders in interpreting spirituality afresh to their people, and to the rights-based aspirations that the Christian faith could inspire in the mission-educated.

In this collection we do not deny that we are talking about individual missions at particular times and in specific places — most of our contributions are built up from core missionary archives. But we reinforce the view that these histories are neither peripheral, nor stereotypical; indeed they are dynamic and spectacularly unpredictable, serving to break down the notion of "mission" as a unitary category. Even if missionaries start with a core belief in proselytisation and cultural reshaping, unexpected happenings emerge across different mission fields; the outcomes of missionary activities are not predetermined. Such analysis of missions has wide ranging implications for core historical narratives of modern world history, whether those of globalization, multi-faceted racial interactions, modernity, science and technology and the identity formation and political mobilization of local peoples. Each chapter signals how missions impacted on national stories.

The collection has coalesced around certain key themes. First is the explanatory power of intimate relations and gender, what we can learn from them and how these relationships worked out in the mission community. As an historian recently wrote, the concept of the "Christian Home", however malleable, was viewed both as "a means and goal of Anglo-American missions".[7] Day-to-day interactions between missionaries and indigenous peoples, and among other groups of people — settlers, traders, migrants of colour — who interacted with the mission, emerge here imbued with multiple meanings.[8] Second is the role of indigenous Christians in the spread of the faith and the creation of religious communities, a fact that, among others, historians of previously missionized countries have brought strongly to the fore. That they seldom left written records is just one reason for their relative absence in earlier mission histories.[9] Third is the social and geographic context for missions: the nature and power of the political structures in which they were situated, their interactions with other Europeans in the vicinity, and their response to the broader geographical and climatic environment.[10] The core of missionaries' values could be undermined, even shattered, because their own material, spiritual, cultural and political positions might be rendered so contingent.

The first four chapters that follow are primarily concerned with advancing the explanatory power of intimate relations, domestic tragedies and the broader sociology of life on mission stations. In "Mother's Milk: Gender, Power and Anxiety on a South African Mission Station, 1839–1840", Elizabeth Elbourne undermines any generalized notions of the stark authority and brute confidence of the missionary in the field. She cautions against extrapolating the quotidian as the broader history of Christianity in the region. Opening the volume with a case study of the death of a newborn child of white missionaries on a South African mission station in 1839, she enables a much more complex and fruitful reading of what she depicts as the contingent social relationships of people, who, in living in close and constant contact, could not help but change one another. Here the authority, and ultimate success or failure of missionaries, were much more precarious than is often depicted, depending as they did on the fragile interpersonal ties between missionary and would-be missionized, and on inconsistent and unpredictable readings of appropriate class and gender roles. Missionaries performed complex negotiations with native power brokers in order to curry favour, glean resources, establish reputations and wield authority. They also trod warily through unsteady physical and social landscapes. Their lives were mediated through unanticipated meanings attributed to their actions; gossip and scandal, Elbourne tells us, could have telling repercussions on their physical and moral wellbeing. In this topsy-turvy world, missionaries themselves may not have been all-powerful instruments of cultural change, but the institutional roles they assumed, legitimated or which were undermined by native support or opposition, could be extraordinarily transformative for missionaries and indigenous peoples alike.

The moral certainty with which many missionaries viewed the degradation of non-Christian families did not of itself mean that they were unable to learn anything from them, or were not changed by them. Intimate relations in the mission field were worked out in a variety of ways, sometimes unpredictably. Missionary views of indigenous sexual morality and proscriptions about indigenous sexual practice, as well as sexual impropriety by or amongst missionaries themselves, have begun to be analyzed by historians less as a one-way exercise of conquest and control, and more as a complex collision and contestation over competing codes of propriety in which neither one side nor the other inevitably prevailed. This complex reality of intimate negotiation and reformation is observed in Angela Wanhalla's chapter, "'The Natives Uncivilize Me': Missionaries and Interracial Intimacy in Early New Zealand" on intimate relations between missionaries and Maori in New Zealand. Wanhalla observes intimacy from the viewpoint of missionary attitudes to the institution of marriage itself, whereby contemporary discussions about marriage can be read as significant indicators as to the propriety of particular sexual or racial behaviours. While this chapter establishes the nexus between the experience of affection and intimacy and the success or failure of a mission, public scandals surrounding missionary misconduct and interracial sexual relationships are further linked to the reputation of the colony itself, not just to the standing or circumstances of individual missionaries. Temptation and transgression are ultimately regarded as the rule, rather than the exception, of missionary experience.

Household arrangements, and gender relations on mission stations more generally, are key sites of cultural conflict. Elizabeth Prevost in "Contested Conversions: Missionary Women's Religious Encounters in Early Colonial Uganda" continues the important preoccupation of mission history with the relationship between women and the exercise of colonial power in her chapter on East Africa in the late nineteenth century, at a time when women were entering what had previously been a patriarchal mission field in increasing numbers. This process is well exemplified in her study of female Church Missionary Society missionaries in colonial Uganda. Her analysis illuminates this transition under the spotlight of interchange between missionaries and indigenous people, with surprising conclusions about the ways in which female missionaries were able to blur taken-for-granted male and female roles when it came to traditional missionary activities of conversion and institutional support. She further observes this mission field as a "point of collusion" between female missionaries and indigenous women. Missionary women were highly dependent on African women, and as elsewhere in the volume, the processes of missionization and colonization are seen to be highly political, embedded in particular local exigencies of power and patronage. These women's exercise of Christianization informed unanticipated political outcomes in which their message was sometimes taken up in quite unexpected ways.

Prevost points to the ways in which the religious and cultural character of the missionaries themselves was transformed as a direct consequence of the feminization of mission work. Myra Rutherdale in "'It is No Soft Job to be Performed': Missionaries and Imperial Manhood in Canada, 1880–1920" counsels the mission historian that gender and race need to be analyzed in concert if the mission movement is to be properly understood. The concept of the Christian home was, as much as anything, a patriarchal one, and Rutherdale's chapter on missionaries and imperial manhood in Canada explores the ways in which missionary manhood was constructed on the home front as well as in the field. Like Prevost, Rutherdale is concerned with reading the ways in which gendered understandings were reshaped through interactions on the ground. These chapters confirm that key new insights are being derived from a focus on the roles of indigenous men and women, as both subjects and as agents of the mission process.

Any understanding of the relationship between missionaries and indigenous peoples is complicated by the difference between the daily lives and activities of individual missionaries as recorded at the time, and the ways in which later reportage put particular readings on these activities. In this respect, Peggy Brock's chapter on one indigenous Christian's views of missionaries in Canada is an important corrective to the predominantly missionary perspectives on their interactions with indigenous peoples. In "An Indigenous View of Missionaries: Arthur Wellington Clah and Missionaries on the North-west Coast of Canada", Brock is concerned with Clah's insights into missionary worlds, including their personal weakness and inadequacies. In his journal — remarkable for the rarity of such preserved texts — Clah recorded the ways missionaries struggled to live up to competing demands, as they attempted to mediate between First Nations peoples and various colonial authorities. Here, the missionary was seen as a person to cultivate, whose potential as an ally could serve local interests. One of Brock's key insights is to assert the ambivalent ground between missionary versions of their roles and relationships with local communities, and the ways in which indigenous converts refashioned and subverted these expectations.

The writers of the following three chapters advance their interest in language and translation as a medium of Christian evangelism and cultural interchange, when indigenous Christians served as cultural informants. Andrew May in "The Promise of a Book: Missionaries and Native Evangelists in North-east India" places the work of the Welsh mission in north-east India from the 1840s in a longer lineage of native Christian evangelism with its roots decades earlier in William Carey's Serampore mission. May asserts the strategic importance of missionaries operating within local political hierarchies and intellectual circles, both indigenous and European. Engagements with indigenous language, literacy, orthography and oral culture were the building blocks of missionary practice. The Welsh missionary Thomas Jones, like many missionaries, played both a religious and secular role in translating the Bible into the local indigenous language. Such a task may have facilitated evangelical success, but it also provided a means for indigenous cultural expression, in which indigenous informants could surprise the newcomers with their linguistic and cultural sophistication.

Following on from May, Jane Samson in "Translation Teams: Missionaries, Islanders, and the Reduction of Language in the Pacific" and Helen Gardner in "Practising Christianity, Writing Anthropology: Missionary Anthropologists and their Informants", extend the analysis of linguistic colonialism as not simply a one-way process of colonial hegemony, with indigenous people as passive receptors. It was, rather, a literacy process in which indigenous peoples played active, and sometimes subversive, roles. The complex dynamics and legacies of language "retrieval", "reduction" or "rendering" can be explored therefore less as racism or mimicry, and more as negotiated and collaborative exercises. As in other contributions to this volume, missionaries are seen to be decidedly dependent on the patronage of high-ranking native chiefs. The theological anthropologies of missionaries were also shifted in seismic ways; enmeshed in the cultures they sought to change, they were sometimes able to challenge entrenched Eurocentric views of indigenous inferiority. Gardner highlights this uneasy position occupied by missionaries as they attempted to retain objective distance while at times becoming ineluctably implicated in local power relations. Converted indigenous informants, too, provided missionary anthropologists with intelligence filtered and complicated by their liminal intermediary position between cultures. Without denying some of the fundamental inequities and lamentable consequences of the missionary project, Samson demands that any reading of the relationship between missionaries and indigenous peoples must restore both native agency and missionary insight.

The final four chapters examine several sites of missions in ways that reveal how differing political regimes shaped the policies that missionaries could sustain, while continuing the exploration of indigenous peoples' agency and the intimate and domestic arena of intercultural exchanges of the previous chapters. The first example is from southern Africa; the other chapters in part, or whole, single out Australia for especial focus. In "Missionaries, Africans and the State in the Development of Education in Colonial Natal, 1836–1910", Norman Etherington focuses on the means by which the indigenous converts to Christianity, such as the men who figured in the chapters of Brock, May, Gardner and Samson, acquired the education that enabled them to become effective evangelists, translators and informants for western projects. His concentration across nearly seventy-five years on the educational efforts of Protestant missionaries in the British colony of Natal offered him the opportunity to examine the dense and complex set of circumstances that served as a context for the missions. The missionaries in Natal were drawn from a number of faith traditions and originated from a considerable number of European countries and the United States. Etherington teases out their aspirations for their proteges, ranging from basic learning to an ambitious liberal curriculum. But he also shows how, whatever the missions' intentions, the external power structures under which they operated shaped the outcomes of their work. In the early phase the African peoples had their own wishes for the training of their children that missionaries could not ignore if they wanted children in their class-rooms. Missionaries who favoured a rounded education discovered that as British colonial officials spread their authority, it was industrial and domestic training that was prized if the missions needed state support. As settlers assumed increasing polit-ical influence any benign attitudes to African education diminished: they wanted very little education for Africans at all and were not prepared to subsidize it. Settlers did not want Africans as rivals of whites in skilled employment, but, rather, as labourers and domestic servants. Missionaries who persevered with the education of Africans did so without the material backing of governments.

Etherington thus alerts us to the fact that crucial cultural exchanges took place not only between missionaries and African peoples, but also between colonial governments of differing biases and settlers with varying stakes in Africans' education. These pres-sures provided constantly evolving boundaries to mission agendas and could indeed extinguish them. His findings resonate with those of Felicity Jensz in "Colonial Agents: German Moravian Missionaries in the English-Speaking World". She works from a different perspective, through a case study of the global outreach of the small but renowned United Brotherhood, or Moravians, based in Herrnhut in Germany. The Moravians' mission activity started in the early eighteenth century with a firm commit-ment to keeping their spiritual goals separate from political engagements. Their enterprises expanded with the wave of British imperialism in the nineteenth century including several sites in North America, southern Africa and Australia. In each case Jensz shows that although the missionaries wanted nothing more than conversions of souls and shared a training that upheld certain common practices, missionaries in the field were obliged to concede ground to local political authorities or face the abandon-ment of their cause.

Jensz ends her coverage of Moravian missions with the example of the relations of Moravians and the colonial government in the south-east Australian colony of Victoria. The last two chapters continue the exploration of the politics of missions in Australia, a site where missions had a distinctive historical trajectory. In its origins Australia was an exception among the settler colonies because of its birth as a penal colony, the denial of land rights to the indigenous people and as new colonies formed, their early acqui-sition of elected settler governments. Surveillance from the Colonial Office on the treatment of indigenous people faded rapidly as settler regimes supported ruthless land appropriation at the expense of the local owners. The great British missionary bodies left the task of spreading the Gospel to the white colonial churches but, in fact, local volunteers were few, and many missions became the work of Continental Protestant or Catholic religious bodies. Missions, except for a very few small ventures in the first decades, became virtual arms of the colonial states in their drive to marginalize Aborigines.

First, Joanna Cruickshank and Patricia Grimshaw in "'A Matter of No Small Importance to the Colony': Moravian Missionaries on Cape York Peninsula, Queensland, 1891–1919" offer another illustration of Moravian dilemmas about spiritual and temporal affairs. The northern Queensland mission venture that they examine grew out of the earlier Moravian initiative, which Jensz describes. In the north, however, the Moravians faced novel challenges. Frontier violence there was recent and extreme; the traders who plied the coast and pastoralists who wanted cheap labour cared little for indigenous people's needs or rights, and settler governments had mixed commitment to missions. Missions extended the provision of protection and basic material needs and might be said to have relieved politicians' consciences about the dispossession and killings, rather than to represent a commitment to providing a good education or healthy environment. In time, as legislative controls on Aborigines tightened, the missions became a convenient location for mixed descent children summarily taken away from their Aboriginal mothers; politicians considered such children, usually with absent white fathers, deserved a European upbringing that might allow them to merge into the settler population. Amidst these tensions the Moravians, nevertheless, sought to educate and convert Aborigines, and to find ways that Aboriginal Christians could form self-sustaining families and communities. The missionary caring came with harsh edges, and their withdrawal from the field was accompanied by disappointment.

The Moravians on Cape York had separated the children from parents by placing them in dormitories, the better to persuade their young charges to adopt western religion and culture. The second Australian study is the only chapter to examine similar Catholic segregation practices that were common in circumstances where missionaries gained undue authority. Its impact is the key issue that Christine Choo and Brian F. McCoy discuss in their chapter on Catholic missions: "Mission Dormitories: Intergenerational Implications for Kalumburu and Balgo, Kimberley, Western Australia". Their analysis reverberates with the widespread practice in Australia of the removal of mixed descent children from their families to missions, orphanages, training institutions and foster families. Aboriginal children were often taken a great distance from their lands, and frequently grew up in ignorance of their origins, or even that they were Aboriginal. All this was to facilitate, as administrators thought best, their assimilation into white Australia.

This heartless and cruel child removal policy was the subject of a national apology from the newly-elected Australian Labor Party Prime Minister, Kevin Rudd, on 13 February 2008. As Choo and McCoy indicate here, however, many more children were kept from their families through the system of dormitories, which damaged many people by alienating them from their heritage. The spiritual, cultural and educational exchanges of western missionaries in Western Australia, as more generally within the politicized sites of British imperial expansion, shaped the life chances of many peoples and many emerging nation states. The case studies of *Missionaries, Indigenous Peoples and*

Cultural Exchanges contribute in diverse ways to the unravelling of these remarkable histories.

Notes

1 For recent important studies of mission history see Brock, ed., *Indigenous Peoples and Religious Change*; Etherington, ed., *Missions and Empire*; Porter, *Religion Versus Empire?*; Comaroff and Comoroff, *Of Revelation and Revolution;* Stanley, *The Bible and the Flag;* Stanley, ed., *Christian Missions and the Enlightenment*; Thorne, *Congregational Missions*; Cox, *The British Missionary Enterprise Since 1700*; Carey, (ed.), *Empires of Religion*.
2 For a discussion see Etherington, "Missions and Empire".
3 For a discussion see: Evans et al., *Equal Subjects, Unequal Rights*, Chapter 1.
4 See Frankenberg, *White Women, Race Matters*; Frankenberg, ed., *Displacing Whiteness*; Anderson, *The Cultivation of Whiteness*.
5 See, for example, Haebich, *For Their Own Good*.
6 See Brown and Louis, eds, *The Twentieth Century*; Gifford, ed., *The Christian Churches and the Democratisation of Africa*.
7 Robert, "The Christian Home as a Cornerstone of Anglo-American Missionary Thought and Practice".
8 For discussions of gender, family and intimate relations surrounding missions see: Semple, *Missionary Women: Gender, Professionalism and the Victorian Idea of Christian Mission;* Wanhalla, *In/Visible Sight: The Mixed Descent Families of Southern New Zealand*; Rutherdale, *Women and the White Man's God;* Langmore, *Missionary Lives: Papua, 1874–1914*; Hunter, *The Gospel of Gentility*; Grimshaw, *Paths of Duty*; Grimshaw and Sherlock, "Women and Cultural Exchanges"; Grimshaw, "Faith, Missionary Life, and the Family"; Erlank, "Sexual Misconduct and Church Power on Scottish Mission Stations in Xhosaland, South Africa, in the 1840s"; Chuchiak IV, 'The Sins of the Fathers"; Brouwer, *New Women for God*; Bowie, Kirkwood, and Ardener, eds., *Women and Missions*; Robert, ed., *Gospel Bearers, Gender Barriers*. See also Cooper and Stoler, eds, *Tensions of Empire*; Stoler, ed., *Haunted By Empire*.
9 For indigenous Christians' assistance to missionization see: Munro and Thornley, ed. *The Covenant Makers;* Brock, ed., *Indigenous Peoples and Religious Change*; Singh, *Gender, Religion and the "Heathen Lands"*. See Nelson, Smith and Grimshaw, eds, *Letters from Aboriginal Women*.
10 See, for example, Elbourne, *Blood Ground*; Hall, *Civilising Subjects*; Huber and Lutkehaus, eds., *Gendered Missions*; Robert, ed., *Converting Colonialism*; Grimshaw and McGregor, eds, *Collisions of Cultures and Identities*; Barry, Cruickshank, Brown-May and Grimshaw, eds, *Evangelists of Empire?;* Swain and Rose, eds, *Aboriginal Australians and Christian Missions*; Perry, *On the Edge of Empire*; Neylan, *The Heavens Are Changing*.

CHAPTER TWO

Mother's Milk
Gender, Power and Anxiety on a South African Mission Station, 1839–1840

ELIZABETH ELBOURNE

During the last days of December 1839 a newborn child died, seemingly of hunger, on the South African mission station of Kuruman. The deaths of African children from hunger were tragically common at a time of drought and precarious harvests, and doubtless frequently went unremarked in the missionary archive. This baby was, however, the child of white missionary parents, and her death occurred on one of the flagship stations of the London Missionary Society (LMS) in southern Africa, made famous by Robert Moffat, father-in-law of the even better known explorer David Livingstone. Furthermore, the death occasioned bitter controversy. The subsequent archival traces shed unexpected light on the social world of a southern African mission station.

The dead baby did not belong to anyone well established at the station. Her mother was Lydia Philips, the young wife of an Irish missionary doctor, Robert Philips of the Church Missionary Society (CMS). The baby was a month premature, her early birth caused by a "blister" applied to the mother's side a few days previous, or so colleagues believed.[1] The baby's name is nowhere noted in the archival record, and it is even possible that she died without one. With only a couple of exceptions, the many letters and statements about her death, even those written by her parents, refer to the baby as "it". She does not seem to have ascended to more than the fleeting possibility of personality and presence. Nonetheless, her death caused a furor that helped end the brief CMS mission to South Africa. The scandal would also reveal the brittle social relations of a mission station in a precarious position, drawing back for the historian the polite veil usually draped in missionary correspondence over the nitty-gritty of mission station social life and the uneasy dance between missionaries and the would-be missionized. The death sheds light on what was expected by Africans from a male missionary who hoped to succeed in the difficult conditions of the early nineteenth-century southern African interior, and on what were seen as appropriate gender roles among both whites and Africans. Not least, writing and testimony by women show struggles over issues such as how to raise children, whether doctors or mothers knew best, and what kind of knowledge was needed to manage children. There were also occasionally unexpected alliances across lines of race, class and gender, although African perspectives are muted in the archives. Missionary messages about not only motherhood but also fatherhood and gender roles in general were, I want to suggest, surprisingly far from uniform in this period.

Place and Context

The Philips were in Kuruman in the first place because of the fledging, indeed fragile, nature of the CMS mission to southern Africa. Part of a small group of recently arrived CMS missionaries, the Philips were due to start a new station further north among seTswana speakers. The CMS had in fact only been in South Africa since 1837. Already its first major mission, to the Zulu, had collapsed in the maelstrom of regional power struggles as Zulu, Afrikaner and British competed for power in modern-day Natal. On 6 February 1838 the traumatized mission head, Francis Owen, had watched the followers of Zulu chief Dingane killing about a hundred members of Piet Retief's party from the Cape Colony, Afrikaner migrants and their Khoekhoe dependents, whose land hunger the Zulu feared.[2] All the CMS missionaries were doubtless tense and uncertain.

Kuruman was one of the few well-watered areas on the borderlands of the Kalahari, now in the Northern Cape region of South Africa, but then beyond the confines of the British Cape Colony. The station was aimed at seTswana speakers, but it sat at the crossroads of travel by diverse peoples at a turbulent, hungry time.[3] It also served as a base for white missionary enterprise in the region. The station was relatively crowded in 1839. The station head, Robert Moffat, accompanied by family members, was in England, arranging for the publication of his seTswana translation of the Bible, drumming up funds for the mission, speaking to the faithful and generally positioning himself as a missionary hero.[4] Nonetheless, there were an unusually large number of white individuals on the station. These included the aged Mr Hamilton of the LMS, who had lived with the Moffats since his wife left him in the 1820s; game hunter and trader David Hume, his wife Margaret and their children; Roger Edwards, a former carpenter turned LMS missionary, and his wife and children. Mr and Mrs Lemue of the Paris Evangelical Missionary Society and their children were not living on the station, but they paid a visit at a crucial moment, as did Wallace Hewetson, an Irish former soldier and blacksmith, now employed by the CMS, and his family, including his heavily pregnant wife, who doubtless still thought often of the death of their own much-loved young son in Cape Town in 1837.[5] Not present at the time of the baby's death, but arriving shortly thereafter, was the Reverend Francis Owen, the head of the Southern Africa CMS, travelling in the company of his wife, a botanizing sister, and a servant from Britain named Jane.[6] It is Owen's subsequent investigation, including lengthy written statements from Mr and Mrs Edwards, Dr Philips's response and Owen's summation of his questioning of other mission residents, both black and white, that provides the bulk of evidence discussed below.

The white missionaries were accompanied by a large number of African servants and assistants. It is difficult to know exactly how many, but various references in missionary papers suggest that Philips thought of four men per wagon as the minimum number required to travel safely, that builders and ploughmen were essential to setting up a station, and that missionary families employed servants, including nannies, house servants and, if need be, wet nurses. The mission also required translators and, some-times, African catechists. A translator, named in the missionary records as "Jacob", worked at Kuruman, for example, also helping certain missionaries learn seTswana. If the station was well equipped and the missionaries had food, a mission station was a major source of food and money in a time of economic difficulty. In addition to those directly employed by the missionaries, there were the Tswana, who lived in the town in the vicinity of the station and might occasionally come to religious services, and who relayed gossip and news across information networks stretching hundreds of miles. There was little privacy in the claustrophobic atmosphere of a mission station, and a large potential audience for missteps.

Milk and Care: The Politics of Nourishment

Mrs Edwards had been away from the station, but returned on 23 November to find to her surprise that Mrs Philips had delivered some ten days ago. "[T]ho the child was small, it was quite perfect and remarkably strong in voice, & likely to live". Conflict quickly arose between Mrs Edwards, an experienced mother, and the neophyte Philips over child-rearing techniques. Mrs Philips was too weak to wash and change the child, and so Mrs Edwards offered to relieve Dr Philips of a task she clearly thought of as female. On her first visit, however, she "found their way of managing a child very different to my own, or what I had ever seen, & was of course extremely awkward & jokosely [sic] said some things in reference to the clothing etc of an infant which I ought to have kept in, not suspecting the characters I had to deal with". Mrs Philips asked Mrs. Edwards "not to trouble myself any more about washing & dressing the Infant", and Mrs Edwards in consequence visited them only once a day thereafter.[7] Although we do not know exactly what the different views of Mrs Edwards and Dr Philips were, this is the first of several pieces of evidence that suggest that the interfering Mrs Edwards had strong views about childrearing, emphasizing, as we shall see, co-sleeping, sole reliance on breast feeding and frequent contact between parents and child, while the more upper-class and doubtless better-educated Dr Philips had what he probably saw as a more "professional", detached and scientific approach. He also took upon himself tasks that the mission women tended to see as women's work.

The following week, on a Wednesday morning, Mrs Edwards called on the Philips. To her surprise she "found both Mr. and Mrs. P. in the hall and heard soon the cry of the Babe in the chamber; on inquiring after it Mrs. P. told me very coolly it had been crying that way for more than two hours and nothing would pacify it". Perhaps suggesting more traditional ideas of bodily intimacy, Mrs Edwards rushed to the child and put it to sleep by giving it her own breast. In response to Mrs Edwards's comment that the child's sighs suggested it had "cried much", Mrs Philips observed "it had not cried tears". She also made what Mrs Edwards described as "rather strange" remarks about how she would manage the baby on the forthcoming journey that "startled" Mrs Edwards.

It became clear over time that the baby was not getting enough food. Mrs Philips was unable to breastfeed the baby. She said her nipples were too hard; her husband said that she was too ill. The couple had hired a Tswana wet nurse for two shillings a week. The wet nurse was not, however, Dr Philips complained, giving the baby enough milk. Mrs Edwards knew the nurse, whose husband had worked in the service of the Edwards family, and she told the Philips "this was not to be wondered at", as the nurse was "destitute of proper food, all she lived upon then, being I believed only a little milk; and that even if she got one meal during the 24 hours it was taken at night according to Bechuana custom".[8] The doctor refused to believe the woman was hungry, as she looked "strong and robust". He did, however, ask Mrs Edwards to find him a vial and a sponge so that he could feed the baby with some of Mrs Philips's milk drawn by a breast pump mixed with goat's milk and some from the nurse. Mrs Edwards went home to get them. On her return she found the baby still crying with the parents taking tea in another room. Dr Philips asked her to interpret for the wet nurse, who was accompanied by her husband and wished to speak with Philips:

> She said the Dr. had been finding fault with her that afternoon for not giving his child milk enough: that she had told him, she had no food, her corn was still green, and that to her own child she gave goat's milk, as well as the breast, and she had only one breast to suckle both the children with, the other had been so injured by an ulcer as to cause it entirely to dry up: and again she repeated she had no food and that the Dr. and his wife had told her they had no food to give her. I briefly stated to the Dr. the substance of what she had said, upon hearing which Mrs. P. came up to me and said "But we have no food, what can we do?" (tho' she had just risen from a table on which there was a good loaf of bread). I replied Mrs. P. I would give the last mouthful I had in my house, but my child should have milk, and remarked further that the people thought it strange, a Missionary had no food! They wonder I said and you will get a bad name among them.[9]

A missionary was expected to be a provider. Furthermore if the Philips came from a culture that valued thrift and individual economic accumulation, for many of the Africans with whom they lived, generosity with food and other goods was both a social good and an economic necessity. Early missionaries were often besieged by requests to share belongings when travelling; as Jean and John Comaroff suggest, this was often taken as begging by disgruntled missionaries but might have been seen by Africans themselves as a means to compel socially acceptable behaviour.[10] It was particularly essential to share with kin, while masculinity was defined in part by the capacity to provide for dependents — which was, in itself, an essential prerequisite for gathering followers in relatively fissile societies.

The Philips clearly violated expectations and social norms over property and generosity in a number of ways, and this was equally clearly a subject for criticism by station residents. Roger Edwards began his own statement by remarking: "I am aware there is at this station, and in other places, in the neighbourhood and at a distance, a very strong prejudice against Mr. Philips and his wife, partly I think from a rather harsh and suspicious manner towards the natives, and his apparent selfish temper, and his devotedness to the veriest trifles of a domestic kind in the kitchen, pantry, bedroom, etc. . . . "[11] He observed Philips's "servant woman" railing loudly to a group in the street against what she called "those 'strange people'", complaining about their "unfeeling conduct to the infant which she declared they did not love, and was left alone to cry and suffer hunger, and holding up to their view a few ounces of rice, her rations for the day, exclaimed against their niggardly disposition which would not allow them to make any at least suitable provision for the support of the babe".[12] "I know there are reports the most disgusting respecting Mr. and Mrs. Philips which arose from their excessive meanness and these reports have spread far and wide", Edwards attested further, averring that the doctor worsened his reputation "living as he did with closed doors and windows, as if among those he could not trust, and putting others out of his house least they should steal his belongings and appearing ready to suspect individuals as thieves or something of the kind".[13] For Francis Owen, the mission head who tried to make sense of events, "there is in this gentleman's character an excessive thriftiness, which has the aspect of meanness": he felt that Philips was simply incapable of taking the nurse into his home and properly feeding her.[14]

Tellingly, Dr Philips responded to accusations such as those of the Edwards by pointing out that Hamilton and the Edwards themselves had given them accounts of the "pilfering propensities of the natives" when they first met. He also argued that it was crucial to husband resources when it was impossible to get new supplies and when the people to whom they were to travel were reported to be starving. Perhaps misreading an accusation of meanness for an accusation of inappropriately gendered behaviour, he further stated that he paid minute attention to domestic detail because his wife suffered from extreme debility, and they were unable to communicate with the servant woman.[15] Most tellingly, he argued that the Africans on the station backed up the Edwards because of their own hope for material gain.

Philips's thriftiness and his suspicion of the motives of Africans appear to have made it hard for him to trust the wet nurse: "he said if ever he gave her food, she would let her own child have all the milk; and what moreover was he to do? since he paid her so much per Week for suckling his child? was he to give her that money? and food too?"[16] Ultimately, however, Dr Philips reluctantly agreed to give food to the wet nurse on a trial basis, saying that he would dismiss her if she did not produce enough milk. Over the next few days, the couple harassed her to milk out her breasts before leaving, to allow Dr Philips to feed the baby himself. "I was present", Mrs. Edwards later stated, "when the woman after suckling the child for about ¼ of an hour was leaving and Mrs. P. went into her room, brought out a metal drinking cup, and putting her hand on the woman's breast desired her to milk again into it: the woman looked at her with surprise and told her she had none."[17] Dr Philips also begrudged the nurse the fact that her family came to share the food he gave.[18] Later, he claimed that she was still not giving enough milk and was unable to satisfy the baby, although the testimony of others contradicted him on this vital point. Owen thought that he suspected the nurse of giving all her milk to her own child.[19]

Meanwhile, the women of the station attempted to get Mrs Philips to nurse. Again, one sees different ideas of intimacy and of boundaries between bodies: Mrs Edwards brought her own son, Roger, to nurse at Mrs Philips's breast, to get her milk flowing, although the child refused to feed at a strange breast. Within a few days, Mrs Philips announced that her milk had almost completely dried up. In this atmosphere of suspicion, the baby's condition worsened. It cried constantly and suffered (as Philips later attested) from frequent diarrhea.[20] The parents placed the child in a different bed from their own, to the shock of Mrs Edwards and Mrs Lemue.[21] They also often placed her in a separate room of the house, on a pair of chairs, while they were awake.

On Tuesday 3 December Dr Philips came to see Mrs Lemue at the Edwards' house in order to vaccinate the Lemue children, following this up by some remarks on vaccination. He then informed Mrs Lemue that he planned to see her at the station of Molito in about ten days. When asked what he would do with the baby he said (according to Mrs Edwards) "oh [. . .] we think of giving it to a native woman to take care of for 6 or 7 months, and at the end of that time return to see it". Mrs Lemue answered "But your child will die!" Very clearly, the missionary women believed that it was Mrs Philips's duty to take care of her own child. In the ensuing furor, the other missionaries stated that the Philipses must leave their child with a missionary wife, not a "native", who would not be able to take care of it. Dr Philips countered that native children were very healthy. He also, interestingly, insisted that: "Mrs. P's milk was bad for the child, that it disordered its bowels". Mrs Edwards and the doctor then plunged into a confrontation about how best to feed a baby, in which the far less educated mother challenged the doctor's medical knowledge. Mrs Philips must persevere, Mrs Edwards urged. Her own milk had caused her own baby to retch for months, but she had continued:

> It was perhaps, not so much Mrs. P's milk as the three different kinds of milk, combined, which the child was in the habit of taking daily, viz its mother's milk and goat's milk, in this, he differed from me, and said "he could not possibly conceive how three good things combined could produce one bad effect, when taken into the stomach. I answered, that he was not yet certain they were all three good, that, from the nature of the nurse's food, her milk might at times disagree with the child, and that perhaps he had not ascertained whether the goat's milk was in its first or last stage, which also made a great difference [. . .] Mr. E. and I then advised him to confine the child to one kind of milk, as a trial, either its mother's, the nurse's, or the goat's, and after some further remarks, of the same nature, he came to the conclusion of dismissing the wet nurse, and feeding the child on its mother's milk and that of the goats.[22]

Later that day, Mrs Lemue and Mrs Edwards returned to the Philips's house, so that Mrs Lemue could (however reluctantly) pay her respects before leaving. The baby was lying in the "forehouse, on two chairs, with some clothes laid under it, but without a pillow [. . .] the poor infant's eyes were turned up, the face blue, and convulsed and its cries thrilling!!" Mrs Edwards picked it up. The doctor said it had been crying that way for two hours and nothing would pacify it. When Mrs Edwards urged him to call for the dismissed wet nurse he angrily refused. Mrs Edwards asked if she was to lay the baby on the chairs again and leave it there; Dr Philips answered "yes lay it down there it shall lie there". Seeing, as she put it, the father "shut up all bowels of compassion towards his infant child", Mrs Edwards "turned towards the Mother and asked her if she had no motherly feelings". At that, Dr Philips angrily began to shout at Mrs Edwards: "Come, come. I'll have no more of this. We have had enough of your hints every day, I won't stand it Mrs. P's feelings shall not be insulted in this way". The two quarrelled fiercely as he threw her out of the house. "'I would not witness such a scene without making my remarks'" cried Mrs Edwards. "'I won't stand it and I wish you would give us less of your company in future'" replied Dr Philips. "I'll take care of that", said Mrs Edwards. Mrs Philips had, her husband insisted, "as much affection for her child as any other mother, and had shewn as much." "I should be very sorry", Mrs Edwards replied, "to have such feelings as Mrs. P.". By now, Philips had walked with a raised hand to the door where the two women stood. He apologized to Mrs Lemue, who hastily left. "And I am to consult your feelings and the whims and feelings of the people on this place am I. It is a pity I ever came into contact with such people as you". Mrs Edwards threw back: "it is a pity such people as you ever came to a heathen land". Throughout, the child continued to scream, while Mrs Philips walked about rubbing her hands and saying: "yes indeed, yes indeed".[23]

All day long the child continued to cry. "The child has just got to sleep, being quite killed with crying", remarked the servant woman to her friends late in the afternoon.[24] Throughout the week the crying went on. Jacob, the interpreter, who was also teaching Dr Philips seTswana, dropped in on the Edwards to report that the child was "left alone to cry in another room while the parents give themselves no concern on the subject. They have just put it in water, & it is now gone to sleep". As Mrs Edwards walked through the village with Jacob later that evening on the way to see a sick child, a woman cried out "'Is the child still left alone to cry' — 'Yes, just as always' was his reply". By the 13th, the parents called on Mrs Hume, the trader's wife, to report that the child was ill and to ask her to see it; by the following day they did not expect the baby to live. They still proposed, however, leaving it "with a native woman & Mrs. Hume to see it once or twice in the week". On the 15th the child was very weak, but Mrs Hume still believed it could recover. The parents still did not send for a wet nurse. On Sunday night Mr Hamilton called and saw "as usual" the child in one room and the parents in another. On the following day, the 17th, the baby died alone, "at least", according to Roger Edwards, "such was the testimony of the servant woman who said that when the parents went to feed it, they found it was dead".[25] Throughout the village, the inhabitants condemned the Philips, saying the child had died from hunger. "*Gasi bathu*", "not human", was what they were saying of the Philips, reported Matscaubana to Mrs Edwards.[26]

Aftermath

The story did not end there. Several days later, the Philips attempted to proceed to their long-desired station. The news of Philips's neglect of his child had preceded him and clearly made him an undesirable missionary. "The character of Mr. P. has sustained an irreparable injury, not only at Kuruman but at Molito & even amongst the Baharutse on the Harts River, a hundred miles from hence", wrote Owen to the home society.[27] The Barolong chief at Molito, Mochuana, asked Lemue who Philips was and on learning he was a doctor said "away with such a doctor; we cannot trust him for any help; God will help us & not that man; no, no, away with him!"[28] As soon as Philips arrived at Molita on his way to Mosika, Mochuana came to see Lemue to insist that Philips return, "saying that he was not a man, &c". Furthermore, he informed Lemue that the Baharutse chief Mokatla had sent Mochuana a message to stop Philips from proceeding. Mochuana went to Philips's wagon to deliver the unpleasant message but the driver, Mebala, dissuaded him and the Philips continued, nonetheless, to Mosika.

For his part, the thoroughly disconcerted Owen, having concluded his investigation, decided to dismiss Dr Philips from the mission and to urge him to return home to Britain, even though he had not yet heard back from distant London. By now Philips had quarrelled with other missionaries who, he felt, failed to defend him, including Wallace Hewetson. Philips agreed to leave, but he presented the rupture as his own decision. In the meantime, he wrote furiously to London to defend his reputation, as well as writing letters to missionaries involved.

In his letters Philips describes an exhausted couple struggling to care for a child with a severe inflammation of the bowels who was unable to keep food down. He also, however, underscores the class dimensions of the conflict. He claimed he had been persecuted by those beneath him. Better behaviour was hardly to be expected from "unsanctified and worldly minded spirits like his [Hewetson's] and Edwards, who were all originally low in life, and are consequently puffed up by the familiar contact and access which their present situation affords them". They needed to be taught "the vanity of that equality with those whom God has placed above them at which in their unsanctified state they are so prone to aim".[29]

In all of this, Mrs Philips's voice is largely missing from the archives. Owen described her as ineffectual and lacking in energy. Her husband defended her in his letters, saying rather that she was extremely ill and constantly tired, unable to feed her child in consequence. Indeed, he had once shocked other missionaries by declaring that the life of a mother was far more valuable than that of her child. It comes as a jolt, then, to read a letter of 19 May 1840, from the missionary Wallace Hewetson to the home society, in which Hewetson defends himself against the accusations of Philips, knowing that Philips had written home to criticize him. Dr Philips, it turns out, hit his wife.

Here is the relevant passage. Mrs Philips stayed with the Hewetsons for ten days once while her husband travelled. She told Mrs Hewetson, Wallace recalled (I preserve his punctuation):

> that she was truly miserable, that the Dr. and her were cousins, they knew each other
> from childhood & yet they were but a very short time married when Mr. P. displayed
> his jealous temper by striking her for speaking to a friend whom she met coming out
> of Church, this recurred (Mrs. P said) while in London previous to sailing his conduct

was so strange on board ship that when Mrs. P. was confined no person would go to see them & help them while Mr & Mrs P were at Sidbury with Mr. Owen's family he accused Mrs. P of freedom with Young Judge brother to Mr. Judge & ever since he has made himself so unpopular that Mrs. P. says she is truly miserable.[30]

Was this then the explanation for the closed doors and windows, and even for Mrs P's illness and retreat to bed? It seems impossible to know. What we do know is that Owen knew all along that Philips tightly controlled his wife and had struck her in the past, because Mrs Owen told him. He evidently did not feel able, however, to do more than hint delicately at the doctor's "habitual tyranny" in his correspondence with London. There were multiple levels of power relations on the mission stations of southern Africa, and not the least of these related to gender.

When Owen at last received a reply to the avalanche of correspondence with which the London committee had been deluged, it was to announce that the southern African mission was being shut down. There were doubtless a number of reasons, although this case was probably the final straw. The Zulu mission had failed amid great bloodshed. Hewetson and Owen's new station was now collapsing because of mass hunger and the reluctance of the Baharutse to come and settle there. The CMS support group in Cape Town was foundering and in debt. And now Philips's Tswana mission had fallen apart as well, and several of those associated with the scandal were exhausted and demoralized. "I cannot express to you the horror I feel at the whole transaction which has led to Mr. Philips' retirement", wrote Owen in November 1840 after he had received word of the termination. "Words cannot describe what I have felt, during the whole process of this shameful affair [. . .] I cannot think of it without shuddering". The CMS had suggested that Owen move to West Africa in order to help pioneer a new mission there. Owen pleaded instead to be allowed to leave the missionary profession: he could not imagine the waste of time involved in starting again, not least in learning a new language and struggling to pioneer a new mission at his age. He was also appalled at the amount of time he had spent on material rather than spiritual concerns. "I feel that I have lost so much time, that I dare not without pausing encounter the risk of losing more [. . .] Life is passing away: sinners are hurrying to the tomb: I have been set apart for the work of the ministry: and what am I doing? What have I been doing?"[31] Owen never went to West Africa and left the missionary service.

The Meaning of a Death Foretold

What are to we to make of this domestic tragedy in terms of the themes explored in this volume? Does it tell us anything larger about the relationship of Africans to missionaries in early nineteenth-century southern Africa? I would suggest that it does. At the most obvious level, the story underscores the precarious physical environment in which missions in the Northern Cape region operated and the daily tragedies confronting many. Hunger was a constant fear in an environment without enough water. In 1839, many were starving as they waited for corn to ripen, even though this year is not remembered in the historical record as particularly worse than any other. The Philips's wet nurse was trying to feed two children on a single drink of milk a day. Missionaries with a loaf of bread and a cow were rich. The political upheavals of the earlier nineteenth century and the tragic episodes of famine, exile and warfare that had accompanied them were calmer by the late 1830s, and yet there was still great political uncertainty and food insecurity, coupled with the disruptive incursions of emigrant farmers and British imperial designs.[32] This created a role for missions.

In this environment African polities were inherently fissile. Power lay in the capacity to gather people and to accumulate resources. To survive, people needed to move to where the resources were. New polities were frequently formed by powerful men (and sometimes women), usually with a claim to chiefly authority, who were able to accumulate warriors, cattle and fertile women. Moshoeshoe, the iconic founder figure of modern Lesotho, was such a leader, for example, gathering together refugee groups in a secure mountain-top environment. So too, as Norman Etherington's revisionist history of the southern African interior suggests, were many of the chiefs who led trading and raiding groups across the lands of the interior during the earlier conflicts of the so-called "mfecane" period.[33] In this environment successful missionaries surely functioned at least in some respects like successful chiefs. They too accumulated people and indeed cattle. They too integrated their followers by creating new identities and new foundational myths tied to the identity of the ruler. Kuruman, for example, only began to flourish at the very end of the 1820s when it picked up many refugees from conflict and hunger.[34] Alternatively (and sometimes in tandem), missionaries became the protégés of chiefs and great men who were able to clear the path to their settlement in the region, and who sought, in turn, to benefit from missionary goods and diplomatic access, or indeed from the power of Christianity itself — which is not to say that such mentors actually obeyed missionaries or saw them as their superiors. Missionaries could not function without access to people and to resources. Indeed, the mission that Hewetson and Owen were struggling to establish failed at least in part because the missionaries could not provide resources (they were too far from the supply lines of Kuruman and their crops failed); in turn, they could not attract people and, without men, were unable to plant properly, completing a vicious circle.

Women's fertility was a symbol not only of the ability of chiefs to lead, but also of the capacity of missionaries to produce good things and to provide protection. Is it too far-fetched to see in the failure of a missionary to protect his baby a symbol of his failure to protect and provide more broadly? Not to provide milk was a powerful symbol, not only of lack of femininity but also — and perhaps more powerfully — of a failure of masculinity. To milk cows was a male role in Tswana society, just as cows, the main form of wealth, were signs of masculine power. "God will help us and not that man!" exclaimed Mochuana. Indeed, it is interesting that an earlier scandal at the station in the early 1820s had also involved the fertility and bodily comportment of dependent white women. On that occasion, the mission community had again been racked by conflict when Ann Hamilton, the wife of Robert Hamilton, had refused to have sex with her husband. Robert Moffat had attempted to have Ann Hamilton repent publicly and confess in church. She, on the other hand, had not only stated that her husband repelled her, but also hinted that she did not want more of the children who (Doug Stuart speculates) were interfering with her missionary career.[35] Here too it strikes me that the ability of missionary women to bear and nurture children was, among other things, a sign of male power, but also that missionary women sometimes resisted the roles laid out for them.

Whether unwilling or unable to provide, Philips could not nurture the alliances necessary to be accepted as a missionary. He failed to meet Tswana conventions of civility, generosity and sociability. The spread of information about these failures suggests that mission stations were caught up in webs of "gossip" and information exchange and that these networks mattered. Missionaries were often painfully aware of what Africans thought of them (or, at least, what they believed Africans were thinking) and worried about it. At the same time, Africans and whites alike exerted considerable powers of censorship and interference in one another's lives. If missionaries were trying to impose their own views of appropriately gendered behaviour and of social relationships on Africans, at least some Africans were attempting to do the reverse. The Philips's "servant woman", as we have seen, stood in the street displaying her meagre rations in order to denounce the Philips's lack of generosity. It mattered to Edwards that "she exposed the matter repeatedly and likewise told others that she had more than once attempted to excite Mrs. P's concern for the neglected and suffering infant".[36] The papers in the case are full of other examples of African censure. An unnamed "native woman" came to Mrs Edwards as the baby lay dying and asked her "if those people [. . .] had no repentance for their conduct now that death was looking them in the face"[37] Words flew rapidly through the countryside. Roger Edwards likened the Tswana to the Athenians in their love of news and gossip: "the people of this station have much intercourse with Molito Town and other places as well as with the Baharutse, all of whom are like the Athenians spending much of their time in telling or hearing some new thing, the Dr. furnished them with much new matter of a new kind indeed".[38]

The missionaries were divided about whether or not it mattered what "the natives" thought. Indeed, Philips was particularly shocking because he so boldly affirmed that he did not care at all what Africans thought of him. Tension over this point and the extreme anxiety of most of the missionaries over what the Philips were doing to their reputation, suggest a personal sense of insecurity. As a number of historians have suggested in a variety of contexts, Christianity may have been powerful but individual missionaries were not necessarily so — unless and until they were placed in positions of institutional power, such as running schools or working for the imperial state, as the advent of formal colonialism changed missionary status. The recent example of Owen's complete (and unsurprising) failure to negotiate with Dingane underscored this. In the case we have examined, relationships were fragile enough that most missionaries were convinced that nothing could be accomplished without a good reputation. This in itself established certain parameters within which they needed to remain.

A growing body of work examines gender and sexuality in missionary history. A particularly key point has been the importance to missionaries of modelling domesticity and appropriate gender relations.[39] Such modelling was all the more important because both Christian missions and colonialism more widely were often justified among the British by reference to the supposed oppressive gender relations and domestic cruelty of the "heathen". Indeed, Owen pointed to the Tswana practice of killing one of two twins and disabled children at birth as evidence of their need for Christianity. His anxiety over poor missionary parenting practices was, doubtless, all the greater. Despite the importance of this overall observation, it is still true that missionaries themselves were not always in agreement about what constituted appropriate gendered behaviour. This is evident in the debates over childrearing that we have seen playing out at Kuruman. Roger Edwards even cast the debate as in some ways opposing maternal nature to "professional" knowledge, exclaiming at one point: "the Dr. however appeared to trust to his professional skill and counteract the evil arising from the want of its mother's breast [. . .] medicines and warm baths cannot supply a mother's milk, which he must have known with all his knowledge of medicine".[40] Certainly Mrs Edwards challenged and rejected Dr Philips's claims to superior knowledge and, just as clearly, he deeply resented her intrusions and her lack of respect for his class and education. British ideas about childrearing and the relative roles of professionals and mothers (to take just one example) were scarcely fixed. In this context, there was the possibility of agreement between the views of certain Africans and certain whites on subjects such as the importance of constantly holding babies and keeping them in the same bed, even if the broad cultural contexts were very different. Motherhood was not a fixed idea, and there was room for debate about what constituted being a "good" mother. My work also suggests that inextricably linked to debates about good motherhood were debates over good fatherhood.

There was some room for struggle about appropriate economic behaviour. The Protestant missionary message tended to stress economic individualism and the benefits of accumulation. This was always a message that sat uneasily with strictly moral ideas of the economy, especially in an era in which economic ideas were in fact very much about the creation of a moral society. How much individual accumulation was too much? This example suggests that structural circumstances, African pressure and missionary concerns for their reputation might urge missionaries into adopting African economic practices, such as a greater degree of sharing goods. Owen thought that the Philips ought to have, if need be, taken not only the wet nurse into their family home but also her family, and fed all of them. This did, in fact, echo the economic practices of both Afrikaners and wealthy Africans of having entire families of dependents, including children, associated with their own families, and available for work, in exchange for subsistence. At the same time, the case also suggests that missionaries stepped into upper-class roles, from a British perspective, in part because they had the resources to employ Africans. Once the power of chiefs was diminished by the colonial state, the power lent to missionaries by patronage and paternalism would more effectively come to the fore.

I want finally to suggest that this type of micro study focuses attention on the mission station as an institution in itself in relation to a much larger picture. There were many intermediaries who attended missionaries. These included servants, but also mission catechists. In the case of missions to the Tswana, these intermediaries also

21

included people from the Cape Colony, many of whom were of Khoekhoe descent, as well as members of powerful local Griqua powers. The dependence of missionaries on such intermediaries even on mission stations seems symbolically appropriate. In fact, as I and others have suggested elsewhere, Africans accomplished most conversions.[41] News of Christianity travelled along the same networks of information exchange that had born criticism of the Philipses. Networks of preachers from Khoekhoe stations in the colony were in fact crucial in bearing Christianity across the Orange River. Much of the action, in other words, was outside the purview of the station and often outside the ken of missionaries. The sociology of the mission station should not be confused with the history of Christianity in Africa.

Nonetheless, Africans sometimes wanted and sometimes tried to use mission stations, in contexts of considerable political and economic insecurity. Not surprisingly, they also tried to contain their power and to limit the capacity of missionaries to interfere in the details of their lives. People, all the same, lived in close proximity to one another and could not avoid changing one another. The mission station was, in its own way, a place of intense and often anxious interaction. It was also a place about which the rosy presentations of missionary magazines were often misleading. Although the mission station may not have done what missionary societies tended to think it did, if one digs beneath the surface of the archival record, its anxieties, tensions and dense social relationships reveal much about wider relationships of power on many levels.

Notes

1 M. A. Edwards, "A Statement respecting Mr & Mrs Philips", Church Missionary Society Papers, University of Birmingham, South Africa Mission, CA 405; a copy with a couple of small deletions is also reproduced in C A4/M1, Mission Book, 1836–1843. I will mostly refer to this latter copy as it has page numbers. CMS South Africa hereafter CMS SA.

2 Rev. F. Owen's journal, December 29–March, 1838, CMS SA, C A4/M1, Mission Book, 1836–1843, pp. 104–36, especially entries for February 6 and February 7, 1838, pp. 121–9; Kuper, "The Death of Piet Retief", *Social Anthropology*, 4(2), 1996, pp. 133–43.

3 On various aspects of Christian missions to the Tswana in this period: Landau, *The Realm of the Word: Language, Gender and Christianity in a Southern African Kingdom*; Comaroff, *Of Revelation and Revolution*, vols 1 and 2; de Gruchy, "The Alleged Political Conservatism of Robert Moffat, pp. 17–36.

4 On discourses of missionary heroism, inter alia, Stuart, "'Of Savages and Heroes'"; Anna Johnston, *Missionary Writing and Empire*; de Kock, *Civilizing Barbarians*. See also Moffat, *Missionary Labours and Scenes in Southern Africa*; Moffat, *The Lives of Mary and Robert Moffat*.

5 Schoeman, *A Thorn Bush that Grows in the Path*; Stuart, "'Of Savages and Heroes'"; Elbourne, "African Missionary Wives"; Wallace Hewetson to the Secretary, Cape Town, December 21, 1837, CMS SA, C A4/M1; Journal of Wallace Hewetson, 1837–38, C A4/04/2-3. On the former employment of Edwards and Hewetson as carpenter and blacksmith respectively, R. Philips to the Lay Secretary of the CMS, April 29, 1840, CMS SA, C A4/M1, Mission Book, 1836–1843, p. 417. Hewetson also had a stint as an enlisted solider in the Lancers.

6 "Owen, Miss M.C." in Gunn and Codd, *Botanical Exploration of Southern Africa*, pp. 268–9.

7 Edwards, "A Statement", CMS SA, C A4/M1, p. 462.

8 Edwards, "A Statement", p. 463.

9   Edwards, "A Statement", p. 464.

10 Comaroff and Comaroff, *Of Revelation and Revolution*, vol. 1.

11 Roger Edwards, "R. Edwards' Statements", CMS SA, C A4/M1, p. 470.

12 Edwards, "R. Edwards' Statements", p. 472.

13 Edwards, "R. Edwards' Statements", p. 476.

14 Francis Owen, "Statement of Facts", CMS SA, p. 4.

15 "Mr. R. Philips' Reply to the Revd R. Edwards", July 25, 1840, CMS SA, C A4/M1, p. 443.

16 M.A. Edwards, "Statements", CMS SA, CA 4M1, p. 445.

17 M.A. Edwards, "Statements", p. 445.

18 "Mr. R. Philips' Reply to the Revd R. Edwards", CMS SA, C A4/M1, p. 445. "Her husband and children very frequently came at the regular hour of meals to share in her food — and it is not then to be wondered at that she should sometimes complain that she did not get enough to eat, but notwithstanding the extra mouths thus brought to bear on her rations, she became fat and well liking while in our employment".

19 Francis Owen, "Statement of Facts", CMS SA, p. 4.

20 R. Philips, "Reply to Mrs. Edwards's Statements", Mosiza [sic], April 7, 1840, CMS SA, C A4/M1, pp. 440–1.

21 M.A. Edwards, "Statements", p. 446.

22 M.A. Edwards, "Statements", p. 447.

23 Edwards, "Statements".

24 Edwards, "R. Edwards' Statements"; Owen, "A Statement of Facts", p. 9.

25 Edwards, "R. Edwards' Statements", p. 474.

26 Edwards, "R. Edwards' Statements", p. 474.

27 Owen, "A Statement of Facts", p. 12.

28 Edward, "R. Edwards' Statements"; Owen, "A Statement of Facts", p. 12.

29 R. Philips to the Lay Secretary, Mozika [sic], April 29, 1840, CMS SA, C A4/M1, p. 417.

30 Wallace Hewetson to the Lay Secretary, May 19, 1840, CMS SA, C A4/M1, p. 413.

31 Francis Owen to the Secretary, Kuruman, November 20, 1840, CMS SA, CA 4M1, pp. 485–7.

32 On debates about the so-called mfecane, Hamilton, ed., *The Mfecane Aftermath*.

33 Etherington, *Great Treks*.

34 Elbourne, "Robert Moffat".

35 See the references in endnote 5 above on the Hamiltons.

36 Edwards, "Statement", p. 471.

37 Edwards, "Statement", p. 474.

38 Edwards, "Statement", p. 476. For innovative work on gossip and rumour, White, *Speaking with Vampires*.

39 For a trenchant overview of key work: Grimshaw and Sherlock, "Women, Missions and Cultural Exchanges".

40 Edwards, "R. Edwards' Statements", p. 473.

41 A point stressed by Norman Etherington in his introduction and by contributors in Etherington, ed., *Missions and Empire*, as also by Maxwell, "Writing the History of African Christianity".

CHAPTER THREE

"The Natives Uncivilize Me"
Missionaries and Interracial Intimacy in Early New Zealand

ANGELA WANHALLA

In evidence before an 1838 House of Lords committee on New Zealand, Joel Polack, a settler at the Hokianga, claimed "the Conduct of One or Two" of the missionaries "has been such as to undo much they could have done themselves, and to have thrown Dishonour upon their Names".[1] Dandeson Coates, secretary to the Church Missionary Society (CMS), questioned about the nature of intimate relations between missionaries and Maori in New Zealand before the same committee, claimed there "has been no Instance of Intermarriage of any Persons connected with the Mission with the Natives".[2] Questions about missionaries, marriage, and interracial intimacy arose in this context because of the misconduct of male missionaries in the colony, amongst them Thomas Kendall in 1822, William White in 1835 and William Yate in 1836. But why should the 1838 House of Lords committee take such close interest in the conduct of missionaries in New Zealand, particularly their sexual relationships?

Intimate relationships were of interest, just two years before New Zealand was annexed by the British Crown under the Treaty of Waitangi, because, as Kirsten McKenzie has eloquently demonstrated, public scandals about very private affairs were as much about the reputation of a colony as they were about the individual, and, in 1838, the stability and standing of the missionary project.[3] In New Zealand some mission families created ties to Maori through "regular marriage", and others were the subject of scandal, gossip and rumour throughout the colony. An unmarried missionary was of particular concern to London and Sydney authorities. Any rumour of sexual impropriety quickly spread to the metropole, and became subject to investigation, proving Adele Perry's claim that there is a "tangled relationship between intimacy, power and scandal".[4] Indeed, colonial power and authority was bound up with intimate affairs and "shaped by the production of sentiments".[5]

Missionary men who transgressed undermined missionary claims about the excesses of "renegade" settlers in pre-1840 New Zealand, exposing the vulnerability of the missionary project in early New Zealand, as well as the colonial project as a whole. The alacrity of intervention into intimate and private affairs by mission authorities, as well as representatives of the British Crown, gestures towards the fragility of the colonial project during the 1830s and 1840s. In 1838 the House of Lords was determining the possibility and nature of British intervention into New Zealand, while witnesses of leading missionary organizations were attempting to protect their position in the colony; sexual encounters with indigenous women, and the collaboration of missionary men with traders and whalers, were potentially harmful to both missionary and imperial interests and agendas. Exposing sexual scandals in such a public forum could potentially undo careers, families, and colonies.

When the first CMS "mechanics" arrived at the Bay of Islands, they encountered a social world where interracial encounters of an intimate nature were a reality. While missionaries deplored the effect of "white strangers" upon Maori, they could do very little to prevent the continuation of such encounters except to encourage "regular unions". Missionaries were living in a Maori world where Maori were engaged in mutually beneficial economic and social relationships with traders and whalers. How missionaries managed affective ties had an important bearing on their acceptance into Maori communities, as well as their ability to access the "newcomers", or "white strangers" who required "conversion" to Christianity as much as Maori. Some, like the Roman Catholic brothers, used traders to mediate with Maori. Building up good and close relationships with the traders in Tauranga, for instance, gave the Catholic orders a foothold in interracial communities.[6] My focus, however, is on the CMS and Methodist missions in early New Zealand. I demonstrate that the acceptance of interracial relationships by missionaries in early New Zealand depended upon the status and reputation of the newcomer involved. Following Tony Ballantyne and Adele Perry, I argue that missionaries sought to encourage sex within marriage, the creation of "regular" and moral unions, and to sanctify relationships that encompassed respectable masculinity.[7]

Marriage, Morality and Masculinity

Interracial relationships, as Perry notes, were part of the "fabric of colonial life" in British Columbia and in other parts of the British Empire.[8] Missionaries, wherever they were located, attempted to regulate interracial connections and encounters of an intimate or sexual nature. Anglican, Methodist and Catholic missionaries located in early New Zealand all sought to make interracial relationships "regular" through a marriage ceremony, even if some of the intimate encounters they sought to "regularize" were short-term and fleeting by nature. A great variety of sexual intimacies existed in early New Zealand, but in large part interracial relationships were predominately monogamous.[9]

Marriage, and the process of baptism which preceded the ceremony, was the main work of missionaries in early New Zealand. The Reverend Richard Taylor's journals are full of references to marriage. On 25 October 1843 "we stopped some time . . . to speak with the natives especially relative to the illicit intercourse between Europeans and native women".[10] At a whaling station near modern Wellington, he found a European man "living with a native female. I spoke to him on the subject and he listened very attentively."[11] Bishop Selwyn did the same on his visitation to the southern regions of New Zealand in 1844. At Ruapuke Island he had a "conversation with Kelly and Moss about marriage. Explained to the women with whom they had been living. Married them, and baptized their children."[12] At Bluff "much conversation on marriage" ensued between Selwyn and male newcomers.[13] At Stewart Island he spoke to interracial couples, "on the sanctity of marriage and the sin of their mode of life; with reference also to the effect of their example upon their children. Most of them had been living many years with the same consorts, and apparently were resolved to be faithful to them." After talking to the men, he assembled the women and "explained marriage to them", and then sanctified the unions of ten couples.[14]

Just because all mission societies sought to "regularize" unions, did not mean there was widespread support for interracial relationships. Personal documents, such as diaries and letters, do not support such a view. In 1838 John Liddiard Nicholas of the CMS, in evidence before the House of Lords committee, noted that there were many "Adventurers", which he said were "of the most abandoned Description" now living in New Zealand.[15] John Watkins, surgeon, claimed the 400 or 500 men of "low class" in the country were "perfectly lawless" and a mischief to the missionaries whom they ignore: "Nothing can be more lawless than the Europeans living there; they frequently lay aside the English Dress, and take up the native Mats, and have promiscuous Intercourse with the Native Women."[16] John Flatt, who worked for CMS missionaries Richard Davis and Henry Williams, described these men as "more degraded than the Natives".[17] Robert Fitzroy, future Governor of New Zealand, visited the Bay of Islands for ten days in 1835, and found eight or ten respectable families living there; the remainder were "ragamuffins".[18] The "ragamuffins" and "adventurers" described in 1838 before the House of Lords comprised a group of newcomers, sometimes called "strangers", who were fleeting visitors to the shores of New Zealand. Interracial relationships formed out of this trade context, and with these men, were often viewed as degrading, brutal, and violent in nature. Condemned as a form of prostitution, missionaries used these relationships to critique indigenous and newcomer masculinity.[19] Nevertheless, missionaries were pragmatic men. Interracial relationships were a thriving and widespread part of early New Zealand where resource economies like sealing, whaling, and trading were centred such as the Bay of Islands, along the eastern and southern coasts of the South Island, in Poverty Bay and the Bay of Plenty. Newcomers encountered a society with its own marriage customs and social regulations in which polygamy was practised and sexual freedom was not unusual.[20] Marriage was a tribal and family sanctioned process, which followed certain cultural and social protocols, and was designed to integrate newcomers into the tribal group. These newcomers could be Maori, in the case of inter-tribal or *inter-hapu* (sub-tribal) alliances, and in the contact era the process was expanded to encompass non-Maori newcomers. Maori society was organised along highly structured kin-based lines, in which status rather than gender was of importance. Bilateral descent meant that women could outrank men and own land and resources, and it was through marriage that political alliances were formed and boundaries redefined.[21]

Prior to contact, it was through the marriage of high-ranking women that political alliances were forged, peace deals were brokered and access to resources gained. Maori women took an active role in forging these marriage alliances within tribal society and in the new post-contact resource economies of sealing, whaling, and trading. In pre-contact and post-contact New Zealand, marriage was absolutely central to the formation of families and new communities, because it brought individuals together and created political and social ties of immense significance. Marriage, therefore, was a private as well as a very public social and community event that functioned to link people to the land, and to draw together political, social and economic alliances into a web of kinship. Economic, political and social relevance did not mean that relationships were not based on affect in Maori society, or with traders and whalers who landed on the shores of New Zealand.[22]

In general, missionaries gave support to interracial unions where newcomers were seen to fit the ideals of respectable masculinity, especially when relationships conformed to "western practices and models of sexual propriety, morality, and respectability, particularly the taking up of monogamy".[23] A mixture of pragmatism and concern for morality is clear in the extensive textual record of the Lutheran missionary to southern Maori, Johannes Wohlers, who arrived in the South Island in 1843 with three trainees of the North German Missionary Society. With the encouragement of the paramount chief, Tuhawaiki, he established a mission station on Ruapuke Island in the Foveaux Strait in May 1844. Ruapuke was the headquarters of southern Maori, but as Wohlers explained, it had certain advantages for a mission site "because it is a sort of gathering place, where everybody, native or European who crosses through these waters comes ashore".[24] He lived at Ruapuke for forty years, ministering to a population on the island and dispersed settlements on the mainland.

On arrival Wohlers noted the considerable number of European men "on the shores of this region [southern New Zealand] and more and more remain here". "All of them amalgamate with the natives" and co-habit "in marriage according to the New Zealand way".[25] By December 1845, the southern coast was "crowded with fisheries and many whaling ships are cruising around here".[26] Economic activity was constant, but permanent settlement was emerging out of the whaling industry, reflected in the mixed descent families arising. At the close of 1845, the Neck, the major settlement on Stewart Island, was "inhabited by Europeans who are married to New Zealand women" who had fathered, claimed Wohlers, at least 100 "half-caste" children.[27] Just two months later, Wohlers claimed 150 such children lived "in the surroundings of Foveaux Strait".[28]

Missionaries frequently commented upon the mixed descent population produced from relationships undertaken during the whaling era in southern New Zealand. Wesleyan missionary James Watkin viewed interracial marriage as a trade relationship describing it as "the practice of selling", denying any female agency in such encounters or an interpretation of them as romantic or meaningful connections.[29] Watkin saw the "practice of selling" as central to the demographic decline of Maori in the southern regions during the 1840s, when inter-tribal conflict, introduced disease and epidemics, were more culpable. Wohlers, by contrast, believed the "Europeans with their mixed offspring are going to continue the line of the thin population of this region."[30] Depopulation and eventual disappearance dominated colonial musings on indigenous peoples and are persistent tropes "in the fantasies of contact".[31] Wohlers supported and encouraged interracial marriage, in part, as a temporary solution to Maori depopulation.

But bringing Christian marriage to Maori was as much about controlling newcomers as it was about celebrating the successful conversion of Maori to Christianity. In northern New Zealand, noted the German naturalist Ernst Dieffenbach, "the missionaries seem to have been actuated by a desire to check the influence of bad characters who may thus connect themselves with a tribe".[32] Missionary practice was no different in southern New Zealand. Exasperated by the behaviour of former whalers, Wohlers claimed they "don't lift a finger to civilise their wives. The most they do is buy them a European women's dress, whether it fits or is becoming or not."[33] Just seven months later, in December 1845, Wohlers recorded some success, noting how the men, "especially those who already have several children", were seeking to have their "families baptised and to get married to their wives in the Christian way".[34] Wohlers sanctioned and supported, through the rites of baptism and marriage, a particular type of masculinity that encompassed permanent ties to a community, an absence of violence and heavy drinking, clean homes, and in general, those who worked to "civilize" their wives. Public expression of Christianity was of particular importance to Wohlers, as was the status of the newcomer men.[35] William Sterling was "one of the most important local people" at Bluff, and James Spencer "an important trader" there, while John Howell of Jacob's River was "the most important man of the place".[36] Wohlers took pleasure in sharing the company of men of a similar social position to himself, and took care to remark upon the gentility of their domestic life, while also celebrating these men's public support of his mission work. Howell, for instance, allowed Wohlers the use of his home for religious services.

But Wohlers was also a very pragmatic man. While he sanctified the unions of men who were willing to conform to monogamy — particularly those men who gave up their transient life for domesticity — he was very aware of the realities of marriage in the region, especially given the nature of employment available. Expressing delight that after only two years at Ruapuke women insist on being officially married, Wohlers noted it "shows certainly an especially strong religious feeling, although", he admits, "it might also be the precaution of tightening the bond as firmly as possible, so that the man cannot leave them again. For marriage is shunned by those who do not want to stay at the place for the rest of their lives."[37] His pragmatism is also expressed in other ways. Wohlers often relaxed the committee's rules, which allowed a couple to marry only if both parties had been baptized.[38]

Temptation and Transgression

Missionaries sought out relationships with newcomers, particularly with traders as intermediaries, especially in the early phases of the mission. Much has been made of the difficulties of the early CMS and Methodist missionaries in northern New Zealand, particularly during the formative period of the missions during the 1820s when their numbers were few, the resources stretched thin, financial support virtually non-existent, and conversions a rarity. A similar story existed in the southern mission stations, but is rarely remarked upon in the standard mission history of early New Zealand. The men who ministered to southern Maori in Otago and Southland were embroiled in scandal before their arrival in New Zealand. James Watkin and Charles Creed, most notably, were entangled in interracial liaisons while stationed in the South Pacific and both ended up at the Waikouaiti Mission Station, located near the Otago Peninsula. Wohlers was not associated with any similar indiscretions, but his extensive archive reveals an intense awareness of the possibility of falling into such a relationship, which was heightened by his extreme isolation and poverty. Marriage was at the forefront of his mind: his early reports to the Bremen Mission authorities pleaded for financial support so that he could engage in a suitable marriage. Unless he did so, Wohlers feared he could not minister to the female population with any success.

Missionaries lived in close proximity to Maori, and the relationships they developed were often ambiguous. A lack of social distance, and an isolated mission, brought forth a fear of physical and spiritual transgressions. In his early letters and reports to the Bremen authorities, Wohlers often expressed his intense fears and anxieties about the dangers of temptation. He was acutely aware of the isolation of his mission station, and a lack of social distance between the missionary and his flock. Wohlers announced, "I am not the man to civilize them, on the contrary the natives uncivilize me."[39] In May 1845 he noted: "it is not quite without danger for such an old bachelor as me to come into such close contact with the young New Zealand women who are not invariably amiable".[40] Moreover:

> What should one do for instance with the local females who throw themselves on you all the time to be told what they are to do. You must not get embroiled with young women because they might easily imagine things. Older women are trying to use their advantages which the position of an unmarried missionary offers and which causes for him such violent struggles regarding carnal temptations that he has to fight down.[41]

A potent mix of isolation from European settlement and lack of social distance is evident in Wohlers' description of the young girl who cleaned his house and had responsibility for domestic management while he was away at Stewart Island: "she is a very modest girl. Now, that I am back again she does no longer show herself. Otherwise there is no scarcity here of coquettish wenches."[42]

By July 1849, the temptations on offer to a single man at an isolated mission station became too much. It is "no longer possible to carry on the mission work with only bachelor missionaries", wrote Wohlers to the Bremen Mission authorities. He pleaded for them to "provide the means for me to marry".[43] His marriage to Eliza Palmer of Wellington took place in September 1849, and the relationship brought a noticeable change in the tone and content of his reports. No longer was Ruapuke a sexually tempting or dangerous place for him. It did, however, remain a lonely and distant mission, and in 1858 he wrote of the effects of isolation upon his mind and beliefs.

Angela Wanhalla

After fourteen years at Ruapuke, "I have lived for so many years among the Maori (hence) I am feeling awkward in my sermons as well as in my manners in social intercourse and I feel more at home with the Maori."[44]

Wohlers was not the only missionary to feel intensely the temptations of an isolated life. Similar situations existed elsewhere in the British colonies. In India, Kenneth Ballhatchet found that missionaries "played an ambiguous part on the imperial stage" as "uncomfortable members of the ruling race, criticizing British as well as Indian immorality".[45] In British Columbia, CMS missionary William Duncan opened a mission house for Aboriginal girls in 1862, to regulate their sexuality and to restrict intimate encounters with newcomers. Because the unmarried Duncan lived in the house in "intimate proximity" to the women, he became the subject of rumour and innuendo.[46] Stories of inappropriate sexual relationships across racial boundaries, particularly the belief circulated in settler society that Duncan fathered a child by one of the mission girls, troubled mission authorities enough to prompt them to send someone to investigate Duncan's conduct. Authorities urged Duncan to resolve the situation by marrying a white woman who could act to constrain his immorality, monitor standards of respectable masculinity, and aid in the mission proper.[47]

Duncan was not the first missionary to be the subject of rumour about his sexual behaviour; similar stories are common to the Pacific mission and in western Canada. Interracial sexual relationships were subject to social scrutiny and debate at Red River, the settlement established in 1821 for retired fur-traders, many of whom were high-ranking officers who had Aboriginal or mixed descent wives and large families. John West, Red River's first missionary in 1820, publicly criticized the leading men of the settlement for engaging in immoral relationships. West's career in Red River was a short one, but his departure did not witness the end of public debate about interracial relationships at the settlement. Intimate relationships continued to be very public in several court cases concerned with questions of legitimacy and inheritance.[48]

Missionary men lived in a world in which they were dependent upon the traders and sailors, as well as Maori for their existence, survival, and patronage. This was particularly true of the first CMS "mechanics" who established the Reverend Samuel Marsden's Rangihoua mission at the Bay of Islands in 1814. William Hall, John King and Thomas Kendall had an acrimonious and competitive relationship, in part because of the isolation of the mission, the inability of Marsden to provide adequate financial support for its "civilisation first" goals, and the consequent dependence of the mission upon Maori.

The London Missionary Society (1795), the CMS (1799) and the Methodist Missionary Society (1813) all followed a policy of sending married missionaries into the overseas mission field.[49] Samuel Marsden, catalyst for the arrival of the CMS mission to Maori, advocated strongly for missionary wives to accompany husbands into the field, especially in Polynesia, not only to assist in the labour of the mission, but, as Hilary Carey claims, primarily to limit the possibility of moral "backsliding" by male missionaries.[50] Marsden's views about married missionaries were reinforced by the care and close attention he paid to the domestic life of his employees: he refused to support applicants to go into the field unless they married, arranged marriages for missionaries, and played patron to the careers of missionary children.[51] Marsden's policy did not, however, solve the problem of "backsliding" missionaries.

Thomas Kendall came to the attention of authorities because of his intimate economic and social ties to whaling captains and traders: a set of relationships he needed to foster in order to gain the patronage of Maori chiefs, and for economic survival. Gunrunning, drunkenness, collaborating and socialising with traders and ships' captains, drew Marsden's ire. Kendall's affair with Tungaroa, the daughter of a high-ranking chief, which came to light in 1822, confirmed Marsden's view that Kendall was engaged in a pattern of sin and vice. In 1823 Thomas Kendall attracted further notoriety, and condemnation from Marsden, for sanctifying the first mission and church-sanctioned interracial marriage in New Zealand, between Maria Ringa and Norwegian trader Peter Tapsell. Kendall's dismissal from the mission attracted reprisals from northern Maori, who enacted raids against his former mission station: a visible expression of Maori support for Kendall, and a warning that the mission's survival depended upon the patronage of the leading chief, Hongi Hika.[52]

Sexual scandals and whispers of misconduct were not limited to heterosexual relationships. Kendall's was the first case to come to the attention of mission authorities, but his was followed by an investigation into claims against William Yate, CMS missionary, about whom gossip circulated amongst New Zealand mission communities from 1832. In 1836 Yate was accused of improper sexual contact with Maori boys. These accusations arose as a result of charges Marsden levelled against Yate of an inappropriate relationship with Edward Denison on a return voyage to Australia that year. Yate was eventually dismissed from the CMS in 1837, although nothing was ever proved against him. Marsden and fellow missionaries marshalled evidence against him, but Yate had his supporters and sympathisers in England, where he waged a public campaign to prove his innocence. He was eventually reinstated because his actions could not be proven to be criminal.[53] Yate commented on the accusations and investigations in his diary, concluding that "I have gained a friend though, I may thereby have lost a name."[54]

Rumours about missionaries were incited by their employees, often as a result of a personal grievance, or an acrimonious relationship, and sometimes because mission employees engaged in interracial relationships in defiance of their authorities. William Duncan dismissed an employee from his mission for developing an affective relationship with an Aboriginal convert, and violating norms of respectable masculinity. Similar cases appear in the New Zealand mission field, where isolated missions and their employees were positioned in close proximity to Maori settlements. During the mid-1840s, with the support of Governor George Grey, the Reverend Morgan (CMS) established a school in the Waikato region, near Otawhao, for "half-caste" children. Morgan's school took in orphans and the children of "poor parents who have large families such as William Turner of the Waipa".[55]

Very quickly, Morgan found his school at the centre of multiple claims and counterclaims about inappropriate conduct by John Edwards, who "formerly lived with me as a Servant". In his defence, Morgan explained that Edwards had "made an offer of marriage to one of the Half Caste girls, which was rejected. From that time he has shown the most malignant feeling towards her and I have since been obliged to discharge him for insolence." After his dismissal, Edwards incited local Maori and settlers to work against the school. He "sent messages or went himself to several of the Parents of the Half caste children to persuade them to remove their children, on the grounds that the School was improperly conducted, [because] I refused to dismiss Girls, [such] as Matilda Moncur, from the establishment. The investigation will prove his motive towards this poor girl, who had rejected his offer of marriage."[56] The claims made against Morgan and his school came only a month before those against Thomas Power in January 1852. Power, formerly an agricultural instructor at the school, had perpetrated physical violence against some Maori men, threatened others, and committed adultery with the wife of another.[57] Maori attempted to exact *muru* (plunder) for these offences by seizing his horses.

Mission servants accused their employers of misconduct, as did Maori communities. A great variety of intimate encounters, involving violence, coercion, adultery, and love, that eventually ended in marriage for some, took place across the New Zealand mission. Accusations against William White of the Methodist Mission, who had spread rumours amongst settlers, Maori and mission authorities about William Yate, demonstrate that a variety of intimate encounters took place between men and their female converts. White was accused of adultery with a Maori woman, as well as the attempted rape of a chief's wife. The records concerning an investigation into the claims against White are listed as "missing" at Archives New Zealand, but the description of their contents are tantalizing. In December 1835, Thomas McDonnell informed the British Resident, James Busby, that he was "now investigating with a committee of chiefs a charge of rape against a missionary. The evidence is only too clear."[58] In the end, William White was dismissed from the mission.[59] Christopher Davies, husband of Marianne Williams, the daughter of CMS missionary Henry Williams, was accused of adultery in 1853. On investigation further sexual transgressions came to light, demonstrating the extent to which Maori had full knowledge of the impropriety of the CMS missionaries. Christopher Davies, it was alleged, sexually abused a Maori woman while performing a medical examination upon her, while Marella Davis, William Colenso, and another missionary, Barker, were all named by Maori as engaged in adulterous relationships.[60] Maori tolerance for sexual indiscretions involving women from their communities was limited, and often involved an immediate response based on Maori custom and justice, such as raiding parties.

Elizabeth Colenso (née Fairburn), a second-generation missionary wife, married to the CMS printer William Colenso, was "greatly scandalized as a consequence"[61] of her husband's affair with their servant Ripeka Meretene who gave birth to a son, Wiremu, in 1851. Bishop Selwyn suspended William from the CMS for he had, admitted William, "deviated from the path of morality". Based at Ahuriri/Napier, and like other missionaries subject to claims of sexual misconduct such as Duncan and Kendall, William was a difficult man, widely viewed by his colleagues and peers as intolerant and dogmatic. Elizabeth's passionless and cold nature has been implicated in his fall, but as Jeanette Cottier demonstrates, the correspondence between William and Elizabeth indicates a loving relationship.[62] William's indiscretion attracted the intervention of church and colonial authorities when Bishop Selwyn and Governor George Grey attempted to return Wiremu to Ripeka's family in 1853. Elizabeth took Wiremu to Auckland when negotiations failed. On arrival in Auckland, Wiremu was refused entry into the Fairburn household by Elizabeth's father, William Fairburn.[63] Ultimately Wiremu's public arrival in Auckland, and his rejection by the Fairburns, forced Elizabeth to surrender her role as protector in light of the wide social disapproval Wiremu's presence in the town attracted.

Elizabeth's case demonstrates that sexuality and intimacy were not absent from missionary texts, both in their public and private forms. In the pages of letters and diaries "marriages between couples of different denominations and races attracted comment, sometimes simply curious, other times condemnatory".[64] George Kissling described the Colenso situation in a letter to Archdeacon Alfred Brown as "the most afflictive and disgraceful shock which our poor Mission has sustained", and a "truly painful case" for all involved.[65] Thomas Grace, CMS missionary at Taupo, noted in his diary the "painful fall of Mr Colenso; it has thrown a gloom over our work here the evils of which have yet to come . . . May God protect His infant Church in this land, and may those of us who think we stand take heed lest we fall."[66] The wider CMS community were well aware of the details of the case, as were settlers and Maori. To Ripeka's community, William Colenso had committed adultery and they were "inclined towards making a great matter of it — to distinguish between right and wrong and because he has endeavoured to keep us down and to raise himself up".[67]

Concluding Comments

Intimate relationships entered into by missionaries, whether they involved the absence of a wife, a difficult relationship with a partner, or sexual encounters across racial and moral boundaries, suggest affection and intimacy were implicated in the success or failure of a mission. Public, official, and political interest and intervention into cases of interracial intimacy, particularly in the cases of Colenso, Kendall, Yates and White, demonstrate the fragility of the colonial project in early New Zealand. There were limits to the acceptance of interracial relationships. Broad missionary practice was to accept interracial unions where they conformed to monogamous relationships and western understandings of respectability. But the official reaction to Kendall and Colenso reveals how far interracial relationships were tolerated: the appropriate place for sexuality was within the bonds of marriage, and only the most degraded men (not married missionaries) engaged in adulterous relationships. Maori leaders tolerated and accepted interracial relationships for a variety of reasons, but like the mission authorities they would not accept the abuse of Maori women, and enacted appropriate and immediate retribution. Interracial relationships took place in numerous British colonies, suggesting a shared colonial experience. Likewise, claims of missionary misconduct, like interracial intimacy, are typical of the missionary experience rather than exceptional to New Zealand.

Interracial intimacy remained of interest to the various missionary societies after the annexation of New Zealand in 1840. In 1856 Bishop Selwyn, who had investigated claims against Richard Morgan in 1851 and sought to intervene in and resolve the scandal surrounding William Colenso in 1853, presented evidence before the Board of Inquiry in Native Affairs in New Zealand. Along with Selwyn, representatives from all mission societies gave evidence before the board, whose committee was particularly interested in how best to deal with mixed descent children, and to encourage loyalty to the government amongst what was claimed as a "new and important class" of people.[68]

Concerns about illegitimacy and inheritance were at the heart of the evidence presented. Governor Grey's proposal of 1847 to enter into relationships of trusteeship for the children, in order to ensure their land rights in case of future abandonment, was given support. The Reverend John Whitely of the Wesleyan Mission at Kawhia proposed that if land grants were made "there should be a difference made between the half-caste children born in wedlock and the illegitimate children. In giving Crown Grants to half-caste children, I think the parents should be required to marry."[69] Not all mission societies agreed on how to deal with interracial intimacy. Before the same Board of Inquiry the Anglican missionary at Opotiki argued that no distinction ought to be made between "those children born in wedlock and otherwise" because in "the eye of the Maori law all these half-castes are legitimate".[70] In general, the views of missionary representatives sat well with Grey's broader policy of racial amalgamation in which Maori were to be assimilated into British institutions, culture and values through capitalism, commerce, and marriage. Interracial intimacy would continue to be of interest to New Zealand and British authorities throughout the remainder of the nineteenth century.

Notes

1 Evidence of Joel Polack, 6 April 1838, Report from the Select Committee of the House of Lords, appointed to Inquire into the Present State of the Islands of New Zealand, and the Expediency of Regulating the Settlement of British Subjects therein (hereafter, Select Committee, 1838), *Great Britain Parliamentary Papers*, 1837–40, p. 83. The author would like to gratefully acknowledge the support of a Royal Society of New Zealand Marsden Fast Start Grant, which enabled the research for this chapter to be completed.
2 Evidence of Dandeson Coates, 14 May 1838, Select Committee, 1838, p. 264.
3 See McKenzie, *Scandal in the Colonies*.
4 Perry, "The Autocracy of Love and the Legitimacy of Empire", p. 262.
5 Rodman, "The Heart in the Archives", p. 296.
6 See Tremewan, "French Tupuna: French-Maori Families".
7 Ballantyne, "The Reform of the Heathen Body", p. 32. Perry, "The Autocracy of Love", p. 282.
8 Perry, "The Autocracy of Love", p. 267.
9 See Stevens, *"Gathering Places"*.
10 R. A. Taylor Journal, 25 October 1842, Special Collections, Auckland City Library.
11 Taylor Journal, 22 April 1843.
12 Bishop Selwyn, Journal of Visitation, 28 January 1844, reproduced in Howard, *Rakiura*, p. 374.

13 Selywn, Visitation, 2 February 1844, in Howard, *Rakiura*, p. 375.

14 Selywn, Visitation, 5 February 1844, in Howard, *Rakiura*, p. 376.

15 Evidence of John Liddiard Nicholas, 3 April 1838, Select Committee, 1838, p. 5.

16 Evidence of John Watkins, 3 April 1838, Select Committee, 1838, p. 19.

17 Evidence of John Flatt, 6 April 1838, Select Committee, 1838, p. 51.

18 Evidence of Robert Fitzroy, 11 May 1838, Select Committee, 1838, p. 161.

19 Perry, "The Autocracy of Love and the Legitimacy of Empire", p. 268.

20 See Biggs, *Maori Marriage*.

21 See Heuer, "Maori Women in Traditional Family and Tribal Life, 1769–1840", pp. 448–94.

22 Binney, "'In-Between' Lives", pp. 93–118; Salesa, *Race Mixing*; Wanhalla, *In/visible Sight*; Stevens, *"Gathering Places"*; Wanhalla, "'One white man I like very much', pp. 34–56; Anderson, *Race Against Time*. Riddell, *A 'Marriage of the Races'?*

23 Perry, "The Autocracy of Love", 269.

24 Johannes Wohlers, Travel Report, 1 May 1845, Wohlers Papers, 0428-04a, Alexander Turnbull Library, Wellington, hereafter ATL.

25 Wohlers, Travel Report, 1 May 1845, Wohlers Papers, 0428-04a, ATL.

26 Wohlers, Travel Report, 31 December 1845, Wohlers Papers, 0428-04a, ATL.

27 Wohlers, 31 December 1845, Wohlers Papers, 0428-04a, ATL.

28 Wohlers, 19 February 1846, Wohlers Papers, 0428-04a, ATL.

29 Journal of James Watkin, 8 March 1841, MS-0440/04, Hocken Collections, Dunedin, hereafter, HC.

30 Wohlers, Ruapuke Report, 31 December 1845, Wohlers Papers, 0428-04a, ATL.

31 Kelm, *Colonizing Bodies*, p. 15.

32 Dieffenbach, *Travels in New Zealand*, p. 42.

33 Wohlers Report, 1 May 1845, Wohlers Papers, 0428-04a, ATL.

34 Wohlers, 31 December 1845, Wohlers Papers, 0428-04a, ATL.

35 See Stevens, *"Gathering Places"*.

36 Wohlers, 19 February 1846, Visitation, Wohlers Papers, MS-Papers-0428-04a, ATL.

37 Wohlers, Travel Report, 30 June–17 July 1846, Wohlers Papers, MS-Papers-0428-04a, ATL.

38 Wohlers, 5 June 1855, Wohlers Papers, MS-Papers-0428-05a, ATL.

39 Wohlers, Ruapuke Report, 2 February 1845, Wohlers Papers, 0428-04a, ATL.

40 Wohlers, Ruapuke Report, 1 May 1845, Wohlers Papers, 0428-04a, ATL.

41 Quarterly Report, 1 July–30 September 1848, Wohlers Papers, MS-Papers-0428-04b, ATL.

42 Ruapuke Report, 31 December 1845, Wohlers Papers, 0428-04A, ATL.

43 Wohlers to Bremen Mission, 19 July 1849, Wohlers Papers, MS-Papers-428-04c, ATL.

44 Wohlers, fragment of letter, 1858, Wohlers Papers, MS-Papers-0428-05a, ATL.

45 Ballhatchet, *Race, Sex and Class Under the Raj*, p. 4.

46 Perry, "The Autocracy of Love", pp. 269–70.

47 Perry, "The Autocracy of Love", p. 278.

48 Perry, "The Autocracy of Love",, p. 263. See Backhouse, *Colour-Coded*.

49 Johnston, *Missionary Writing and Empire*, p. 16.

50 Johnston, *Missionary Writing and Empire*, p. 49. Carey, "Companions in the Wilderness?" p. 230.

51 Carey, "Companions in the Wilderness?" p. 230.

52 Binney, *The Legacy of Guilt*, p. 19.
53 See Brickell, *Mates and Lovers*, pp. 23–30. Binney, "Whatever Happened to Poor Mr Yate?" Also see Wallace, *Sexual Encounters*.
54 Brickell, *Mates and Lovers*, p. 29.
55 R. A. Morgan to George Grey, 31 December 1849, in Grey: New Zealand Letters, Special Collections, Auckland City Library.
56 Morgan to Grey, 31 December 1851.
57 Morgan to Grey, 14 January 1852.
58 Thomas McDonnell to James Busby, 24 December 1835, BR 1/2, Archives New Zealand, Wellington, hereafter ANZ-W.
59 Macdonald, Penfold and Williams (eds.), *The Book of New Zealand Women*. Cottier, *Elizabeth Fairburn/Colenso*, p. 131. Some of William and Elizabeth Colenso's letters, as well as correspondence between other CMS missionaries about the Colenso scandal, have been published in Porter and Macdonald (eds.) *'My Hand Will Write What My Heart Dictates'*.
60 Cottier, *Elizabeth Fairburn/Colenso*, pp. 136–7.
61 Elizabeth Colenso to William Colenso, 27 May 1854, in Porter and Macdonald, *'My Hand Will Write What My Heart Dictates'*, p. 301.
62 Cottier, *Elizabeth Fairburn/Colenso*, pp. 19–22.
63 Cottier, *Elizabeth Fairburn/Colenso*, pp. 137–43. Elizabeth Colenso to William Colenso, 19 December 1853, in Porter and Macdonald, *'My Hand Will Write What My Heart Dictates'*, p. 300.
64 Porter and Macdonald, *'My Hand Will Write What My Heart Dictates'*, p. 190.
65 George Kissling to Alfred Brown, 28 October 1852, in Porter and Macdonald, *'My Hand Will Write What My Heart Dictates'*, p. 297.
66 Diary of T. S. Grace, 7 January 1853, Grace Family Papers, MS-Papers-4760-2, ATL.
67 Hoani Niania to Donald McLean, 24 July 1852, in Ross, *Women with a Mission*, p. 115.
68 Evidence of Bishop George Selwyn before the Board of Inquiry into Native Affairs, 8 April 1856, G 51/1, ANZ-W.
69 Evidence of John Whitely before the Board of Inquiry, 7 April 1856, G 51/1, ANZ-W.
70 Evidence of J. Wilson, 5 May 1856, G 51/1, ANZ-W.

CHAPTER FOUR

Contested Conversions
Missionary Women's Religious Encounters in Early Colonial Uganda

ELIZABETH E. PREVOST

The first British women missionaries to Uganda arrived in 1895 amidst a seeming victory of British colonialism and Protestant Christianity. The creation of a British Protectorate had solidified the mutual interests of the Ganda oligarchy and the Church Missionary Society (CMS), stabilizing prior political upheaval and enshrining the success story of Christian mission which had garnered a legendary reputation in metropolitan missionary literature. This narrative recalled the dedication and self-sacrifice of early missionaries and Ganda Christians under the persecution of Mwanga's regime in the 1880s, which culminated in the famous martyrdom of Bishop Hannington in 1885 and the expulsion and death of many Ganda Christians in the second half of the decade — events that were widely recounted in Britain and other mission fields. Missionaries' representation of the Baganda's particular spiritual and intellectual receptivity to Christianity commended the speed with which indigenous evangelists had spread the Gospel, the fortitude of their faith under persecution, and the sincerity of people's adherence to Protestantism, exemplified by impressive numbers of baptisms and a seemingly inevitable progression towards a native church.[1] The missionary women's own arduous journey 800 miles inland and the overwhelming reception they received in Mengo (the capital) seemed to confirm that they were poised to play a role in a great drama of the globalization and indigenization of Christianity.[2]

Yet this teleological narrative did not presage the real experience of Uganda's first Protestant women missionaries. As they began work in the capital and provinces, British women encountered not a triumphal march of the Gospel but rather a messy religious, social, and political terrain in which the terms and meanings of Christianity were still very much being worked out. The boundaries of converted and non-Christian politics and identity were far from clear, and the social and political privilege that became attached to conversion incited concern among missionaries that the colonial Protestant state was in fact a haven for secularism and materialism, leading missionaries to try to regain control of the Christian message. The fact that white women had not been part of this mission before presented these new missionaries with a challenge as well as an opportunity to shape the terms of this process. However, as missionary women themselves encountered Christianity in unexpected ways, they also quickly realized their dependence on African women in navigating an unfamiliar social and ideological landscape.

The rich literature on the relationship of religion and empire in East Africa has not focused on women's role in brokering this unstable mission and colonial culture.[3] By comparison, those who have investigated the gendered dimensions of colonial and missionary encounters in this region have largely concentrated on domesticity, motherhood, education, and medicalization.[4] This scholarly focus reflects the historical bias of Protestant mission organizations, which assigned women's work to the "cultural" sphere of evangelism, but does not take into account the informal ways in which women asserted religious authority. Although more overtly cultural programs were crucial to feminizing the missionary endeavour, they should not obscure the equal importance of religion as a medium of dialogue. Nor should tracking the terms and meanings of female Christianity assume a forgone hegemony of gendered bourgeois values and discursive forms.[5] The case of Uganda shows that early missionary women did not have the upper hand in these negotiations, and were not in a position to impose a western form of Christianity; instead, local factors compelled them to re-evaluate their strategies in collaboration with indigenous women.

This chapter, therefore, suggests one way in which missionaries themselves might be considered products of the mission encounter, by showing some of the religious consequences of the feminization of mission work. Although missionaries initially "read" the African landscape through preconceived social categories, they were forced to re-think some of these markers as they came face to face with the inadequacy of evangelical norms of conversion, metropolitan narratives of the indigenization of Christianity, and institutional gendering of missionary spheres. Missionaries' interactions with Ugandan women highlighted the problems of bifurcating "real" and "nominal" conversion and offered new ways of interrogating the spiritual and practical manifestations of Christian persuasion.

The Uses and Limits of Conversion

The CMS had begun operating in Buganda in the late 1870s, after *Kabaka* Mutesa[6] extended an explicit invitation (via Henry M. Stanley) to Protestant Christian missionaries.[7] Unlike other parts of East, West, and southern Africa, where missionaries had a longer-established presence in conjunction with or independently of older forms of colonialism, the extension of Anglican evangelism to Uganda overlapped with Britain's part in the "new imperialism" of the late nineteenth century. The conflicts over kingly succession in the 1880s which mapped Muslim, Christian, and traditional religious identities onto older regional political rivalries — culminating in the famous martyrdoms — prompted British assistance, and the 1894 Protectorate and the 1900 Uganda Agreement established the British colonial presence within the framework of Ganda Protestant Christianity's dominance over competing politico-religious factions.[8] Protestantism was crucial to extending the kingdom's political hegemony over outlying districts, and the new Ganda succession mobilized the symbolic utility of

Protestant Christianity in legitimating membership in the new political order. The outward markers of conversion — baptism, literacy and education, church participation, material culture — signified allegiance to the *Kabaka* as much as to Christ. At the same time, the civil wars had eroded the authority of the office of the *Kabaka* and ultimately strengthened the Ganda Protestant oligarchy.[9] Evangelism became a way to solidify the chiefs' stake in the royal succession and courtly political culture, as well as providing non-elites with an entree into and leverage within that establishment. The large-scale, expeditious spread of Christianity by Ganda evangelists in Buganda and into neighbouring kingdoms, therefore, signified political incentive and social mobility as much as it did evangelical motivation.[10] Although this hegemony exacerbated political relations outside Buganda, evangelism also provided competing factions with a way to leverage their position within inter-kingdom and colonial configurations of power. While stationed in Bunyoro between 1902 and 1906, Elizabeth Chadwick received a visit from a deputation from another northern province who "came to demand a missionary for their tribe; why should the Baganda and Banyoro be taught, and they be left in ignorance?"[11]

Missionary expectations about indigenous Christianity, however, did not always cohere with political ones. In the mid-1890s missionaries began to display uncertainty about the conditions out of which these numbers grew and to re-evaluate the motivation behind peoples' adherence to Christianity, questioning the validity of many conversions. The CMS charged missionaries with the task of redirecting Christianization away from what it called "nominal adhesion" or "fashionable profession" of Christianity and instead toward "practical" Christianity, whereby outward manifestation of religious affiliation would reflect inner devotion. Protestants were not content to establish a Christian state in name only, but rather aimed to create a comprehensive Christian society — manifested not in European material culture, but in moral, social, and religious practices. Of course, missionaries' means of signifying the spiritual dynamic were often the very markers of confessional identity which became increasingly unreliable in the face of political and social utility: baptism and confirmation, church attendance, proficiency in scripture, evangelistic careers, and certain lifestyle changes. Furthermore, the manifestations of godliness missionaries sought to denote converts' inner conviction — humility, repentance, piety, moral rectitude — proved just as liable to the conditionality of outward appearance.

The CMS's decision to send women to Buganda and surrounding provinces was inseparable from these developments. Women's entrance into the Uganda mission field formed part of a larger program of consolidating the mission church after the first wave of evangelism in the 1870s and 80s. The infrastructure that accompanied Britain's annexation of Uganda made this possible: major developments in transportation overrode the perceived liabilities of female travel to and life in the interior, and provided the final impetus for the CMS to dispatch single women beginning in 1895. By the time these women missionaries began to arrive, the mission was moving away from the evangelical revivalist mode of the earlier years and towards formalized programs in literacy, baptism and confirmation preparation, healthcare, and lay and clergy evangelist training.[12] After the establishment of the first generation of Ganda Christians, missionaries generally preferred to let African evangelists take charge of the apostolic dynamic of conversion while they devoted their attentions to institution-building. Missionary women's role in this phase of mission work was a varied enterprise. The CMS divided women's work into evangelical, educational, and medical branches, with separate women in charge of each; among the 1895 party, Edith Furley and Mary Thomsett were charged with evangelistic and "spiritual instruction", Eleanor Browne and Elizabeth Chadwick assumed school teaching, and Eliza Pilgrim worked in a medical capacity.[13] In practice, however, there was a high degree of ideological and practical fluidity among these categories.

Women missionaries initially encountered a CMS bias against working with African women who had not already converted, reflecting an operative missionary ideology of gendering evangelistic spheres. Men were entrusted with introducing Christianity while women were charged with solidifying it through cultural institutions after converts' baptisms. Those women missionaries whose work was deemed "evangelistic" were expected to train evangelists or to prepare those who had already been admitted as candidates for baptism. The CMS instructed the first party of women that the advanced state of evangelization in Uganda merited a focus on Christian women:

> In some fields the Missionary who finds herself called upon to work among Christians chafes at being kept from touch with the actual heathen. In this mission, at least, any such thought would be a serious temptation . . . Here you will often find them, to your hands, ready won, and the many earnest but as yet little-skilled workers are daily winning more. Your privileged lot will be to guide and train them as Christian witnesses and workers.[14]

These instructions put forward a simplistic idea of conversion as a definitive and irrevocable condition that baptism would seal; women were meant to step into the process at this point and leave earlier stages of evangelism to male missionaries and African catechists.

This theoretical separation of converted and non-converted could not be sustained in the Ugandan mission field, however, because Christian and non-Christian cosmologies and social contours were too fluid for missionaries to be able to separate their work among women. The CMS was the most evangelically-inclined of the three Anglican missionary societies operating in Africa; this Protestant theological bent traditionally assumed a watershed moment in every convert's experience whereby sin was confessed and repented, and the old life and mindset left behind.[15] Missionaries dichotomized the Christianizing process between temporal and spiritual dispositions, treating the outward practice of Christianity as a cultural, intellectual, or moral condition that reflected inward purity and strength of conviction. Yet the evangelical requirement of renouncing one religious system to adopt another and instilling an exclusive "belief" in God ran counter to the fluidity and selectivity of African cosmologies. British women encountered Christians and non-Christians alike who felt that adherence to a single object of worship or source of revelation was tantamount to denying broader sources of protection for oneself and one's community. Chadwick spoke of how acts of nature could either endorse or condemn Christian credibility. On her first visit to the compound of the Nyoro queen sister, the missionary party was entering the compound when "there was a slight earth tremor, and the gateposts, each composed of three or four stout poles stuck in the ground and encased in polished reeds, seemed to bend as if saluting us and then stood upright again. The great lady's retainers, and indeed she herself also, regarded us with considerable awe and veneration on account of this." On the other hand:

> less auspicious was another slight earthquake which occurred just as we had pitched tent on one of our first visits to a country village for a weekend. Here the peasants, in spite of anything the young catechist could say, were convinced that the spirits were furious at our invading the district, and none of them dared come round to welcome us or listen to our words on that occasion.[16]

Cosmological and temporal pragmatism were not necessarily at odds in Uganda, where religion functioned as a source of political utility and as a guard against natural disaster and physical malady.

The diversity of the social landscape mirrored the cosmological one: Protestants, Catholics, and non-Christians shared the same political, familial, and healing spaces. Chadwick wrote of a visit to Mutesa's tomb where she encountered an eclectic group gathered for singing: "All the women of the neighborhood, heathen, R[oman] C[atholic]s and Protestants collected in Mtesa's tomb drumming and chanting some of their queer songs in high good humor while a couple of young girls in turn danced in the open space in the middle." The music bridged the divergent religious expressions that the *lubiri* (royal residence) encompassed, although Chadwick also qualified that "there are very few real Christians inside that lubiri, though a good many nominal ones".[17] Mission centres also provided medical and social services for non-Christian as well as Christian women. When Nabunya, a non-Christian wife of Mwanga, gave birth to his sickly second son, the Katikiro arranged for an annex to be built in Namirembe's mission compound so that Misses Timpson and Taylor could provide constant care.[18]

To offset the potential detachment of the Christian message from Christian institutions, these medical missionaries tried as much as possible to tie healthcare directly with the Gospel, and the Gospel with literacy. While lending a hand at a mission stopover in Kenya, Beatrice Glass commented on the modus operandi of her host Miss Bazett's medical visitations: "She was armed with a Gospel and hymn book and lint and ido-form and boracic acid and a good big syringe."[19] Free medical treatment was usually contingent upon participation in reading classes and hospital worship services. Ruth Hurditch related the policy of the Mengo hospital that required the outpatients to attend a half-hour service and hour-long reading class in the outer court before they would be treated, and shut the gate to any "late comers who might care for the medicine without the service".

Hurditch later instituted this policy in her Toro dispensary.[20] Yet Chadwick's medical itinerating in Hoima revealed that Africans' interest in mission services far exceeded the interest in evangelization: "if you find half a dozen baptized in a meeting of seventy or eighty it is quite wonderful".[21] Missionaries had difficulty reconciling pragmatic uses of mission institutions with their own hope that belief in God and personal uprightness would constitute their own reward rather than a means to material status, prosperity, or safety.

In the absence of clear demarcations of social space around Christian and non-Christian, and Protestant and Catholic identities and practices, and in the midst of suspicion about "nominal Christianity," the first women missionaries used prior frames of reference around class and gender to map Christianization on to Ganda womanhood. Some missionaries construed levels of Christianization along a gendered gradation, whereby baptism functioned as a marker of domestication and feminization only when it was accompanied by true inner sanctity. During her first days in Mengo, Edith Furley contrasted her reception by King Mwanga's chief wife, Lois Rose, a baptized Christian, with that of the *Namasole*, his non-Christian queen mother. Her first impression of Lois Rose was that of an accommodating woman with a docile demeanour, seated on the floor among other Christian women whose "real joy at our arrival was one of the most touching things I ever saw". The *Namasole*, by contrast, she described as:

> a regular heathen Princess, with a grim hard face that made one quite believe her capable of all the many acts of cruelty which they say she has committed. She was seated in state on an embroidered Indian rug spread on the ground, holding a large knife in her hand, made of copper and brass mixed, and was most autocratic in the way in which she ordered us to stand up and sit down, that she might get every possible view of me. One could not help contrasting her with the Christian women here, the difference is most marked. Some of the latter are sweet women, it is a pleasure to know them and be their friends.[22]

Furley cast the *Namasole* as despotic, untamed, and warrior-like (marked by her independence from and resistance to Christianity), against the example of the Christian women's affectionate and ladylike qualities. Chadwick similarly contrasted the warm and gracious welcome she received on her visits to Sara Bweyinda, a member of a local chief's household on Lusaka hill, with her inhospitable reception on the other side of the hill where the *Namasole* lived. The *Namasole* converted to Christianity later in life, but while Chadwick knew her she characterized her heathenness as masculine barbarity, typified by an infamous story of her killing a young child who had violated one of the household rules.[23]

Yet it did not always work to divide converted and non-converted status along neatly gendered lines, particularly in missionaries' day-to-day encounters. Some missionaries, for example, encountered Christian predispositions outside the formal boundaries of conversion, in cases where indigenous women were not at liberty to convert. Beatrice Glass commented that she met women who were "Christians at heart and lack the courage to confess in baptism, but their homes and their children are very different to heathen homes and children. I visited two side by side today and saw."[24] Ruth Hurditch, on the other hand, separated the marked improvement in Christian lifestyle from what she saw lacking in the Banyoro's spiritual union with Christ. For her, lifestyle changes could not exist in a vacuum; inner conviction made the difference between outward appearance as cultural expression versus moral behaviour. Cultural change was a byproduct rather than the object of Christianization:

> As to the religious condition of the people, one finds after a while that true deep spirituality is little known among them. Of course there are some grand exceptions — Religion seems to effect a moral change in their lives — their heathen practices are abolished, bigamy discountenanced, and for two years they will come regularly to church, reading of the Gospels, then they will go on into the other classes, but vital union and fellowship with Christ is scarcely manifest.[25]

These examples illustrate missionaries' frustration with how to identify and foster true Christian intention when neither baptism nor behaviour offered a dependable indicator. Questioning whether conversion and Christianization constituted the same process, missionary women began to re-evaluate different vehicles of catechesis and their meaning for African women as well as themselves. In the process, early groups of women missionaries depended heavily on the assistance and initiative of Ganda Christian women in feminizing Christianity.

Mediating the Word

The first wave of Christian evangelism and church leadership in Uganda was tied to the political consolidation of the Ganda Protestant oligarchy. Moreover, the prevention of white women's presence in Uganda before 1895 meant that the first female Christianizing efforts came from African women's incentive. Many prominent Ganda women had become Christians before white women's arrival; by the time women missionaries began operating in Mengo and provincial mission centers, a significant core of royal women and chiefs' wives were involved in evangelistic efforts to spread Protestant Christianity.

British women's class-oriented perception of the local social fabric influenced the strategies and relationships they formed with African women. Missionaries sought elite Ganda women as evangelistic partners on the assumption that their political networks would best facilitate the dissemination of the Word. Women of royal and chiefly households were also among the first to convert, and they were most receptive to missionaries. The King's chief wife, Lois Rose, was one of the first to greet the five women missionaries in 1895.[26] By the following year, ten of the King's wives had been baptized and were under the instruction of the first female mission party, as were Damali (Mwanga's queen sister), the attendants of Mutesa's tomb at Kasubi, and the members of the household of Mwanga's queen mother (*Namasole*), even though this went against her own wishes before she herself converted.[27] Every *Kabaka* took his own queen mother and queen sister upon accession, and women in these offices held their own courts in separate *lubiri* (royal compounds). The status of royal women rendered the security of the

Elizabeth E. Prevost

Ganda Protestant establishment equally important to women's work as it was to other mission and colonial politics. Remarking on the changes in women's positions that accompanied the new infant king Daudi's installation in 1897, Furley remarked on the importance of having Protestant women in key offices, albeit ones whose version of Christianity was in line with that of missionaries: "[Agari's] retirement no one can regret as, though baptised, her life has been a disgrace to the religion she professed. We are hoping to get a good Christian woman appointed to take charge of Uniya and her household until she is of an age to govern herself."[28]

Equally central to early mission work were chiefs' wives, because of their bases in outlying regions and their mobility between those regions and the capital, which enabled them to train and teach for a time in Mengo, before taking up work in their own districts. This sometimes rendered the work force in Mengo itself sporadic: the war of succession and "Sudanese rebellion" in the late 1890s temporarily stalled mission work in the capital, since chiefs' wives and their attendants had to return to the countryside to help secure their landholdings, which in turn depleted large numbers of teachers and students. But these political instabilities also provided new opportunities for Christian wives to move to the forefront of evangelism in country districts. Women took up the bulk of evangelistic work in the absence of husbands who were engaged in military campaigns, such as Emma, the wife of a chief near Mitiyana, who took refuge in Mengo but returned to her own region when she realized there was no other catechist to carry on mission work.[29] After the war a new generation of Christians took up work in the wake of displaced chiefs, and the missionaries placed high hopes on the calibre of their wives who would serve as teachers. When a new Christian chief in Singo assumed power after the fall of one of Mwanga's followers, Furley highlighted on the teaching of Labeka, the new *Mukwenda's* wife, as a lynchpin in the evangelization of the region.[30]

Elite women were, of course, in a better position to engage in unpaid work that was not tied to seasonal labor, but missionaries assumed that their adoption of evangelism would require them to forgo other duties and revoke traditional gender roles. In 1902 Hurditch commended the first deputation of licensed women in Toro, which included several prominent women from the royal household. Among them were: Ana Kageye, an "important woman chief" and head of the King's household; Minka Kabaheta, the King's cousin and a member of the queen mother's court; Basimasi Wenkeri, also a member of the Royal Court; and Mai Gatoma, a former wife of the King. She remarked:

Our first ten women missionaries from among the Batoro have been dismissed. We had a very large farewell meeting and it was very touching to see these brave women rise and testify to all their willingness to leave home and loved ones for His sake and the Gospel's. What this means to them we can scarcely understand, for the Batoro women have always led such a sheltered and dependent position.[31]

In Ankole and Buganda, the structuring of women's royal households (*lubiri*) rendered evangelistic work among women reminiscent of *zenana* visiting in India, which may have been a more familiar physical framework for some missionaries (from either missionary literature or experience) in which to foster an exclusively female association.[32] There were reportedly twenty-eight *lubiri* housing former kings' tombs in Buganda at the turn of the century, the older and less prominent of which Chadwick said were "in a state of great decay and the women in abject poverty, so that the fences had become very black spots for drink and immorality." At the other extreme was Kasubi, the compound housing Mutesa's and Mwanga's tombs, which was "kept up in considerable state" by seven principle widows and many more "inferior wives and slaves".[33] Chadwick held regular women's classes here assisted by Damali, Mwanga's queen sister and a prominent catechist who lived in a *lubiri* on the other side of the hill. Damali always hosted meals at her *lubiri* after the classes, during which Chadwick relied on Damali's lady-in-waiting, Juliya, to guide her in the unfamiliar Ganda etiquette of washing and eating rituals.[34] With the start of girls' formal education around 1900, girl pupils who were members of various *lubiri* provided other missionaries an entree into these enclosures and helped them navigate unfamiliar customs that accompanied their visits, such as cautioning them which beverages were alcoholic and which were *Mubisi* ("temperance drink").[35]

No evangelistic forum revealed missionaries' reliance upon African women's guidance more than linguistic training. The CMS made clear to missionary women before they even began their service that the success of Christianity was at stake in missionaries' linguistic capability. Advising at least eight months' study in the field before taking up serious work, the CMS warned that "by using a language foreign to the people you might delay and even permanently injure your intended usefulness, which can only be at its best when you have adequately learned Luganda".[36] Women experienced this contingency all too keenly, and occasionally complained that this language policy did not reflect the vernacular realities of the field. Ruth Hurditch felt at a disadvantage when she was required to spend time preparing for a Luganda exam, which she wouldn't actually use in her teaching in Bunyoro.[37] Only upper-class men and a few women understood it, and none of the labouring classes; moreover, privileging Luganda fuelled the tensions of Ganda evangelism. Luganda catechesis, therefore, met with significant opposition, which Hurditch felt was well-deserved: "it seems that until these people can have their own religion and reading in their own tongue, Christianity will remain more or less outside their actual lives".[38]

Thus, missionaries knew all too well how important linguistic proficiency was to their evangelistic credibility: fluency in local tongues accorded authority over the direction of the Christian message. Edith Furley felt perpetually self-conscious about her weak language aptitude, which she considered an evangelistic impediment that undermined her authority in baptism and confirmation classes:

> Oh friends do pray definitely about this language difficulty, for it is a real difficulty to me; when you have spent a long time over your preparation and taken great pains to try and get your words right, and you come out from your class utterly small and humbled, knowing that any one of those women you have been trying to teach, could have taken the class infinitely better than you have done![39]

Furley's comment indicated how, in the midst of these kinds of vulnerabilities, British women came to acknowledge their concurrent dependence on African women.

At the same time, language study became a medium for forming closer relationships among women. Beatrice Glass preferred the help of Africans in practising her conversation skills, seeking them out through informal visitations because she felt less self-conscious with Ganda women than with Europeans.[40] Furley, having worked in Mombasa before joining the Uganda party, spoke some Swahili and appreciatively grasped the few chances women provided her of interpreting Luganda through that medium. Furley acknowledged her debt to the wife of Henry Wright Duta (one of the first ordained Anglicans in Buganda and a prominent church leader):

> Sarah Duta has been an immense help to us; when we were first left with only servants to whom we could not speak a word, she used to come in every day, and . . . acted as interpreter between myself, and Hannah, and the children. I don't know what we should have done without her those first days, she truly was a friend in need, ready to do anything, and an immense help in many ways.[41]

Furley also spoke of Mirembe, her first Luganda teacher, as someone whose role took on a nurturing and spiritual character as their relationship developed: "She loved to come and sit on a mat beside me, holding my hand, and several times we read the Testament together, she correcting my stumbling reading." When she and Furley fell ill simultaneously, Mirembe improved first and visited Furley throughout her convalescence: "She sat down on the mat by the bedside, she stroked my hand, she measured my wrists between her finger and thumb, and mourned over my loss of flesh. She passed her hand over me, and over the bedclothes; evidently she thought that I had no body at all . . . Now that I am better, she is greatly rejoiced; yesterday she took me for a walk."[42]

Scriptural and linguistic training went hand in hand, and multi-sided pedagogy was often the result. Confirmation preparation became a site for linguistic and evangelistic collaboration between Furley and her Ganda teacher, Ada Lumonde, prompted by the failure of over twenty candidates on the examination:

> When they came back to me in the school, I said to my great friend among the teachers Ada Lumonde 'What shall we do with this big class, there is no teacher unless you will take them?' She answered 'You must take them and I will help you' and somehow we came to this arrangement to take the class between us, she enlarging on my words and explaining them to the class; and it is a great encouragement to me to feel that it is easier to me now to speak than when we began, and I know by the way she repeats what I say when I have spoken correctly and my meaning has been clear.[43]

Furley reported the initial failure as a jointly empowering experience in which each brought different areas of expertise to an evangelistic endeavour, advancing Furley's language skills and Lumonde's teacher training while also benefiting the confirmation class. She further described the inspiration that came to her and Ada, as well as to the students, as a result of their collective engagement with the book of Romans:

I don't think I ever felt so strongly before the difference between the 7th and 8th chapters of Romans and I can't forget Ada's bright face as she looked up at me and repeated my words to the class that 'now we had come out from under the law and stood in the grace of Jesus Christ.' As we began to read Romans VIII — we have been three days over this chapter and it has been a wonderful chapter to both teachers and class — we had a very interesting talk one morning on the 'Redemption of the Body' (Rom. VIII:23) which showed a new thought to some of them, and one woman told me afterwards that now she should understand better what we meant in church when we said 'I believe in the Resurrection of the <u>Body</u>.'[44]

The student's new understanding gratified Furley because she felt it deepened the theological and devotional meaning of the passages for each of them. In the end, every single student who had previously failed the examination passed it the next time, a source of great affirmation for Furley as well as the confirmands:

The same party of women came tearing down the hillside to meet us, clapping their hands and shouting for glee, they had all passed, every one, or as they expressed it, they were 'all healed,' a much more expressive expression. I did rejoice with them most heartily, not only because of their joy, but because it showed they had understood, what I felt I had so lamely and so stumblingly tried to teach them.[45]

Yet women like Furley always qualified these signs of encouragement with the caveat that the possibility for converts' regression was never far behind, citing some baptized Christians who were "falling away into great sin" (in this instance, intemperance) after their initial enthusiasm and moral rectitude.[46] This conditionality led women to examine more closely the nature of the baptismal commitment itself. Women working in Buganda and Toro gave detailed descriptions of what a baptismal course entailed, including catechism classes and a corresponding exam, regular interviews with a catechist, classes covering Matthew and John which were then examined by a Ganda clergyman, and then a final interview with a European missionary; moreover, in the weeks before someone's baptism, banns were read in church to give anyone the opportunity of opposing the person's candidacy.[47] This rigorous training assumed a high level of dedication, suggesting that the commitment would not have been taken lightly by either candidates or catechists. Ruth Hurditch, however, commented that the literacy requirement was problematic. On one hand, it ensured that no one would take up Christianity lightly, but on the other it was subject to different interpretation by Africans, and put those who did not already read at a disadvantage:

Besides these hundred and thirty [recently baptized], many, many more are finishing the reading requirements and will soon be ready for questioning. You will see that there are drawbacks to this method, it means a long time if people cannot even understand the alphabet, which involves going to school first. A chief or a very ignorant peasant must possess a very real desire if they are willing to go through all this, but there are many. Then, also, there are those who mistake Christianity for some standard of learning, and think if they can only read Matthew and John they are quite entitled to baptism. We have had long talks over this, but cannot decide yet as to a better test . . . It would be dreadful to enroll converts more speedily if the practical life of Christianity were nothing more than a structure with a heathen basis and embellishment.[48]

Hurditch acknowledged the difficulty of finding viable alternatives that would ensure both accessibility and serious commitment to the baptismal covenant. Some missionaries encouraged confirmation as a regular aspect of conversion, rather than as an extra step for the truly committed. Confirmation presented a ready way of rendering the baptismal commitment a more meaningful institution, since confirmation candidates went through a similar process as those preparing for baptism. Women missionaries considered it a particularly spiritually charged sacrament, and they recommended the eve of confirmation to be a fruitful moment to approach candidates with a "special appeal" about conducting evangelistic work.[49] Baptism's repeated critique as an appropriate marker of conversion prompted women to scrutinize the institution itself as well as to seek out supplemental mediums of religious expression.

Thus, women construed Christianization as a multi-faceted spiritual endeavour that could neither be neatly divided into stages nor declared at a definitive end after baptism. They were also forced to acknowledge their own limitations and accommodate those limitations constructively to the larger evangelistic process. Many missionary women represented their role as merely facilitative and celebrated the fact that African women's capabilities more than compensated for their own failings:

The work here grows more interesting and wonderful every day, especially when one considers the smallness of the means that has been so used to the feeding of these multitudes . . . indeed what has already been done in this way without much organization and the competency of those already teaching fills us with wonder more than anything else . . . [50]

Missionary women thus acknowledged the ways in which their own weaknesses opened certain opportunities for African women.

Concluding Comments

British women entered the evangelistic arena in Uganda at an explosive historical moment when religious identity carried intense political import. Protestant Christianity provided a point of collusion between the various players on the colonial stage, a means to political and social advancement and a way of solidifying British and Ganda colonial interests. Yet missionaries found themselves in the tenuous position of sharing a convenient infrastructure with the Ganda and British political establishment while disagreeing with their ideological deployment of Christianity. The Uganda mission's broader uncertainly about what constituted Christianization put women missionaries in a peculiar position between the evangelical imperatives of heartfelt conversion and institutional consolidation. Female missionaries' own wariness of conversion as a stable category arose from their experiences with both baptized and unbaptized women who belied traditional understandings of how the Christianizing process should unfold in social terms. Since missionaries were not in a position to claim total authority over the Christian message and its manifestations, their evangelistic goals depended on women who had already converted as well as allowing the conversion process to become itself a medium of two-way knowledge.

More broadly, the case of Anglican women in early colonial Uganda signals how missionaries' encounters with African women informed attempts to claim a new female evangelistic space. Alternatively engaging with and circumventing prevailing understandings of Christianity's function in colonial society, women also enacted new vehicles for female empowerment in an evolving mission church that was ostensibly patriarchal. Investigating the collaborative underpinnings of female religious authority and its intervention into the contested meanings of conversion and Christianization might therefore offer ways of exploring further how evangelism mediated African and European cultural expression.

Notes

1   By 1897 the Church Missionary Society (hereafter the CMS) listed 200 churches and native clergy, 200 native teachers, 500 local contacts for itinerant evangelists, 800 attendees at the monthly Mengo missionary meetings to hear reports of returning evangelists, and 13,211 Testaments and portions of Scripture sold in one ten-month period. Stock, *Story of the Year*, 1895–6, pp. 20–1; Stock, *Story of the Year*, 1896–7, p. 25; and Stock, *Story of the Year*, 1900–1, p. 19; Stock, *The History of the Church Missionary Society*, vol. III, pp. 410–27; CMS Archives, University of Birmingham G3 A7/O/1900/153; Acc. 167 F3/8.

2   Stock, *Story of the Year*, 1895–6, pp. 17–18. For further exploration, see Prevost, *Feminizing Missions*.

3   Hansen, *Mission, Church and State*; Pirouet, *Black Evangelists*; Twaddle, "The Emergence of Politico-Religious Groupings"; Strayer, *The Making of Mission Communities*.

4   One notable exception is Hodgson, *The Church of Women*. On medicalization, maternalism, and/or domesticity in East and Central African missions, see Beidelman, "Altruism and Domesticity"; Summers, "Intimate Colonialism"; Musisi, "Colonial and Missionary Education"; Musisi, "Morality as Identity"; Musisi, "The Politics of Perception"; Hunt, *A Colonial Lexicon*; Predelli, "Sexual Control and the Remaking of Gender."

5   On the missionary "colonization of consciousness" and its critics, see Comaroff, *Of Revelation and Revolution*; Landau, *Realm of the Word*; Elbourne, *Blood Ground*.

6   Mutesa is also referred to as Mtesa and M'tesa.

7   Stock, *History of the Church Missionary Society*, vol. 3, pp. 94–102; Low, *The Mind of Buganda*, p. 5.

8   The colonial and ecclesiastical boundaries of "Uganda" basically overlapped. Under Lugard's treaty in 1892 which ended the civil war of succession and laid the groundwork for the Protectorate, various politico-ethnic groupings were reassigned both within and outside Buganda: kingdoms became "districts", more generally grouped together as provinces (the western, northern, and eastern provinces surrounding the Buganda province). The Diocese and Protectorate of Uganda encompassed Buganda and the neighbouring

provinces. See Hansen, *Mission, Church and State*, pp. xvi–xix, 48–51; Low, *Mind of Buganda*, pp. 9–41. Outside Buganda, the most important districts for women missionaries' early work were Toro and Ankole to the west, Bunyoro to the north, and Busoga to the east.

9 The Protestant victory over competing Muslim and Catholic factions still required solidification, particularly as it was in a minority position in numerical terms (Catholic adherents far outnumbered any other). The rebellion of 1897 by the ruling King Mwanga against the British Government and its Ganda supporters briefly threatened the Protestant ascendancy; Mwanga's attempt to mobilize support in a Catholic province failed, however, and rival chiefs' and colonial armies suppressed the rebellion one month later. Mwanga's infant son, Daudi Chwa, was installed with Apolo Kagwa, the *Katikiro* (Prime Minister), as his chief regent. The 1900 Agreement endorsed this arrangement, but also transferred the burden of financial tribute from royal fealty to colonial hut tax. CMS G3/A5/O/1897/273&369; G3 A7/O/1900/132. See also Hansen, *Mission, Church, and State*.

10 Pirouet, *Black Evangelists*; Hansen, *Mission, Church and State*.

11 Jane Elizabeth Chadwick papers, CMS Acc. 167 F2/1-2.

12 CMS G3 A7/O/1901/153.

13 "Instructions delivered on May 16th 1895 to the Misses E. M. Furley, M. S. Thompsett, E. L. Pilgrim, E. E. Browne, and J. E. Chadwick, proceeding to the Uganda mission," CMS G3/A5/L7/1895/366-73.

14 "Instructions delivered on May 16th 1895," CMS G3/A5/L7/1895/366-73.

15 Pirouet, *Black Evangelists*, pp. 22–6.

16 Chadwick papers, CMS Acc. 167, F2/1-2.

17 Chadwick to Ethel McGowan, 6 April 1899, CMS Acc. 167, F3.

18 Furley journal-letter, 21 March 1898, CMS G3 A7/O/1898/122.

19 Glass journal letter, CMS G3 A7/O/1900/68. Travel to the interior and the mission stopovers en route were formative to many women's conceptions of the Christianizing process.

20 Hurditch journal letter, 20 April 1900, CMS G3 A7/O/1900/132; 23 July 1900, reprinted in *Footsteps of Truth*, December 1900, 383, CMS G3 A7/O/1900/197.

21 Chadwick to Ethel McGowan, 19 May 1904, CMS Acc. 167, F3.

22 Furley journal-letter, CMS G3 A5/O/1896/67.

23 "Chadwick papers", CMS Acc. 167 F2/1-2.

24 Again, Glass made this observation at a Kenya mission en route to Uganda as a new missionary. Journal letter, CMS G3 A7/O/1900/68.

25 Hurditch to parents, 10 June 1900, CMS G3 A7/O/1900/147.

26 Stock, *Story of the Year*, 1895–6, p. 18; Furley, 7 October 1895, CMS G3 A5/O/1896/67.

27 Stock, *Story of the Year*, 1896–7, p. 26; Chadwick papers, CMS Acc. 167, F2/1-2.

28 Mengo, 13 August 1897, CMS G3 A5/O/1897/369. This forms part of a longer passage explaining the royal offices and the women who filled them, an illustration of how female offices were equally subject to the precariousness of ruling power and religious identity, even within the same royal family unit.

29 Edith Furley, 21 March 1898, CMS G3 A7/O/1898/122.

30 Edith Furley, 21 March 1898, CMS G3 A7/O/1898/122.

31 Hurditch to Miss Jenkins, 16 February 1902, CMS G3 A7/O/1902/79.

32 According to Hurditch, women in Ankole lived "in seclusion as in India, therefore can only be reached by women." CMS G3 A7/O/1902/79.

33 According to Chadwick, Mwanga was unconventionally buried at his father's *lubiri* rather

than his own because the infant King had not moved to a new compound at his accession. CMS Acc. 167, F2/1-2.

34 Chadwick papers, CMS Acc. 167, F2/1-2. Juliya later went on to become an evangelist in Bunyoro.

35 Glass journal-letter, 27 November 1900, CMS G3 A7/O/1901/73.

36 "Instructions delivered on May 16th, 1895," CMS G3 A5/L7. Edith Furley also referenced the Finance Committee's new eight-month recommendation two years later (CMS G3 A5/O/1897/128).

37 Ruth Hurditch, 9 July 1900, CMS G3 A7/O/1900/161.

38 Ruth Hurditch to parents, Kabarole, 10 June 1900, CMS G3 A7/O/1900/147.

39 Mengo, 1 August 1896, CMS G3 A5/O/1896/313.

40 Glass journal-letter, 8 July 1900, CMS G3 A7/O/1900/163.

41 7 October 1895, CMS G3 A5/O/1896/67.

42 7 October 1895, CMS G3 A5/O/1896/67.

43 CMS G3 A5/O/1896/209.

44 CMS G3 A5/O/1896/209.

45 20 May 1896, CMS G3 A5/O/1896/226.

46 5 October 1896, CMS G3 A5/O/1897/3.

47 Glass CMS G3 A7/O/1900/153; Hurditch to parents, 23 July 1900, reprinted in *Footsteps of Truth*, December 1900, 384, CMS G3 A7/O/1900/197. In 1903, women missionaries resolved to standardize female baptismal preparation throughout all diocesan districts. Minutes of Conference of Lady Missionaries, Mengo, 13 May 1903, No. 20, CMS G3 A7/O/1903/124.

48 Hurditch to parents, 23 July 1900, reprinted in *Footsteps of Truth*, December 1900, p. 384, CMS G3 A7/O/1900/197.

49 Minutes of Conference of Lady Missionaries, Mengo, 4 July 1899, No. II.1, CMS G3/A7/O/1899/198.

50 Elizabeth Chadwick to home secretary, 15 June 1896, CMS G3 A5/O/1896/256.

CHAPTER FIVE

"It is No Soft Job to be Performed"
Missionaries and Imperial Manhood in Canada, 1880–1920

MYRA RUTHERDALE

Recent attention to gender history has produced a rich body of literature on the subject of socially constructed gendered behaviours in a wide variety of historical contexts around the globe.[1] This literature has begun to shape new directions in missionary history, both because it has led us to better understand how men's and women's missionary identities were constructed, and because it has helped us to come to terms with how race and gender must be analyzed together in order to grasp how mission movements operated. The study of gender allows us to probe how missionaries were expected to behave in the mission field and how those expectations were either fulfilled or remained illusive. Recent studies on gender and mission have paid particular attention to women, but the history of the mission enterprise during the age of high imperialism can also be understood when a mix of masculinity, empire, and mission are put under the microscope. According to Alison Twells, the connection between all three becomes clear when the relationship between fatherhood and mission is considered: "Good Christian men, as members of a missionary movement for global change, were expected to manage, guide, discipline and nurture 'other' males identified by missionary philanthropic discourses as objects of reform, and in need of careful steering from 'heathen' childhoods to Christian maturity."[2] Part of reaching "Christian maturity" was to embrace the western model of patriarchal household formation. In her assessment of gender and mission Patricia Grimshaw argues similarly that "missionaries had few qualms about asserting to non-western peoples the virtues of their own ideal gender arrangements, with the Christian family as their crucible".[3] Other studies of gender, masculinity and empire have suggested that, at least for those in late-Victorian England, the mission field was frequently seen as a male domain, a place where fantasies created by boyhood adventure novels could be played out, or muscular Christianity reinforced.[4] However, this is not the contention of Mary Taylor Huber and Nancy Lutkehaus who maintain that "no matter how 'muscular' missionaries attempted to be, they were feminized by their ambiguous local alliances and domestic ideals."[5] In a more recent treatment of the topic, Anne O'Brien argues that missionaries "do not feature much in recent writing on imperial masculinities". She seeks in part to correct this imbalance with her discussion, set in northern Australia, of missionaries and the homoerotic gaze during the late-nineteenth and early-twentieth centuries.[6]

Here, I will explore the connection between missionaries, masculinity, and empire in the context of western and northern Canada in the same time period. The missionaries featured here were largely British-born Church Missionary Society (CMS) or Society for the Propagation of the Gospel (SPG) missionaries who came to Canada with the goal of converting Canada's Aboriginal people to Christianity, and at times were meant to work in newly settled western Canadian communities with a mix of Newcomers to Canada and already established Native Canadians.[7]

This chapter interrogates meanings of manhood in three different ways. First, I analyze how missionary manhood was constructed from the home front, or how those recruiting male missionaries described the job. I then consider how the male missionaries themselves reinforced certain ideas of manhood when they were in the field. The third part of the chapter will discuss how missionary men viewed their own masculinity in light of Aboriginal manliness. In this section I will also assess how Aboriginal manhood was constructed. Questions concerning male missionaries' relationships with the natural environment and the outdoor life are also considered. For example, how did missionary men measure their manliness in relation to Aboriginal men in the context of travelling by canoe, procuring food and knowledge of the natural world? Was there a sense of competition, or did Newcomer men hope to learn from Aboriginal male guides? What can encounters between missionary and Aboriginal men tell us about reshaping masculinity in the mission field, and about white male missionaries, who were sometimes portrayed as "wilderness saints?" The chapter thus takes into account race relations, imperial manhood and location and draws from diaries, letters, official correspondence and autobiographies.

Manly Men Wanted

In order to encourage Anglican missionaries to sign up for work in Canadian mission stations, the London-based Church Mission Society (CMS) and the Society for the Propagation of the Gospel sent appeals to church newspapers and Sunday church bulletins. They also arranged for missionaries who were on furlough to tour Britain and provide lectures and sermons promoting the great potential for mission work in Canada. In their recruiting efforts, the mission promoters conveyed the message that the type of men they wanted should possess a blend of the "muscular Christian" and a true propensity to enjoy the outdoor life of the rugged backwoods.

The emphasis on Christian manliness, or muscular Christianity, was particular to, but not exclusive to, western and northern Canada. In fact, the idea of the shooting parson or the outdoors gentleman clergy was a characteristic aspect of masculinity in England.[8] So too was the connection between missionary men and muscular Christians to be found throughout the British empire, as Anna Johnston makes clear:

Intrinsically tied to the development of muscular Christianity . . . missionary men both discovered and invented their masculinity through encounter with other, colonized cultures. Vigorous but pious British manliness was contrasted with depraved native masculinity, and missionary texts anxiously but assertively represented the world in these terms.[9]

Manliness had to be rough and assertive but also pious. Christian missionaries may also have shared some similarities with those whom John Tosh highlighted in his study of men who went "pioneering" in Australia, western Canada and other colonial settings. Many of Tosh's men expressed a desire to be independent from women and to be with men in a "mateship" model of masculinity. These men strove to continue to live in the homosocial world that they had become familiar with in public school: "For the soldier, the administrator, the trader and the frontiersmen, the empire was a site where comradeship was valued"[10] Certainly, most of the men in this study were bachelors when they arrived in Canada. They lived with other men when they were starting out on their first mission assignments. They, however, were aware that they would be working to convert both men and women, and they were, no doubt, also conscious of the fact that it was very useful to have a wife as a partner in the mission enterprise.

While ambiguities existed in the forms of masculinity, there was little doubt in the minds of mission promoters about the type of men wanted for the job. A fine expression of the desired type of man was offered by Bishop Frederick DuVernet, who in 1904 was consecrated Bishop in the Diocese of Caledonia, an expansive diocese that occupied almost all of present-day northern British Columbia. His vision of the best male missionaries for this vast region had much to do with their ability to "tramp the trail":

> they must be men of the right kind. Men who are willing to tramp the trail in advance of the train. Men who can find a joy in carrying the Gospel to the lonely settler. Men who with simple reverence can lead in the worship of God a congregation of ten in a neighbor's shack. Men who can count it a privilege to be pioneers for Christ and His Church.[11]

This was a job for a vigorous parson.

This message was reinforced in Sunday sermons in churches at home in England. The Reverend Martin Holdom was intrigued when he heard a sermon from the Bishop of Calgary, William Pinkham, who was struggling to maintain enough clergy for the ever-expanding population of Alberta in the boom years of the first decade of the twentieth century.[12] Holdom was born into a privileged family: his father was an estate administrator and was able to provide first a governess and later, a public school education for his son. After attending the All Saints Public School, Oxfordshire, Martin attended Oxford University where he completed a Bachelor of Arts and later a theological degree. Upon his ordination, he was appointed assistant curate in Leicester where he served for two years before he met Pinkham. He was keen for excitement and adventure, and thought that was just what Pinkham had to offer. The Canadian Church was careful not to mislead those who might show interest:

It is no soft job that is to be performed. Indeed, for men trained in England the life involves considerable hardships, physical as well as spiritual. A clergyman in the West must be ready to do for himself things which he has been accustomed to have done for him. He must be strong, manly, 'gritty,' and ready to adapt himself to new conditions. That he is a clergyman will not count for much, it is what he is as a man that matters.[13]

Manly men were wanted in Canada. They had to be "gritty" and tough. Their education or clergy collar would not impress the hardy folks of the backwoods or the northern climes, but their manliness could. Any romantic notions about the softness of the job or the promise of adventure were dispelled by this honest approach. Like hundreds of others who responded throughout the Victorian and Edwardian years, Holdom was not deterred. He left England for Castor, Alberta in the fall of 1909 as a young twenty-five-year-old, recently ordained Oxford graduate.

Sporting Parsons

Male missionaries who wrote letters home, sent newsy correspondence into mission publications, or kept diaries, often reinforced the conflation between hardy masculinity and mission. This image invoked an integral part of mission identity at a time when the field was rapidly feminizing. Masculine discourse figured strongly because the context of a re-settling society prompted responses that drew on comparisons between the homeland and the perceived newness of the geographical spaces and physical features of western and northern Canada. Each missionary would approach these new settings in individual ways, but at the same their gendered responses suggest that missionaries sent to Canada would manage based on their strength and endurance, and that men would not hesitate to highlight some of their more "manly" moments.

For example, the Reverend William Collison, a long serving CMS missionary in the Diocese of Caledonia originally from Ireland, used terms that echoed boys' adventure literature when he described the excitement of shooting a sea lion off the North Pacific coast:

Off Rose Spit a large sea lion harassed us by following the canoe, and coming up and down now on one side and again on the other. My crew feared it might upset us, and although we were sailing very fast, we could not overdistance it. So, acting on their advice I seized my rifle, and as it again emerged very close to the canoe, I shot it through the head.[14]

Manly missionaries had to be able to come to terms with the great outdoors, even if it meant hunting down animals. The first Bishop of Caledonia, William Ridley, exhibited the same level of excitement and desire to overcome natural obstacles. A manfully invigorating moment came when he travelled up the Skeena River by a steamer boat that had entered a rather dangerous set of currents: "the swiftness is a difficulty rather than a peril. Not so the whirls and cross currents at the confluence of some of the largest tributaries. At these points skill and nerve are summoned to the contest, and exciting it really is."[15] The capable outdoorsman, someone able to shoot a gun if necessary or steer a boat in rough conditions, was an important part of the self identity and gender formation of male missionaries in northern and western Canada. As the historian of religion, John Webster Grant, observed: "Protestants were more inclined to think of hardships as obstacles to be overcome in the athletic spirit of British Christianity."[16]

Even before Martin Holdom arrived in Castor, Alberta, he was excited about the prospect of a sporting life. Bishop Pinkham convinced him that his territory of 1,600 square miles would offer much in the way of outdoor activity. In one of his many letters home, he indulged in imagining how it would be: "It is also a great sporting country near a large lake, so there will be plenty of duck shooting in off days. It is such a glorious life out here, so free, simple and real."[17] The reality of his surroundings would soon become quite apparent to the young Reverend Holdom. Upon arrival in the community of Castor he immediately faced the fact that there was nowhere for him to sleep since no arrangements had yet been made for his lodgings: "I had to go to a very rough lodging house, everything else let. I shared my bed with a huge Irishman, an awfully good fellow, though rough as you make 'em. He hadn't washed for months but nobody does here. And as for a bath, there is not such a thing in this place."[18] His introduction to Castor may have brought unexpected challenges, but Holdom seemed to see the humour in his situation and over the next few days he found a room for rent. He would meet many "rough" men over the next few years but he was impressed that "they never laugh at a parson out here; they always treat one as a man. I hardly heard a bad word."[19] Being treated "as a man" and not being laughed at was critical for Holdom's sense of who he was and how he wanted to be seen: as a manful clergyman. He could fit in with the "rough" men and prove himself in the sporting field as well.

Men Keeping House

Apart from the very real importance of being accepted in a community, manliness could also be associated with the ability to accept privation and sacrifice without complaint. This capacity to accept harsh conditions was often mentioned by others as a strong attribute and sometimes even the missionaries themselves relished their privations. For example, Charlotte Selina Bompas, the wife of the Bishop of the Yukon, observed that her husband William

> had trained himself to endure hardness as a good soldier of the Cross. His diet was at all times abstemious, almost severely so. To the last he never allowed himself milk or cream in tea or coffee. He was a fairly good cook and breadmaker, and loved to produce a dish good and savoury for his friends, although eschewing all such dainties himself.[20]

Privation was undoubtedly part of the mission aesthetic, but it was often conflated with masculinity and a man's ability to "endure hardness".[21] One aspect of privation, as indicated by Charlotte Selina Bompas, was that male missionaries had to develop new skills in housekeeping and cooking since they sometimes did not have anyone to do this for them. Bishop Bompas married only after eight years in the north, having lived as a bachelor missionary.

The Reverend Martin Holdom was quite proud of the fact that he too had learned to cope on his own as a bachelor on the Canadian prairie. He seemed to retain a positive, if not a purely boosterish, outlook toward his circumstances:

> Thank God the rough life does not seem to worry me at all. I was never better in my life, and there is little hardship in living in a little wooden shack and having to do everything oneself. I haven't one idle moment from getting up to going to bed. The worst of it is chores take up so much of the time that one could devote to prayer and reading.[22]

Holdom was not alone in commenting on the time and effort that went into maintaining mission houses and cooking meals. In some cases, male missionaries entered into new homosocial arrangements as they established housekeeping routines in their new communities. Naturally for the new mission stations, the first job of male missionaries was to build the churches and the mission houses. Once that chore was accomplished, daily routines had to be created. The first CMS missionary to the Inuit of Canada's north-eastern Arctic, Edmund James Peck, noted in the summer of 1898 that he and his fellow workers had just finished expanding their house after their first winter at Blacklead Island: "We are now in the house which we find nice and comfortable, and where we hope to spend many happy days together in the study of language, and in mutual fellowship and brotherly love."[23] Even before the finishing touches were put on to the house, Peck and the other CMS missionary at Blacklead Island had practised their culinary skills. Their first Christmas found them at work making a feast for their Inuit visitors: "Busy preparing articles for Christmas tree, also in cooking for children's feast. Mr. Sampson has undertaken to make the puddings while I make the cakes."[24] Peck's real pleasure was in the culinary art of cooking what he invented as the "Arctic Dumplings" or "Arctic meatballs": "They are made of preserved meat, bread crumbs, cooked preserved potatoes, and a little flour. All the ingredients were first mixed together and made up into a kind of mash, and then formed into balls."[25] These could be taken on Peck's Arctic travels and then easily warmed up in a small frying pan over a traditional seal oil lamp or stove, a *qulliq*. Peck's culinary skill, and his apparent willingness to divide household chores, demonstrate how in these homosocial mission houses men asserted their independence by taking on roles that perhaps would stand in opposition to the image that was advertised. Ironically, in constructing their bachelor lifestyles, male missionaries engendered a sense of pride in both teamwork and independent initiative demonstrated by their abilities to take on what might be considered traditionally women's roles.

Sharing household duties was not always so easy for missionary men. Some had to adjust to the bachelor lifestyle, while others had to learn how to adapt to living with strangers. When Scottish-born Archibald Fleming arrived at the Eastern Arctic community of Lake Harbour in the summer of 1909, he found that his new housemate, CMS missionary Julian Bilby, was somewhat peculiar. His objective was to work toward converting the Inuit to Christianity, but he first had to get his bearings. After the house construction was finished and they moved in together they negotiated their duties:

> We also had to eat, and since the fastidious Bilby would not allow an Eskimo to touch his food this meant that we had to do all our own cooking. He decreed that we should take turns week and week about at this and the housework. For the first week he was cook and provided an excellent table. The next week he suffered my feeble attempts with Christian fortitude. It was a great burden to me for unfortunately I had no culinary skill whatever.[26]

Eventually, after both housemates agreed that "the housework took up far too much time", Fleming convinced Bilby that they should hire a young Inuk boy to help out with the chores. Bilby agreed, with the proviso that he did not have to train him.[27] The result was that they were able to be equally fastidious and, in fact, their homosocial home, particularly during holiday season, turned into quite a formal spectacle. Their first Christmas together included a very well decorated table:

> On this occasion we had a really fine linen cloth on the table, and linen napkins replaced our ordinary cotton ones. A pair of small brass candlesticks, some artificial flowers made by the blind in Glasgow, an embroidered centrepiece, a specially designed menu card bound with a little blue silk ribbon, fruit and candy, gave a festive appearance to the table which surprised and greatly pleased Bilby.[28]

These bachelor missionaries displayed a model of domesticity for the Inuit who would join them at their table, and they did it without the help of women. They constructed themselves as independent men who could both boast about their outdoor travels and also survive individually or collectively in homosocial environments that did not fall apart from disorder.

Manhood in Contact

As is apparent from Fleming's hiring of the young Inuk boy, Joseph Yarley, the masculine assertions of independence or manliness made by men in the mission field were sometimes more complicated. In their navigations through the harsh climate and often arduous travel conditions in western and northern Canada, missionary men frequently relied upon Aboriginal people. Relationships between Aboriginal and missionary men are interesting to contemplate and are significant because they present a fundamental contradiction. In encounters between male missionaries and Aboriginal people generally it was common for a discourse to emerge that tended to dichotomize Christianity and "heathenism", as Aboriginal spirituality was referred to. And it was also common for Aboriginal traditions and rituals to be denigrated by missionaries, who wanted to emphasize their own superiority. While they could be very critical of Aboriginal culture and spirituality, some male missionaries actually acknowledged how profoundly knowledgeable Aboriginal men were when it came to navigating the northern landscape and environment. As a young man from Ireland, the Reverend Robert Renison was travelling on his first mission to the Anishinabee of northern Ontario when he met Solomon, the man he called his "mentor".[29] Their first meeting left Renison feeling inadequate: "I was a complete stranger to the north country and the outfit of my canoe must have spoken inexperience and unimportance to the initiated eye."[30] From the beginning of their friendship in the fall of 1898, Renison felt that Solomon was much more adept in the outdoors. Solomon's "initiated eye" could also see that.

Renison quickly came to depend on Solomon, especially during his itinerant travels out from Fort Albany to visit communities and seek conversions. He always invited Solomon to be his "head guide" on these journeys. He also went out hunting, trapping and fishing with him and claimed to learn from him as if a disciple: "I sat at Solomon's feet on the sea coast day after day to learn the call of the grey goose and the wavy, and to discern from the clouds tomorrow's wind." In return, Renison shared resources with Solomon. Apparently, when Solomon was in need of "new" clothes, he would inform Renison that he "thought I was wearing a shirt too long" and that it should be turned over to him.

Renison portrayed Solomon as a man who was cynical about the European idea of progress. He looked unfavourably on the changes that had occurred since Europeans had arrived. His cynicism was revealed when he was told by a government treaty officer in 1906 that "the white man loves his red brother", to which Solomon acutely replied "He loves the very ground he walks on." Solomon's contempt for modernity, and the pleasure he took in his freedom, mobility and ability to live independently, was portrayed in a conversation Renison had with him:

> As for me I work and I rest as I please. When the sun rises in the morning, if the day is fine I call to my wife and we pack our tent and load our canoe. We paddle forty miles down the stream. When the sun returns to the tops of the trees in the evening I push the canoe ashore with my paddle and in half an hour there is a new tent and a fire.

Solomon was a man keenly aware of his surroundings and perceptive in his calculations of the changes that had been wrought by increased contact with Euro-Canadians. Solomon's knowledge of the outdoors was superior to Renison's. He was a mentor who taught Renison about wildlife, weather, and woodcraft: bush survival skills that proved essential to Renison's ability to work as a missionary.

Archibald Fleming shared Renison's respect for the ability of Aboriginal people, in this case the Inuit, to travel in northern winters and to predict hunting outcomes. Fleming confessed to "being thrilled with the adventure" of travel, and the excitement of bringing the gospel to small Inuit communities on Baffin Island.[31] But he also acknowledged that his head guide, Kidlapik, was extremely capable: "I was also astonished by Kidlapik's ability to continue in a straight line towards his destination over the snow-covered wastes without a single mark to guide him. He could not depend on the wind because it varied constantly. There were no trails — nothing. It seemed as if he traveled by instinct."[32]

Like most of the other male missionaries who travelled out from Britain to work in northern or western Canada, Fleming saw missionary work as an adventure and any of the barriers to introducing Christ were to be overcome. His goal, as he himself maintained, was to "conquer all obstacles in order to win the Arctic wilds for Christ".[33] This statement itself is one of masculine assertion, though it characteristically tends to ignore the fact that the conquest was very much dependent upon Aboriginal men who often led missionaries to where they wanted to go and made sure they were well-fed along the way.

Donald Marsh, who would ultimately succeed Archibald Fleming as the Bishop of the Arctic, also appreciated his guides, one of whom was Joseph Yarley, the same young man hired by Fleming some twenty years earlier. Marsh, who first arrived in the eastern Arctic from England in 1926, recognized the amount of aid given by Inuit guides in the north. He also commented that the key to any successful trip was a willingness to share, a characteristic he felt was particularly evident among the Inuit. He claimed that there was "no better man than an Eskimo" to help out during times of trial.[34] Marsh illustrated this by recounting an incident where he had taken his mitts off to lash something to the sled. They froze immediately: "Without a word your travelling companion draws off his warm gloves, tosses them to you, catches your frozen ones, puts them on his own warm hands to thaw them, and when they're warm tosses them back with a smile."[35] When travelling with an Inuk man, one had to be willing to share resources and help out with the chores. Each partner had to take a turn at running beside the sled while the other steered the dogs. Once the trail was broken then camp had to be established; that too was a shared endeavour. Marsh's view was that the most peaceful feeling during his Arctic travel always took hold after everyone was settled in for the night:

> It's then that one feels a great sense of comradeship. In spite of hundreds of nights spent in igloos, often a hundred or more miles from the nearest habitation, I've never had a sense of loneliness on the trail, but rather the realization that there was a warm-hearted relationship between myself and my guide. I've seldom felt it elsewhere, the comradeship equaled only by boundless hospitality.[36]

To borrow a phrase from Elizabeth Vibert, it was in the "cold spaces of empire" where men could find "warmhearted" intimacy.[37] Archibald Fleming expressed a similar feeling of intimacy toward his Inuk guide, in this case a man named Pudlo. After as long as three months on the trail, Fleming came to appreciate the work and partnership that was shared between them: "It is sufficient to say that with each expedition my love and admiration for him increased."[38] The bond he felt to his guide was expressed in terms of close endearment. Both Fleming's and Marsh's expressions of camaraderie, mateship or homosocial intimacy stands in sharp contrast with the rather harsh claims they sometimes made about Inuit spirituality, or their appearance and lack of cleanliness and hygiene.[39] Yet, while male missionaries emphasized close intimate bonds, there is no evidence of homosexual relations between them and their Aboriginal guides. Regardless, in terms of manhood and masculinity, Fleming and Marsh each emphasized that Inuit men exhibited outstanding competence in the outdoors and that they were masterful companions. They knew how to share resources and they knew the landscape.

Marsh's experiences led him to construct a model of Inuit masculinity. In his estimation the characteristics associated with Inuit manhood were related to one's ability to provide food for one's family and, of equal importance, for others in the community who were in need. A man's willingness to be modest and quietly accomplished was important in affirming his masculinity and, according to Marsh, contrasted with the "white man's" way of selecting manful senior leaders:

> This manner of outlook and leadership made it very difficult for Eskimos to understand the white man's ways of choosing leaders, wherein people apply for a job which is awarded to the man who talks most about himself. The Eskimo finds this inappropriate, because to him the braggart is not the kind of man needed.[40]

A third characteristic that shaped Marsh's construction of Inuit manhood was that Inuit men had a strong sense of independence. They refused to follow directions given by "outsiders". This "trait" Marsh believed came from the necessity to feel confidence on the land: "Eskimos have always had a confidence in themselves, a trait built by the needs of men to feel they can conquer and maintain dominion in a grim and hard country. An Eskimo is a man, an Inuk of the Inuit."[41] Good hunting, modesty and independence were certainly codes of masculinity that were recognized by the Inuit themselves. "A modest person would play down his own accomplishments, be overjoyed and thankful for his catch, and would not gossip about his fellow human beings in his songs", noted Donald Suluk, a Paallirmiut Inuk elder from Eskimo Point (Arviat) where the Reverend Marsh worked. "This type of person is the kind who followed the advice of his grandparents and parents."[42] Another well respected Inuk elder and guide, Etuangat Aksaayuq, described one of his leaders in the community of Pangnurtung (Pangniqtuuq) as follows: "Angmarlik was a real leader. He directed all the hunters in (our) camp . . . He was respected . . . Angmarlik's orders were always carried out, as they were always suitable."[43] Being a good hunter who was willing to share with those who needed food, being modest and being independent were characteristic and fundamental features of masculinity in Inuit communities. Its signs were easily discernible and often admired by male missionaries.

What kind of masculinity did British missionaries model for Aboriginal or settler Canadians? If manhood was defined, by both missionaries and Aboriginal people, as an ability to exhibit competence in the outdoors and share in the intimate spaces of mission houses, tents and igloos, then what kind of manhood was prescribed by male missionaries? Certainly competency was part of what male missionaries wished to exhibit as well, but their sense of accomplishment had a different purpose. They wanted to model their ability in order to convince Aboriginal men and women that they represented a superior civilization and ultimately, of course, to convert Aboriginal people, and others they contacted, to Christianity.

When the Reverend Robert Renison first arrived at Fort Albany to work among the Anishinabee, he recalled a conversation he had with the Archdeacon Thomas Vincent, who was just on the verge of retirement after a forty-year career. Vincent's advice to this junior missionary, as he prepared to depart in the autumn of 1902, was that he must always "remember that you are the representative here not only of the Church, but of the white man's civilization. Never confess that you don't know".[44] On Renison's first day after Vincent's departure an Anishinabee man, Sakabukishkum, came by and complained of feeling ill. Haunted by Archdeacon Vincent's parting words, Renison was perplexed, since, of course, he had no medical training. However, he could not confess this; instead he ordered the patient to open his mouth and gazed down his throat. Telling Sakabukishkum to wait near the mission house with his mouth open, the Reverend ran upstairs in desperation. He later recalled: "I looked in every cupboard but could find nothing that looked like medicine. Finally my eyes lighted on some old bottles covered with cobwebs. Thus I discovered a dark secret in my predecessor's otherwise blameless life. He had a weakness for hair oil."[45] Breathlessly, Renison grabbed the bottle of Rowland's Macassar Oil that had a few inches of residue at the bottom and "hurried down the back stairs to the kitchen with the bottle and filled it with water from the kettle. When it was shaken it turned a fascinating shade of pink . . . "[46] Renison advised his patient to take half of the "medicine" that night and the other half the next morning. Renison believed that he quickly became well known around Fort Albany and surroundings: "My reputation as a great medicine man was made in one stroke, and the news was carried far and wide by every pakater." While he gloried in his new reputation he also felt a sense of dismay: "A cold chill ran down my spine when I realized what could happen if there were a case of appendicitis." He immediately decided to order a "case of drugs of all kinds, dentist's forceps, surgical instruments, and most importantly books to explain how to use them".[47]

Renison's story is significant because his admission that he chose to pretend to be knowledgeable about medicinal remedies suggests a vulnerability that was undoubtedly shared, but not necessarily expressed, by missionaries. As a representative of Anglicanism, and as a man, he felt that he had to demonstrate his knowledge and authority, even if it was an act. The theatrics of empire demanded just such a response. And, of course, clearly Renison believed that he had to establish himself against the authority of the local medicine maker. The sense that there was a competition for authority was prevalent in the discourse of male missionaries. Women missionaries also sought to establish authority and win converts, but the extent of assertion exhibited by Renison in the case above was rarely seen in women missionaries.

Another way in which women and men differed in the mission field was in the field of translation, where men attempted to distinguish themselves by their masculine assertiveness and competency. Anna Johnston has argued in her work on translation in Polynesia that linguistics and authority were conflated. As one of her missionaries claimed: "a missionary's status, among both his own kind and the native population, depended heavily on his fluency in the local language".[48] In the Canadian mission field, women missionaries sought to learn Aboriginal languages, yet they were not involved in the act of translating liturgical texts into Aboriginal languages: men were. And, as a form of masculine assertion and modelling, the acts of translation were acknowledged and valued by home mission societies. When William Bompas went back to England for his consecration to Bishop, after eight years in the Mackenzie River Diocese, he was honoured by the CMS for his translation work in particular:

> You have been there for more than eight years, in labours abundant, and your love has not lessened nor your zeal slackened. You have brought home, the fruit of your labour, portions of Scripture, prayers, and hymns in seven different dialects or tongues. You are ready to take the precious treasure out with you — the translations printed out and prepared by the Society for Promoting Christian Knowledge.[49]

Donald Marsh placed classroom education for children, women and men at the top of his list of priorities and he attributed the ability of many Inuit after several years to be able to read their own language, to missionary's educational work. He observed that "though the educational process may have been arduous for both teacher and student, at least initially, I can state without much fear of contradiction that as the result of mission teaching, almost all Eskimos today can read and write their own language — Inuktitut".[50]

For each man — Renison, Bompas and Marsh — methods of asserting and modelling masculinity to Aboriginal Canadians varied. Renison wanted to be the knowledgeable medicine man; Bompas found power through being able to translate liturgy and prayer into Aboriginal languages; and Marsh found it powerful to educate and be able to teach the written word in Inuktitut. Each one of these men was concerned with demonstrating and sharing knowledge, even if sometimes it was of questionable value. Manhood in the contact zone was negotiated through cultural meanings and knowledgeability and assertion on each side of the religious/spiritual or racial encounter.

Conclusions

Throughout the period under consideration the mission field was rapidly feminizing with increased numbers of women, both single and married, being trained in Britain and sent to the colonies. By 1894 in the Diocese of Caledonia, for example, women missionaries outnumbered men. Eugene Stock, the CMS secretary in London, provided the statistics for Caledonia. He counted "nine clergymen, three laymen, nine wives, and eight other women, total 29."[51] In the same vein the *Church Missionary Intelligencer and Record* reported that women outnumbered men in the mission field worldwide:

> The latest statistics of all Protestant Missionary Societies, British, Continental,

Myra Rutherdale

> American &c., give no less than 2576 unmarried women missionaries. The male
> missionaries are given as 5233, and as these have 3641 wives, the total number of
> women married and unmarried, exceeds that of men by just a thousand.[52]

These changing gender dynamics may have been partially responsible for such a strong
masculinist discourse found in appeals for missionaries and in descriptions of the work,
as portrayed in autobiographical and biographical texts. Perhaps, too, in self-writing
there was pressure to express masculinity so that those at home would not assume it
was a "soft job".

Several types of masculinities emerged in the northern and western Canadian
mission fields. "Muscular Christianity" was prevalent, as were mateship, camaraderie
and self-assertion evident in mission masculinity. At times too there were contrasting
masculinities in the sense that while white missionary men wanted to be perceived as
rigorous and capable in the outdoors, they were in awe of the competency demonstrated
by Aboriginal men. Most significant was the fact that they ultimately had to rely upon
Aboriginal people to guide them, to teach them about life in western and northern
Canada and to interpret for them. Male missionaries chose to perform fancy housekeeping duties and were sometimes forced to share sleeping arrangements with big
"Irish" men or curl up in Igloos with male guides. They willingly admitted that they
felt warm-hearted comradeship, or even love for some of their guides, as they shared
intimate moments in all kinds of contexts. Gendered identities were shaped and
reshaped in efforts to overcome all obstacles in the name of introducing Christianity.

Notes

1   For a small sampling of effective treatments of gender history related to empire see
    MacKenzie, *The Empire of Nature*; Dawson, *Soldier Heroes*; Sinha *Colonial Masculinity*; Vibert,
    Trader's Tales; Perry, *On the Edge of Empire*; Woollacott, *Gender and Empire*; O'Hanlon,
    "Masculinity and the Bangash Nawabs", pp. 19–37.
2   Twells "Missionary 'Fathers' and Wayward 'Sons'", p. 153; On the other hand, some studies
    of mission and empire could be broadened by a gender analysis. See for example Lester and
    Lambert, "Missionary Politics and the Captive Audience", pp. 88–113.
3   Grimshaw, ""Faith, Missionary Life, and the Family", p. 270.
4   Johnston, *Missionary Writing and Empire*; Semple, "Missionary Manhood", pp. 397–415.
5   Huber and Lutkehaus, "Gendered Missions at Home and Abroad", p. 12.
6   O'Brien, "Missionary Masculinities", pp. 68–85.
7   There is now a considerable literature on Christian missions to Aboriginal people in Canada.
    See Grant, *Moon of Wintertime*; Abel, *Drum Songs*; Rutherdale, *Women and the White Man's
    God*; Neylan, *The Heavens are Changing*; Coates, *Best Left As Indians*; Bolt, *Thomas Crosby*;
    Murray, *The Devil and Mr. Duncan*; Christophers, *Positioning the Missionary*; Whitehead,
    "Women Were Made For Such Things", p. 141–50; Whitehead, "A Useful Christian
    Woman", pp. 142–66; Austen and Scott, *Canadian Missions, Indigenous Peoples*; On medical
    missions see Jamie Scott, "Doctors Divine", pp. 13–26.
8   See Dunae, "Boys Literature and the Idea of Empire", p. 120; James, "Tom Brown's
    Imperialist Sons", pp. 89–99. See also Rutherdale, *Women and the White Man's God*, pp.
    9–15.

9 Johnston, "Missionary Writing and Empire", p. 8. In the rather hyper-masculine circles that Murray, a Scottish civil servant in South Africa, travelled in, he sometimes had to hide his poetic talents: "I have always had the feeling that a man might raise chrysanthemums or even play the flute in his spare time, and still have claims to be considered a good business man. But that if his weakness was rhyming he would be set down as a 'feckless' character. Believing this was the general feeling, I have hitherto tried to conceal my weakness from my associates, or if they did get to know of it, I tried to pass off these verses as youthful indiscretions." Quoted in Hyslop, "Making Scotland in South Africa", p. 319.
10 Tosh, *Manliness and Masculinities*, p. 200.
11 Bishop Frederick DuVernet, "News From the Front" p. 51.
12 Voisey, *A Preacher's Frontier*, p. v.
13 Cited in Voisey, *A Preacher's Frontier*, p. viii; From a circular dated February 26, 1910, as quoted in Carter, *Where The Wind Blows*, pp. 24–5.
14 Lillard, *In the Wake of the War Canoe*, p. 75.
15 Lillard, *Warriors of the North Pacific*, p. 217.
16 Grant, *Moon of Wintertime*, p. 228.
17 Quoted in Voisey, *A Preacher's Frontier*, p. 5. Letter from the Reverend Martin Holdom to Edward Holdom, 22 October 1909.
18 Quoted in Voisey, *A Preacher's Frontier*, p. 7. Letter from the Reverend Martin Holdom to Edward Holdom, 29 October 1909.
19 Quoted in Voisey, *A Preacher's Frontier*, p. 8. Letter from the Reverend Martin Holdom to Edward Holdom, 29 October 1909.
20 Quoted in Cody, *An Apostle of the North*, p. 251.
21 Privation was considered a sacrifice worth making for God. This was expressed well by the Reverend Edmund James Peck while he was traveling in the Arctic during the winter of 1898: "However, God's compensations — if I may so speak — far outweigh the seeming crosses and privations, and it is a joy to know that one crosses these frozen seas for the Lord of life and glory — and He is worthy for whom we should do this." Laugrand, *Apostle To The Inuit*, p. 94.
22 Quoted in Voisey, *A Preacher's Frontier*, p. 72. Letter from the Reverend Martin Holdom to Edward Holdom, 17 October 1909.
23 Laugrand, *Apostle To The Inuit*, p. 105.
24 Laugrand, *Apostle To The Inuit*, p. 91.
25 Langrand, *Apostle To The Inuit*, pp. 93–4.
26 Fleming, *Archibald the Arctic*, p. 56.
27 Fleming, *Archibald the Arctic*, p. 65.
28 Fleming, *Archibald the Arctic*, pp. 71–2.
29 Renison, *One Day at a Time*, p. 41.
30 Renison, *One Day at a Time*, p. 42.
31 Fleming, *Archibald the Arctic*, p. 215.
32 Fleming, *Archibald the Arctic*, p. 145.
33 Fleming, *Archibald the Arctic*, p. 392.
34 Marsh, *Echoes from a Frozen Land*, p. 109.
35 Marsh, *Echoes from a Frozen Land*, p. 109.
36 Marsh, *Echoes from a Frozen Land*, p. 110.
37 Vibert, "Writing 'Home'", p. 67.
38 Fleming, *Archibald the Arctic*, p. 179

39 Marsh, *Echoes from a Frozen Land*, p. 29.
40 Marsh, *Echoes from a Frozen Land*, p. 134.
41 Marsh, *Echoes from a Frozen Land*, p. 116.
42 Quoted in Bennett and Rowley, *Uqalurait*, p. 39.
43 Quoted in, Bennett and Rowley, *Uqalurait*, p. 95.
44 Renison, *One Day at a Time*, p. 33.
45 Renison, *One Day at a Time*, p. 35.
46 Renison, *One Day at a Time*, p. 35.
47 Renison, *One Day at a Time*, p. 37.
48 Johnston, *Missionary Writing and Empire*, p. 129.
49 Cody, *An Apostle of the North"*, p. 153.
50 Marsh, *Echoes from a Frozen Land*, p. 28; Stock, "Women Missionaries", p. 343.
51 Eugene Stock, "Women Missionaries in C. M. S. Fields," *Church Missionary Intelligence and Record*, May 1894, p. 343.
52 Stock, *The History of the Church Missionary Society*, vol. 3, p. 384.

CHAPTER SIX

An Indigenous View of Missionaries
Arthur Wellington Clah and Missionaries on the North-west Coast of Canada

PEGGY BROCK

This chapter investigates the interactions of missionaries and Indigenous people from an Indigenous perspective, using the relationship of an early Tsimshian Christian, Arthur Wellington Clah, with Anglican and Methodist missionaries on the north-west coast of Canada in the latter part of the nineteenth century as a case study. I focus on the inherent tensions within that relationship. On the one hand, Clah wanted the approbation, support and friendship of the missionaries; on the other, he was often critical of their liminal role between the colonial state and First Nations people. Sometimes he colluded with the missionaries, while at other times he opposed them. He regarded them as messengers of God rather than as authoritative or morally superior beings. He believed their role was to support and promote the interests of the Tsimshian in spiritual as well as practical matters, rather than to dictate how they should run their lives.

Archival records generally reflect a missionary perspective of their role and relationship with indigenous communities among whom they worked. Mission sources are replete with patronizing and dismissive judgements of the people they hoped to evangelize. On first encounters, missionaries viewed these people as uncivilized savages with immoral and often disgusting habits. Those who became Christians rarely lived up to the expectations of the missionaries and were often represented as weak and easily influenced by others. Missionaries' writings were not only influenced by their racial and cultural prejudices, but by their need to maintain the institutional and financial support of their church or mission society. Mission literature was also popular literature for a distant readership fascinated by the exotic and heroic tales of missionary encounters with remote peoples and environments. Dependence on these missionary-generated sources can result in skewed representations of the relationship between missionaries and the people amongst whom they worked, as historians often do not have access to the views of the people targeted by missionaries.

Clah offers us an independent perspective of mission life through his diary, which he maintained on a daily basis from 1859 until 1909.[1] His view of the missionaries and their role among the Tsimshian and neighbouring peoples on the Pacific coast was not burdened by the expectations of a readership many thousands of kilometres away. Clah's diary was his own record of his life and not for public consumption. While he had strong views, they were his immediate impression of events and not produced for an audience. In this sense they were a more honest appraisal of interpersonal relationships than the missionary reports and correspondence on which historians usually rely. While Clah's observations are not generalizable to other missions or even to all Tsimshian, they offer an important counter to mission-generated views and raise questions about the encounter between missionaries and indigenous people that can be generalized to other mission fields.

The Missionaries

In October 1857 William Duncan, a 27-year-old from Yorkshire, arrived at the Hudson's Bay Company (HBC) trading post at Fort Simpson on the northern coast of what soon would become British Columbia.[2] He was sent by the Church Missionary Society (CMS) to establish the first Christian mission among the Tsimshian. He remained in the region until his death in 1918, the best known, or some might say notorious, of the missionaries on the coast. In 1862 he left Fort Simpson to build a mission village a few kilometres south at Metlakatla, where he could maintain tighter discipline over those who chose to become Christians. After falling out with the CMS and the local Anglican hierarchy, including Bishop William Ridley who was located at Metlakatla, Duncan moved across the Alaskan border in 1887 where he rebuilt his mission settlement.[3]

Duncan was soon followed by other CMS missionaries, who spawned a number of mission villages based on the Metlakatla model. Robert Doolan arrived in 1863 and was sent to the Nass River, north of Fort Simpson, where he first established himself in the village of Quinwoch and then with Robert Tomlinson built a new Christian village at Kincolith (Gingolx). Doolan returned to England in 1867, while Tomlinson later established another mission at Kispoix, before leaving the CMS around 1881 and setting up an independent Anglican mission on the Skeena River at present-day Cedarvale.[4] Two other long-term CMS missionaries on the northern coast were William Henry Collison and James McCullagh. Collison spent periods of time at Metlakatla, Massett in the Queen Charlotte Islands (1876–79) and Kincolith (1884–1922). McCullagh ran a mission, Aiyansh, on the upper Nass River, which had been established by Tomlinson in 1878.

There were other CMS and Anglican missionaries on the coast in the latter part of the nineteenth century, many for short periods; the most notable for his long-term association with Clah and the Tsimshian was Robert Cunningham. Cunningham arrived in 1863 to assist Duncan, but they soon fell out when Cunningham married a local Tsimshian woman with whom he had been having an illicit relationship. After leaving Metlakatla he joined the HBC and then established his own business on the coast as a fur trader and storekeeper.

The other main mission presence on the northern coast was the Methodist Church. Some Tsimshian at Fort Simpson invited the Methodists to set up a mission in their village. The first long-term missionary was Thomas Crosby, who came to Fort Simpson in 1874 and left in 1897. In 1877 Alfred Green established a mission at a new site on the Nass River at Lakkalsap, which became known as Greenville. He remained there until 1890. Crosby, while based at Fort Simpson, spent much of his time as an itinerant preacher up and down the coast, travelling by canoe and later in the schooner, *Glad Tidings*. Green and others deputized for him in his absences. After Crosby left, S. S. Osterhout was based at Fort Simpson for a number of years.

In the early 1890s the Salvation Army became a strong presence on the coast. This was a Tsimshian-inspired movement and not associated with a mission or missionary. Its presence did, however, lead to tensions and conflict with the established churches, particularly the Methodists. Some of these tensions were caused by missionary competition for the minds and souls of the Tsimshian and their neighbours, and some by the internal politics of the Tsimshian.[5]

When William Duncan arrived at Fort Simpson, one of the first Tsimshian he met was Clah, a man of similar age to himself.[6] Clah approached Duncan with a request to join the classes Duncan was running for the families of the HBC staff in the Fort. Duncan found out that Clah had recently killed an old woman whom he blamed for the death of a friend of his, and that others were now planning to punish and possibly kill him in retribution. Despite his misgivings, Duncan soon hired this enthusiastic young man to help him learn Sm'algyax, the Tsimshian language, as he was one of the few Tsimshian with any knowledge of English.[7] Duncan used this opportunity to introduce Clah to Christian precepts:

> & every day I am gaining ground in the language [Sm'algyax]. Today we came to the great fact of the Gospel — Salvation by the death of Jesus. I had a great deal of trouble (rather pleasurable labour) in getting my Indian to comprehend the Mighty truth. I am glad to say however I succeeded. And this is the first instance of my doing so.[8]

Thus Clah became Duncan's first informal convert to Christianity. This early involvement with Duncan was the beginning of a lifelong association with missionaries. Clah and Duncan remained friends (occasionally estranged friends) throughout their lives, but Clah was never formally converted by Duncan, nor did he follow Duncan to Metlakatla or Alaska.

Clah's interactions with missionaries are instructive, particularly as he was on the whole well-disposed towards them and interested in their Christian message, becoming a devout Christian, while never kowtowing or becoming subservient to them. He knew missionaries had more Christian knowledge than he did, but with no more right to that knowledge than he had. He believed Christianity did not come from elsewhere, but was a Tsimshian religion that should replace old ways. Clah viewed missionaries as people to be cultivated, who should serve his interests and those of the Tsimshian, and mediate with the secular authorities on behalf of the Tsimshian.

The day-by-day nature of a diary provides snapshots of Clah's relations with various missionaries. Sometimes he is well satisfied with them, their preaching and behaviour; at other times he is annoyed with them, or disappointed because they have not fulfilled his expectations, or have not adequately protected the interests of the Tsimshian.

Sometimes he views individual missionaries as selfish or greedy, taking advantage of his poor country folk. All the missionaries discussed above appear in Clah's diary. Duncan and Crosby are the most visible, but Green is also frequently mentioned. Clah had a long and quite close association with Cunningham when he became a trader after his short mission career.

William Duncan

Clah's relationship with William Duncan was the most complex and best illustrates the underlying tensions that develop in circumstances in which outsiders move into communities to proselytize and convert. Clah's initial introduction to Christianity was in a sense a by-product of his language sessions with Duncan. The missionary wanted to learn enough of the Tsimshian language to enable him to preach to the people in their own tongue. He therefore needed to translate Christian concepts into Sm'algyax. The process of translation turned into a process of instruction and Clah was very susceptible to this new world view. Clah's introduction to Christianity was thus informal. Over a number of years he came to think of himself as a Christian and began preaching his version of Christianity to whomever he could as he travelled the coastal region, fishing, trading and hunting.

Despite strong pressure from the Anglican Church and the CMS, Duncan refused to become an ordained minister and thus did not baptize anyone, although many Tsimshian he converted were baptized by visiting Anglican ministers. Clah was not interested in the formal accoutrements of Christianity, and was not baptized until 1880 by the Methodist Thomas Crosby. Despite this formality twenty-two years after Clah became interested in Christianity, he never identified himself as Methodist, but participated in services of a range of churches: Anglican, Methodist and later Salvation Army. When he was in Victoria he would also attend Catholic services. Christianity was a personal commitment for Clah, which did not generate loyalty to a particular brand of church. His propensity to distinguish between his own beliefs and that of an institutional allegiance was illustrated early on when Duncan moved to Metlaktala in 1862 and Clah stayed at Fort Simpson. Duncan criticized Clah for remaining at Fort Simpson to improve his status among the Tsimshian. The death toll following a smallpox epidemic in 1862 and the migration of many Tsimshian to Metlakatla, including Ligeex, the chief of Clah's tribal group the Gispaxlo'ots, created the circumstances in which Clah, using resources accumulated through the fur trade, could realize his ambitions of increasing his standing among his people.

Although Clah did not follow Duncan to Metlakatla, he remained a loyal follower, offering his house as a venue for Duncan and visiting Metlakatlan evangelists to hold services. However, Duncan accused Clah of being too emotive in his preaching, reprimanding him on several occasions for his style of preaching: "I hear he endeavours to persuade the Indians at Fort Simpson to give up their sins but he does his work in angry tones."[9] Duncan feared that the Tsimshian could easily be worked up into a frenzy of religious fervour, and so he maintained a measured form of religious service. According to Jean Usher, "Religion at Metlakatla was characterized by sober, earnest attention to scriptural knowledge."[10] Duncan's fears of pandemonium were realized in 1877 when the inexperienced Reverend A. J. Hall relieved him at Metlakatla. Hall worked the people up into a great religious revival that precipitated Duncan's early return after he read of the religious excitement engulfing his mission in the Victoria newspapers.[11]

Duncan's annoyance with Clah's independent activities bubbled over into angry denunciation in early 1874. Duncan made a determined effort to attract Fort Simpson Christians to Metlakatla by inviting them to the 1873 Christmas celebrations. Several canoe loads of Tsimshian responded, leaving a rump of people at Fort Simpson. Clah took the opportunity to rally these people together, preach to them and encourage them to take an unequivocal stand against Duncan's push to split the community by building a bridge to connect the two parts of the village. This was an activity loaded with symbolic meaning as well as a practical outcome, as the bridge connected the two parts of the village that were separated by water at high tide.[12]

According to Clah and more recent accounts, those who returned from Metlakatla were shamed by this display, as he expected.[13] Duncan saw Clah's activities as a direct threat to his own influence. He ridiculed Clah's evangelical activities and Clah's character. But a much greater threat to Duncan's Christian monopoly on the coast appeared a few weeks later when a group of influential Tsimshian invited the Methodists to Fort Simpson. The Reverend William Pollard visited the village and baptized many people, including Clah's four children:

> Mr Pollard Methodist Minister he baptised my children 2 girls and 2 little Boys. he gave them name in Gods name first daughter named Martha, Second named Rebecca Boy 3d named David fourth named Andrew. they all have Gods name Baptized February 26 1874.[14]

Clah reported that Duncan was jealous of the Methodists. There were rumours that Duncan and Tomlinson threatened to send sickness to the Tsimshian or kill them by poisoning them, and that Duncan was going to come to Fort Simpson to blacklist those who had been baptized by the Methodists. In response, the Tsimshian turned against Duncan. Clah held a meeting amongst his house clan at which they decided they would no longer support Duncan.[15]

By December of that year Duncan and Clah were once again friends. Duncan sent word he wanted to see Clah for a witness statement in relation to a matter Duncan was presiding over as magistrate. Clah paddled to Metlakatla: "Our brother Duncan was very kind to us". He took Clah around the village, showed him the new church and they caught up on the latest news.[16] The next day Clah tried to mediate with Duncan over the Methodist presence at Fort Simpson:

> I give advice Old Duncan and all his people. because I had something about between them and Crosby an[d] Duncan jealous. he tells me everything about methodists. . . Mr Duncan you teach us before So what God says in Bible and to keep His Commandment. To Love one another Jesus Christs tells this same love one another.

Crosby teach us and your teach all your people this same. Now you and crosby teach us Bad then we all Bad. I said to him. I think myself everything will breaked up If we all Bad this yours. he says that so.[17]

Such turning of the tables on the missionary, where the new Christian lectures his teacher on Christian behaviour, cannot be found in missionary accounts, in which the missionaries always hold the high moral ground. Clah, however, never perceived the missionaries as morally superior to himself, criticizing them if they travelled on Sundays or broke other rules they imposed on the Tsimshian.

As the two men aged, their names became linked in the history of the introduction of Christianity on the coast. Duncan mentioned Clah as his teacher of Sm'algyax in a book he wrote about his first ten years as a missionary, and other histories expanded on this link, claiming Clah saved Duncan's life when chief Ligeex threatened him in 1858.[18] The last time Clah saw Duncan was when the old missionary invited him to New Metlakatla, his mission in Alaska, in 1907. These two old men had lived through turbulent times together. Clah enjoyed recounting to a wide-eyed younger generation the early days when Duncan arrived on the coast and Clah assisted him in taking his first hesitant steps as a missionary to the Tsimshian.[19]

Thomas Crosby

Clah's association with the other missionaries was never as close as that with Duncan. While Crosby was at Fort Simpson much longer than Duncan, Clah and he had a rather distant and often strained relationship. Clah had been deliberately excluded from the meeting at which it was decided to invite the Methodists to Fort Simpson.[20] He read of Crosby's appointment to Fort Simpson in a newspaper while working on the gold-fields.[21] However, he was happy to have a missionary presence at Fort Simpson, pleased his children were baptized, and he gave generously to Crosby's church-building fund on his return from the goldfields.[22] Although Duncan and Crosby eventually learned to work co-operatively, Duncan was initially upset by the Methodists' move into what he regarded as his territory, particularly as there were many other villages on the Nass and Skeena Rivers where new missions could have been established.

A couple of years after Crosby arrived at Fort Simpson, Clah moved away for several years to try to establish himself on land where he could plant and harvest a garden and to improve his financial prospects, but he had several confrontations with Crosby before his departure.[23] The first was when Crosby, ignorant of the meanings and functions of the Tsimshian potlatch system in which property was given away at special feasts to enhance the status of a person but also as a means of redistributing property, tried to intervene in this redistribution. He wanted people to pay their "debts": "About last night Mr Crosby calling some people to settle old debts. But in our laws when we gave away all our property we not say to friends to take propertys back."[24] Clah was infuriated by Crosby's meddling in the complex Tsimshian system of acquiring and disposing of debt that he did not understand. He did not object to

Crosby's opposition to potlatches *per se*, as he advocated against them himself on many occasions.

Clah's second altercation with Crosby was over Crosby's intervention in a dispute between Clah and some other Tsimshian who accused him of cheating them. The men had gone to the Omineca goldfields and under Clah's leadership built a boat to transport miners and goods along the rivers and lakes of the interior. Clah subsequently bought out his partners. Back at Fort Simpson they complained that he owed them money. Crosby insisted Clah make a payment of $11, which he refused to do. Instead, he went to Duncan and asked him to make a ruling as a magistrate. Duncan supported Clah.[25] This dispute segued into Clah's growing dissatisfaction with Crosby for interfering in Tsimshian matters where he had no right to meddle, while demanding money from the Tsimshian to support his own projects of church building. Clah accused Crosby of stealing from the poor and not paying his workers their full wages. Crosby accused Clah of lying, refusing to shake his hand as he left church.[26] Yet a few weeks earlier Crosby had been holding class meetings in Clah's house. It is difficult to ascertain how serious these disputes were.

While the disputes between Clah and Crosby in 1876 may not have signified a permanent falling out, by the late 1880s Clah was becoming increasingly disillusioned with Crosby over his demands for money from his congregation and his inability to help the Tsimshian over the state's inexorable alienation of their lands. Yet, in Clah's mind, the priest was always separate from the man. However annoyed he might be over Crosby's activities, he still recognized him as a great preacher who could move souls. In 1887 Clah walked around Port (previously Fort) Simpson recruiting people to be baptized by Crosby, although several initially refused because Crosby insisted they go through a Christian marriage first. Clah persuaded Crosby that this prerequisite was unnecessary with the result that twenty people arrived at the church ready for baptism.[27] Two weeks later Crosby led a revivalist meeting: "the great God open our heart. His moving. He was with us in our meeting the Spirit of God was in our meeting."[28]

Crosby, the flawed man rather than the inspiring preacher, antagonized the Tsimshian. They suspected that he kept the money he raised for his personal use rather than providing education for their children or for the church. They accused him of aiding the surveyors who were setting out the parameters of their reserves. The final straw for Clah was Crosby's disregard for protocol when he built a cow shed on Tsimshian land without their permission.[29] Clah was particularly incensed by this as he had written a letter on behalf of the Tsimshian requesting that Crosby desist from building his shed. Despite his annoyance, Clah recorded his ironic riposte to the missionary:

> when I ask him. friend I want to know If you read that letter which I give to you wednesday last[.] he said yes. But I want to know what letter said.
>   so he said to me. because I found no Names on that letter says If I found 2 [or] 3 names on I [would] not built the house. I say well letter dont write himself may be somebodys hand writed [wrote it]. But why not believe what letter said to you.

I said him friend you the priest. But you spoil the people here. you Built the houses every where. you know yourself indians want that land which you built the place on. also one thing I want you stoped about asking mon[e]y in church every Sunday that makes everybodys heart very low. If you [do] that in big city the whit[e] pe[o]ple give you hell. tie you [up]. you the man spoil this place you never teach the people right[.] when I speak to him he speaks very rough to me.[30]

A few days later Crosby left Port Simpson for a visit to Victoria without saying goodbye to anyone in the village and close to tears.[31] In 1895 the Tsimshian wrote to Alexander Sutherland, general secretary of the Methodist Missionary Society, requesting that Crosby be replaced, an action which occurred in 1897.[32]

Through the 1890s Crosby was not only distracted by the perennial problem of a shortage of funds to run the mission, but the appearance of the Salvation Army at Port Simpson. He tried to undermine them, refused to allow them to use buildings at Port Simpson for their meetings and would not baptize their children, marry them or bury their dead.[33] The Salvation Army spread through the north-west coastal region through the agency of local people, which made it very difficult for Crosby to combat its influence, as his efforts to suppress it brought him into direct conflict with the Tsimshian who were factionalized along religious lines.[34] Clah continued his non-aligned position: "some of my friends come to me for why not going any churchs. I have told them I promise to not go any churchs. But I promise to go with Jesus Christ."[35]

Alfred Green and S. S. Osterhout

Clah had a more amicable relationship with another Methodist missionary, Alfred Green, who oversaw the mission on the Nass River from 1877–1890 that became known as Greenville. It is possible that their relationship was less troubled because they lived in different communities. Clah saw Green only when he travelled up the river for fishing or trade. In 1890 Green relieved Crosby at Port Simpson. According to Clarence Bolt, soon after arriving in the village Green criticized the Tsimshian for not leading "godly lives" and for being too concerned with community council matters, while neglecting the Sabbath and indulging in potlatches and drinking.[36] A meeting of leading men wanted to have Green removed for denigrating their status in the community. Clah concurred, claiming Green was working against Tsimshian interests by undermining their confidence in their own autonomy.[37] At other times Green was a supportive friend to Clah. He provided him with medicines when he or his family were sick, and presided over the funeral of one of Clah's sons. Mrs Green offered Clah seeds to plant in his vegetable garden. It was Green, not Crosby, who taught Clah and his wife, Dorcas, the catechism before they were baptized in 1880. Clah maintained friendly contact with Green after the missionary moved to Vancouver Island, calling on him to assist in a legal case in which Clah was enmeshed.

Methodist missionary S. S. Osterhout, who came to the north-west coast in the late 1890s, also became caught up in the internal politics of the Tsimshian. In 1900 the

Methodists and the Salvation Army factions at Port Simpson were at loggerheads. The chiefs and elders of the Methodist church wanted to remove the names of the adherents of the Salvation Army from the church register and abused Osterhout when he tried to prevent them; some threatened they would leave the church if Osterhout persisted.[38] Clah, who was not directly involved in this power play, had an amicable relationship with Osterhout. He asked the missionary to write a foreword in his 1901 diary:

> Memoir of The life of one of Christianity's first converts on the North-west Coast
> Kept with a view to the production of a history of the same region
> See Psalm XC-10
> 'So teach us to number our days that we may apply our hearts unto wisdom'
> S.S. Osterhout[39]

Clah would have liked other missionaries to give their approbation in his diary. In 1903 he complained that the Anglican missionary, William Henry Collison, had kept his "Big Book" for five years without writing in it. James McCullagh, long-term missionary at Aiyansh Anglican mission on the Nass River, gave Clah two books he valued: a copy of William Duncan's *Metlakatlah. Ten Years' Work Among the Tsimshean Indians*; and, on another occasion, a copy of the Bible, presented as Clah was embarking on a gold prospecting trip.[40] Clah was particularly pleased with Duncan's book, which gave official recognition of Clah's role in the introduction of Christianity on the north-west coast.[41]

Robert Tomlinson

Duncan's strong personality and idiosyncratic view of his role as a missionary — refusing to be ordained or give communion — split the CMS and the Anglican church on the northern coast. Robert Tomlinson remained a strong supporter of Duncan, while Collison was caught in the crossfire between Duncan and the new Bishop of Caledonia, William Ridley, who was rather provocatively posted to Metlakatla in 1879.[42] Tomlinson had first come to Metlakatla in 1867.[43] He helped set up the Kincolith (Gingolx) mission in that year and in 1879 he moved to the Skeena River to establish a new mission, but left the CMS in 1881 for England to lodge a complaint against the new bishop, maintaining his independent Anglican mission on the Skeena River. Clah encountered Tomlinson over many years on the Nass River and along the coast, but did not have a close a relationship with him. They did, however, have a couple of personal altercations, and, as with so many of the other missionaries, Tomlinson could be petulant, at least in Clah's eyes, and discourteous. He not only took Duncan's side against Bishop Ridley and the CMS, but also supported Duncan in his initial threats against the Methodists at Fort Simpson. Tomlinson visited Fort Simpson in March 1874 to explain to its citizens the consequences of rejecting the Anglicans and embracing the Methodists:

he says will be no more Maryestrat [magistrate] at FS [Fort Simpson]. If anybody fight no more law no judge and if anyone laying sick give no metisin [medicine] . . . Tomlinson and Duncan very jealous. People says all right. God his the great judge, Jesus Christ he his the great man of war and he his the great Docteur. If anyone believe Him he helping us in His Blood. If anybody laying sick take Jesus [h]is Blood may help pline [blind] people.[44]

Thus were the missionaries' teachings thrown back at them. The Tsimshian did not need the missionaries because God supported them. He was not jealous or acrimonious, but helped those poor blind people in need. The Tsimshian ignored Duncan's and Tomlinson's threats and warnings. By January 1875 the majority of Fort Simpson people had moved to the Methodist church.[45] But the Anglicans' personal animosities quickly dissipated. While Tomlinson refused to shake hands with the Fort Simpson people in January of 1875, by April the following year he was visiting Clah's house and shaking the hands of his erstwhile friends, visiting the sick and providing them with medicine.[46]

Robert Cunningham

In many ways Clah's relationship with Robert Cunningham was the most intriguing. Cunningham barely ranks as a missionary. He arrived at Fort Simpson in 1863 and by 1865 he had been dismissed and was working for the HBC. He married a Tsimshian woman, Elizabeth Ryan, remaining on the north-west coast throughout his working life. While Clah knew him first as a missionary, for most of their acquaintance Cunningham was a trader and storekeeper and later a cannery operator. The two men went hunting and trading together, and Cunningham employed Clah and many other Tsimshian to transport goods for him during the goldrush era. Clah was closer to Cunningham than the missionaries, even though they were long-term residents in Tsimshian territory. Missionaries kept themselves aloof from the local people to main-tain their authority, while Cunningham worked closely with the Tsimshian. In 1866 Clah went to visit Cunningham: "he [is HBC] company and store keep[er] . . . who break Gods word. He use[d to be] Minister before. But now he falling down."[47] We have another snapshot of Cunningham at the time. A visitor to the HBC Fort described "his jolly round face, strikingly white skin and very light curly hair", a man who kept his Tsimshian wife and children out of sight.[48] While Cunningham may have been embarrassed to reveal his Tsimshian family, he continued to have liaisons with many other Tsimshian women.[49]

Despite his continuing fall from Christian grace, Cunningham turned out to be an astute businessman. After working as a fur trader, he took advantage of the burgeoning gold fever by setting up a store on the route to the Omineca goldfields in the interior of British Columbia. In 1871 Clah transported forty-seven cases of liquor, twelve ten gallon casks of liquor, 200 pounds of salt pork, a hundred pounds of axes and ten traps up the Skeena River for Cunningham and his business partner.[50] It took Clah and his crew in a large canoe three weeks through hazardous conditions to complete the journey. The canoe almost overturned several times and was badly damaged, for which Cunningham deducted money from Clah's pay. Clah's acceptance of this business deal was a contrast to his anger over missionary demands for donations for church and mission facilities.

Conclusions: Clah's dream

Clah recounted many of his dreams in his diary, in which missionaries and priests often figured. In one dream two unnamed ministers were preaching God's word on top of the mountain.[51] In another Christ gave Clah passages to read out of the Gospel of Mark 1: 1–8, in which John the Baptist predicts the coming of Jesus Christ, but his reading was interrupted by Cunningham who called him outside because a canoe had capsized.[52] In yet another Clah saw William Duncan, Robert Tomlinson, William Collison, Fred Stephenson (an Anglican minister) and Thomas Crosby.[53] But the most fascinating dream is one in which he encountered Cunningham, as a fallen minister, and three upright Anglican ministers: Arthur Doolan, Duncan and Tomlinson. Doolan took money out of a small box belonging to Clah, and Duncan wound up his broken clock to make it work again. Most intriguingly, Tomlinson gave Cunningham a putrid piece of meat and Clah, a fresh piece, which Cunningham swapped, taking the best for himself.[54] Here Doolan represents the grasping missionary who robs the poor Tsimshian, while Duncan assists them. Tomlinson rewards Clah for being a good Christian while he punishes Cunningham for his sinful behaviour. But opportunistic Cunningham cheats Clah of his due reward. This dream obviously does not represent Clah's actual relations with these three men, but it certainly symbolizes Clah's ambivalent feelings towards missionaries in general. In Clah's view missionaries could be helpful and supportive, but they also stole from the poor Tsimshian. Some were noble, while others were underhand, interested only in their own advancement. In another dream Duncan was working in Cunningham's store selling whiskey, while Cunningham taught Clah how to pray.[55] This suggests a Freudian transference from the bad missionary to the good one. But these dreams do not support Frantz Fanon's claim that the world of the colonized is a Manichean one in which "the dreams of the natives are always of muscular prowess; his dreams are of action and of aggression".[56] Clah's world, as reflected in his dreams, was not a world of stark alternatives; rather he was always hedging his bets as he did in daily life.

Clah gained his religious knowledge from missionaries and learned other important skills, particularly reading and writing, as well as practical knowledge. He relied on them for help and advice over a wide range of issues that he confronted when dealing with the colonial state and society. He rarely criticized missionaries' preaching or services. He himself enjoyed preaching, but if he could attend Sunday services, whatever the denomination, he would do so. He appreciated revivalist services offered by the Methodists, while valuing Duncan's more sober style, and the noise and drama of the Salvation Army. Tensions arose between Clah and missionaries when they stepped out of their religious role to become administrators or mediators between the Tsimshian and colonial authorities. They were expected to be religious leaders, but not demand money to maintain the church. When Crosby first came to Fort Simpson, Clah and the other Tsimshian gladly donated money to build a church. This paralleled their donations to chiefs or heads of households to contribute to the building of a new house that had significance for all the tribal group. But ongoing demands for money, as in the weekly collections at church, were not part of Tsimshian protocols and came to be deeply resented. Clah and the Tsimshian thought the missionaries were lining their own pockets with this money and not putting it to the good of the whole community.

Both Anglican and Methodist missionaries established town councils that they used to impose their own will on the communities. These had the potential for tensions and conflict, which were realized at Port Simpson where the Tsimshian became increasingly disillusioned with Crosby. Many rejected him, moving to the Salvation Army, or offshoots of the Methodist Church — the Band of Christian Workers and the Epworth League — where they were able to exert more control. Missionaries also ran into trouble when they took up a mediation role, particularly over land alienation. Their inability to influence the colonial state was interpreted by the Tsimshian (and neighbouring First Nations) as connivance with the state. On the other hand, Clah continued to consult them and seek their assistance and advice over his personal land dealings. He called on both Collison and Green (but not Crosby) to intervene on his behalf with public servants and lawyers in Victoria as late as 1909, long after Green had moved away from the northern coast.

Clah wanted the missionaries as friends and sought their acceptance and regard, but he did not want them gratuitously interfering in his affairs or telling him what to do or how to behave. As a member of Tsimshian society, he wanted the missionaries to create opportunities for them in the emerging colonial economy and defend their interests, but he did not want missionaries controlling the way the community ran its affairs. In reality it was impossible for missionaries to live up to these different expectations and demands, while remaining responsive to their mission societies and not becoming totally isolated within the settler society. William Duncan managed these differing pressures better than most missionaries, at least until he became old and too set in his ways. He was able to retain the respect of the Tsimshian among whom he lived and died, while maintaining a loyal and influential following in Canada, the United States of America and Britain.

Clah's diary reveals that missionaries were all too human. They could be generous and loyal friends. They tended the sick. They gave advice and assistance to the Tsimshian in communicating with the colonial authorities. At other times they were petty, jealous and vindictive. They sometimes fought amongst themselves and broke the Christian codes they insisted the Tsimshian follow. Many missionaries took on secular roles such as magistrate, Justice of the Peace and head of community councils. They swore in native constables and organized building and maintenance projects in the villages. These myriad roles put them in sensitive situations and conflict with the people they evangelized. Clah's diary enables us to see the missionaries' strengths and weaknesses, their day-to-day movements and activities, not as they would like to have had these portrayed but as they were observed by an Indigenous chronicler.

Notes

1. Arthur Wellington Clah Diary, 140-1-72, Wellcome Library, London, hereafter WL.
2. In the 1880s Fort Simpson was renamed Port Simpson. I use both names in this paper, depending on the period under discussion.
3. Duncan's life and work has been the subject of numerous books and articles, including: Murray, *The Devil and Mr Duncan*; Usher, *William Duncan of Metlakatla*; Neylan, *The Heavens They Are Changing*; Perry, "The Autocracy of Love"; Galois, "Colonial Encounters". Duncan published an account of his early years on the north-west coast, Duncan, *Metlakatlah*, and there were a number of contemporary biographies of Duncan, including: Wellcome, *The Story of Metlakahtla*; Stock, *Metlakahtla and the North Pacific Mission*.
4. For accounts of missions and missionaries on the Nass River among the Nisga'a see Patterson, *Mission on the Nass*; Patterson, "Nishga Perceptions"; Collison, *In the Wake of the War Canoe*.
5. See Brock, "Building Bridges."
6. Clah was born in May 1831 and Duncan on 3 April 1832. Clah Diary, WL, first page; Murray, *The Devil and Mr Duncan*, p. 18.
7. William Duncan Diary, 2 November 1857, 30 November 1857, microform, University of British Columbia Library, Vancouver, hereafter UBC. Clah had previously worked as a servant in the Fort. The fur trade was undertaken in the trade Jargon Chinook. As a result few Tsimshian had a knowledge of English. Duncan Diary, 30 November 1857, UBC.
8. Duncan Diary, 17 May 1858, UBC.
9. Duncan Diary, 3 December 1862, UBC. In 1874 Clah heard Duncan was laughing at his preaching 18 January 1874. See also Brock, "Building Bridges", p. 83, and Neylan, "Eating the Angel's Food", p. 97.
10. Usher, *William Duncan*, p. 96.
11. Usher, *William Duncan* p. 96; Murray, *The Devil and Mr Duncan*, pp. 124–5
12. For a detailed discussion of this episode see Brock, "Building Bridges".
13. Clah Diary, 1 January 1873, 1 December 1874, 3 January 1874, WL; MacDonald and Cove, *Tsimshian Narratives 2*, p. 212.
14. Clah Diary, 26 February 1874, WL. These Christian names are the names subsequently used by Clah in his diary. See also Brock, "Building Bridges", p. 88.
15. Clah Diary, February–March 1874, WL.
16. Clah Diary, 2 December 1874, WL.
17. Clah Diary, 3 December 1874, WL.
18. Duncan, *Metlakatlah*; Johnson, *Dayspring in the Far West*, chapter XII.
19. Clah Diary, 24 November, 6 December 1907, WL.
20. Clah Diary, 12 January 1874, WL. No doubt Clah was excluded because he had shamed Alfred Dudoward, the driving force behind the invitation to the Methodists, by his bridge building activities.
21. Clah Diary, 28 June 1874, WL.
22. Clah Diary, 24 October 1874, WL.
23. Robert Galois argues that Clah left because he fell out with Crosby. Galois, "Colonial Encounters": pp. 105–47, p. 142.
24. Clah Diary, 19 January 1876, WL.

25 Clah Diary, 22–25 February 1876, WL.
26 Clah Diary, 1 March 1876, WL.
27 Clah Diary, 1 January 1887, WL
28 Clah Diary, 16 January 1887, WL.
29 Clah Diary, 3 November 1889, 30 November 1891, 3 January 1892, 24 and 27 August 1892, WL.
30 Clah Diary, 27 August 1892, WL.
31 Clah Diary, 2 September 1892, WL.
32 Clah Diary, 11 February 1895, WL; Bolt, *Thomas Crosby*, p. 92.
33 Clah Diary, 9 December 1894, WL. The Anglican priest Fred Stephenson eventually officiated at the Salvation Army members' funerals; Clah Diary, 18 January 1895, WL.
34 Bolt, *Thomas Crosby*, p.53; Brock, "Building Bridges", p. 95.
35 Clah Diary, 16 December 1894, WL.
36 Bolt, *Thomas Crosby*, p. 88.
37 Clah Diary, 5 February 1890, WL.
38 Clah Diary, 15 August 1903, 5–8 March 1900, WL.
39 Clah Diary, foreword 1901, WL.
40 Clah Diary, 24 July 1891, 14 May 1894, WL
41 Clah Diary, 6 Oct 1882, WL. This seems to be the first time Clah saw Duncan's book and the reference to himself.
42 Murray, *The Devil and Mr Duncan*, p. 140; p. 148.
43 Patterson, "Kincolith's First Decade".
44 Clah Diary, 6 and 11 March 1874, WL.
45 Clah Diary, 15 and 18 January 1875, WL.
46 Clah Diary, 22 January 1875, 4 April 1876, WL.
47 Clah Diary, 3 December 1866, WL.
48 Account of a visit to Fort Simpson nd (*c.* 1868) Duncan papers, microfilm A1720, British Columbia Archives, Victoria.
49 Clah Diary, 7–8 January 1869, WL. On another occasion Clah complained Cunningham was sleeping with many women, including Clah's wife. Elizabeth Cunningham was in a canoe with the Reverend Harold Sheldon and three other people when it capsized and all but one boy were drowned on the Skeena River in 1888; Clah Diary, 23 February 1888, WL.
50 Clah Diary, 11 May 1871, WL.
51 Clah Diary, 6 March 1866, WL.
52 Clah Diary, 17 January 1869, WL.
53 Clah Diary, 7 February 1895, WL.
54 Clah Diary, 20 and 23 February 1869, WL.
55 Clah Diary, 4 January 1872, WL.
56 Fanon, *The Wretched of the Earth*, p. 40.

CHAPTER SEVEN

The Promise of a Book
Missionaries and Native Evangelists in North-east India

ANDREW MAY

From his base at the mission station at Cherrapunji[1] in the present-day north-eastern Indian hill state of Meghalaya, Welsh Calvinistic Methodist missionary Thomas Jones set out in early 1842 on a tour through the Khasi Hills. Jones encountered many villages where the inhabitants had not set eyes on a European in the two decades or so since the British took possession of the region in the 1820s. His visit "caused enormous tumult and fear in the minds of the people",[2] apprehensive as they were of the destruction and persecution that many other villages had experienced at the hands of the agents of colonial power.

Other Khasis he had met elsewhere since his arrival in the hills in June 1841 had recognized him as an Englishman, though an uncommon one; on observing him accomplish a difficult task, some said he could do everything, like a God, others that: "Many people are called English, but we do not believe that they have come from England."[3] By Jones's own account, the hill people were astonished that he could predict the phases of the moon, surprised when he taught them more economical ways to hew wood or burn lime using coal, and were eager to learn English as a means of improving their trading prospects with the plains people or to secure government posts. One small boy came up to Jones, and seeing his library of books, asked for one so he could learn English. Jones replied that he did not have such a book to give him, which puzzled the boy, who thought the Padre Sahib should be able to spare at least one. "He could not comprehend", wrote Jones, "that I had to come here first to learn their language, and then make books for them."[4]

As part of continuing reappraisals of the "unfinished business"[5] of mission history, in which new approaches address the role of the missionary as more than just a "faceless imperial agent",[6] this chapter seeks to inflect the history of one particular mission station with an alternative reading of missionary and indigenous interaction. Both the hagiographies of the insider chroniclers, and the stern and trenchant critiques of the missionary as colonialism's Trojan horse, have together had a marked tendency to undervalue an appreciation of intercultural exchanges. They also all too easily second guess cultural outcomes which may not always be predictable or consistent across time and space, or which may be locally irrelevant or sit uncomfortably with this or that ideological shibboleth.

Thomas Jones was of course a Welshman, not an Englishman, and therefore in a sense he was a colonized colonizer of an area of India that is now 70 percent Christian (in a country where Christians comprise less than 3 percent of the population). An injunction like that of postcolonial critic Ghosh-Schellhorn to read the missionary's impact on the Khasis as "a prime example of Bhabha's concept of 'colonial mimicry'" whereby "Welsh religion, dress, orthography and not the least non-conformism have been rendered ambivalent through transplantation onto a tribal way of life"[7] sits at odds with more recent calls to avoid the kind of paternalism that "would attribute 'false consciousness' to the majority of Christians in the twenty-first century."[8]

A gathering was held in April 2007 at Pynthorumkhrah Presbyterian Church in the Khasi Hills, to inaugurate a program of celebratory events leading up to the bicentenary in 2010 of the birth of Thomas Jones. The President of the Khasi Authors' Society, S. S. Majaw, gave a long speech on Jones's contribution to Khasi literature and education; Meghalaya Chief Minister D. D. Lapang hoisted a flag and launched a small booklet on Jones's life written in Khasi and English; and the Reverend Dr John Tudno Williams, Moderator of the Presbyterian Church of Wales, unveiled a commemorative plaque. The contemporary reality is that many Khasis — whether Christian, or supporters of the Seng Khasi movement (formed in the 1890s to promote indigenous Khasi culture) — celebrate Jones as the architect of the Khasi language, while also able to condemn the hostility of missionaries towards traditional ways of life. [9]

New mission histories continue to excavate the archival record in exciting ways, by the translation of mission sources, and the re-examination of mission publications and documents. This is all the more possible in an era when many Church authorities show some conciliatory willingness for historians to access what is sometimes sensitive documentation that all to easily can show the work of their former operatives in a negative light. Ghosh-Schellhorn might doubt that the Khasis had any idea of the Welsh position in Great Britain — instead conflating them with the mass of British colonial enterprise[10] — yet mission archives might reveal more complex and nuanced readings. Khasi convert U Larsing (1838–1863) travelled to England and Wales in 1861 with William and Mary Lewis, who had joined the first missionary couple Thomas and Ann Jones 18 months after the mission had been established.[11] In travelling to Wales, U Larsing experienced both homecoming and exile, but his letters home clearly reveal an understanding of the Wales/England, Khasi/Bengali cultural dichotomies:

> England is a flat country having only a few little Hills here & there, and is filled with large & small towns. But Wales is a mountainous country. It is like your Jynteah country in many parts, and in some parts like our Khasi country . . . There is not much of jungle, and there is no part of the country without being cultivated . . . All the Rivers glides [sic] smoothly and pleasantly along as if they were silver snakes! But they do not dig the earth away & sink deeply like our rivers in the Khasi country. When I am in Wales, I feel on this account — just as if I were in my own Khasi country. But when I am in England, I feel as if I were in Bengal.[12]

The predominant narrative of both new and old histories of the Khasi mission is the preeminence of Thomas Jones as founding missionary and bringer of the book: the prime architect of the Christianisation of the hill tribes, the *de novo* "father" of Khasi literature in his role as the man who put the Khasi language into written form using Welsh orthography.[13]

When Jones disappointed the small boy who had asked for a book, and then embarked on a process of regularising Khasi language and grammar in written form, Jones in one way established himself as gatekeeper and interlocutor of Khasi culture and thought. Such a claim elided easily with a popular Khasi legend, and drew Jones into Khasi cosmology through a story circulated by mission historians as well as later anthropologists and Khasi scholars. According to Khasi lore, the great God had entrusted a Khasi man and a foreigner each with a sacred book containing his holy law. Returning to their respective homelands, they came to a great river. The foreigner wrapped the book in his long hair and carried it across the flood on his head. The Khasi was short, and though taking the book between his teeth was unable to protect his precious cargo from the swirling waters, and the book was lost. But as this chapter will argue, the heroic version of missionary-as-saviour (cultural or Christian) belies a lineage of debts, relationships and negotiations in which indigenous peoples played an active role in shaping cultural and spiritual outcomes.

The mission brethren back in Wales may have felt Jones had been packed off to the darkest heathen jungles, and Jones himself at times looked every way and saw heathen hordes. Yet the Khasi Hills were neither a blank slate, nor was Jones the only protagonist in the drama of cultural change. Rather than focussing as I do elsewhere on Jones's work as a missionary after his arrival in Sohra,[14] here I am concerned with earlier encounters, and in particular the role of indigenous Christian evangelists (prior to the establishment of the Welsh mission) in intervening in Khasi religious, cultural and linguistic practice. This chapter will firstly set Thomas Jones ashore at Calcutta in 1841, in order to demonstrate both his unpreparedness for the role, as well as the existing network of Christian activity into which he tapped. I then track the influence of William Carey's Serampore mission on the Khasi Hills, with particular reference to the activities of Indian evangelist Chandra Pal, and Anglo-Indian preacher Alexander Lish. The key concern of the chapter is therefore to demonstrate that far from inheriting a blank slate, Jones's work amongst the Khasis was premised on and situated within pre-existing negotiations about power, belief, race and cultural identity.

Missionary Intelligence

William Carey had arrived in Calcutta in 1793 with no intention of ever returning to England, though he could not have dreamt that his work in India would last forty unbroken years until his death at Serampore in 1834.[15] When Thomas Jones arrived in Calcutta in April 1841, he had a similar resolve in mind. His strength of purpose had been hinted at in his application to the London Missionary Society (LMS) in 1839, in which he expressed his missionary calling not simply as the professed duty of any young Christian man, but as a determination "to go whether any Society would send me or

Andrew May

not, and trust to providence for my support and protection".[16] But groomed as he was for the role by the Welsh Calvinistic Methodists, his instructions — such as they were — also gave him licence to make what he wished of the role. After all the preparation and anticipation, and the long sea voyage, as the missionary finally stood on solid ground, the enormity of the task would have dawned on him, and the question of what on earth to do next suddenly became more urgent.

Five days before Jones's ship the *Jamaica* had left port at Liverpool, mission secretary John Roberts had informed Jones that the Foreign Mission Committee found it unnecessary to hand him any formal instructions as to how he might proceed with his work in the Khasi Hills, trusting their missionary to take "the most prudent, & at the same time the most active measures towards accomplishing the important object for which you are sent out". With little information on the country to which they were sending him, they could only advise that his "first business must necessarily be the attainment of the language spoken by the natives", and that Cherrapunji should be the most suitable station for his residence. More than that, Roberts advised, the Committee would be able to form a better opinion when reports were received.[17]

The lack of detailed instructions reflected the inexperience as much as the novelty of the undertaking by the Welsh Society. Other societies proffered far more elaborate orders. The *Calcutta Christian Observer* in June 1837, for example, reported most favourably on the detailed written instructions delivered to four missionaries from the American Board of Commissioners for Foreign Missions, who were about to embark for the Indian Archipelago in the Indian Ocean (in particular, to Java and Sumatra). Key proscriptions included avoiding interference with other existing Protestant missions, not requiring or expecting much from the local government, establishing a safe residence for their families, learning the native languages, raising an indigenous ministry, and ensuring they garnered sufficient local subjects to keep themselves occupied and to encourage home patronage. "Your appropriate sphere of action", it was advised, "is not to be the external and material, but the intellectual and moral world. Your chief concern is to be with thoughts and feelings."[18]

Newly landed in Calcutta, therefore, Jones's first tasks were to tap into the local Christian network, and to figure out how to get to the Khasi Hills. To the newcomer, Calcutta's alluring spectacle of empire was a riot of cultural difference, in which a new sense of order required fashioning out of chaos. Baptist missionary W. H. Denham had described his arrival in Calcutta in 1844:

> In the city are splendid edifices and mud hovels, naked children and half naked adults, various and discordant sounds, mechanics at their employ, vendors sitting by their goods. Innumerable sledges drawn by oxen, fashionable European carriages, buggies, garees, palankins, grooms running to clear the way, in fact, a ceaseless din. Reflection, however, soon dissipated the wonder the scene excited. Degradation and idolatry were around us; 'destruction and misery' walked hand in hand by our side. We may have read — but the reality![19]

For the evangelical missionary, the distancing space between the envisioned heathen horde, so long imagined, and the real Indian subjects that thronged the streets, collapsed in the first encounter. The monolithic category of "savage" could now begin to be renegotiated at an individual level, with room for both evangelising and human-ising (or as Jane Samson observes in this volume, "othering" and "brothering"). In the midst of this disequilibrium, knowing whom to trust was not just a matter of being wary of the natives; it was also a matter of learning how to negotiate with those Europeans who were the missionary's moral or political enemies, as well as those who had perhaps already been subtly transformed by India, perhaps without their own knowledge. Who could you trust in the confusion of a city of a quarter of a million souls? Jones would later write that: "every day convinces me that the further a missionary lives from these wicked Europeans, the better".[20]

The coming weeks that Thomas Jones would spend in Calcutta were an abrupt accli-matisation, and connections from home were essential in stabilising a sense of self and of mission amidst the confusion of arrival. Jones was armed with letters of introduc-tion from former LMS missionary, the Reverend Jacob Tomlin, to various gentlemen in the city,[21] and from Henry Grey of Edinburgh to Scottish missionary, Alexander Duff. Jones kept up a busy round of visiting, garnering the support and approval of many of the missionaries of Calcutta, "who have severally given me a very hearty recep-tion, and hail my arrival in Calcutta as a sign of a revival of religion amongst the Welsh Calvinistic Methodists".[22] On 4 May Thomas Jones was invited to attend the Monthly Missionary Conference:

> I was very warmly received, & offered all the assistance those present could possibly afford me. I might add, what may perhaps be of some consolation to you, that one of their number observed afterwards, though not to me personally, that he never saw any newly arrived missionary, [receive] so general & warm a reception![23]

Calcutta's missionaries had convened Monthly Missionary Prayer Meetings since 1816, and the Baptists, Geoffrey and W. H. Pearce, inaugurated the Calcutta Missionary Conference when they had asked their fellow Protestant missionaries to breakfast in 1829.[24] The Conference became an alliance between missionaries of the various Protestant denominations (Independents, Baptists and Scottish Presbyterians, "together with any others whom they consider as legitimate & worthy missionaries of Christ"). From 1832 their organ — the *Calcutta Christian Observer. Edited by Christian Ministers of various denominations* — published a range of material, from observations and essays on temperance, native manners and customs, education and conversion, to book reviews, essays on the duty of private Christians, and debates around the Romanisation of native orthography. It was here, too, that a monthly digest of missionary and religious intelligence was disseminated, promoting the activities of various missionary societies across the Indian Presidencies, as well as in Malacca, Singapore, Ceylon, Mauritius, Penang, Batavia, Siam, Africa and America. Alexander Duff had spearheaded the Church of Scotland's work in Calcutta from 1830, and was for a time editor of the journal.

Jones fixed his compass in the Christian community of Calcutta. No sooner had he regained his land legs, than the journey to the Khasi Hills beckoned. But before he finally set out, he gleaned further vital information about the area that was to become his home until his death in 1849. In his first report to Roberts from Calcutta, Jones noted that the Reverend Mr Mack of Serampore, who had previously been at Cherrapunji, had paid him a visit:

> and kindly promised to furnish me with all the manuscripts, Books, &c relating to the Cossias & their language, which they at Serampore have in their power to find for me; and (as you are aware) they are able to do more in this way than any body else in Calcutta.[25]

The Serampore Influence and Native Evangelism

The Serampore missionaries were the benchmark of all Indian missions. The Northamptonshire-born Baptist William Carey[26] was inspired to mission by reading in the mid 1780s the accounts of the voyages of Captain James Cook to the South Seas. Publication of his *An enquiry into the obligations of Christians, to use means for the conversion of the heathens* in 1792 inspired the foundation in Kettering in that year of the first evangelical missionary society — the Particular Baptist Society for Propagating the Gospel among the Heathen (later known as the Baptist Missionary Society). Carey exhorted his fellow Christians to take up Christ's commission to his apostles to "go and teach all nations". And there was a plentiful supply of heathens; Carey wildly estimated the world's population at 731 million (including 12 million in New Holland), 431 million of whom "are still in pagan darkness".[27] The practicability of such a mission was confronted by a range of impediments: "either their distance from us, their barbarous and savage manner of living, the danger of being killed by them, the difficulty of procuring the necessaries of life, or the unintelligibleness of their languages".[28]

In November 1793 Carey arrived in Bengal on a Danish ship, with surgeon John Thomas, to commence missionary work. After managing an indigo factory for a number of years, in 1800 Carey set up a mission base at the Danish trading settlement of Serampore, about 30 kilometres north of Calcutta. Together with Joshua Marshman and William Ward (the three became known as the Serampore trio), Carey established a Mission Press (1800), and later Serampore College (1818). Aside from a number of Indian grammars and dictionaries, with assistance from Indian *pundits*, the whole Bible was translated into six Indian languages, while parts of it were translated into a further twenty-nine.

In 1804 Carey wrote to John Ryland, one of the founding members of the Baptist Missionary Society, detailing the *modus operandi* of the Baptist mission. Here the nexus is explicit between Bible translation, education and conversion, as well as the model (influenced by Moravian ideals) of the communal and financially independent mission station supported by native preachers:

> Another plan has lately occupied our attention. It appears that our business is to

provide materials for spreading the Gospel, and to apply those materials. Translations, pamphlets, etc., are the materials. To apply them we have thought of setting up a number of subordinate stations, in each of which a brother shall be fixed. It will be necessary and useful to carry on some worldly business. Let him be furnished from us with a sum of money to begin and purchase cloth or whatever other article the part produces in greatest perfection: the whole to belong to the mission, and no part ever to be private trade or private property. The gains may probably support the station. Every brother in such a situation to have one or two native brethren with him, and to do all he can to preach and spread Bibles, pamphlets, etc., and to set up and encourage schools where the reading of the Scriptures shall be introduced.[29]

On 28 December 1800, after seven years in India, Carey's mission bore its first fruit with the conversion of a Hindu carpenter named Krishna Chandra Pal. At the same ceremony, Carey baptized his 15-year old son Felix in the River Hooghly, in the presence of the Governor and a mixed audience of Europeans, Portuguese, Hindus and Muslims. Pal's conversion was followed by that of his sister-in-law, Joymooni, and wife, Rasoo.[30] Soon after his baptism, Pal had expressed the view that his sights were set on "the salvation of others". With Carey, Marshman and Ward fully occupied with the affairs of Serampore, including the school and the printing office, Pal wished to spread the Gospel throughout Bengal: "I would go to the end of the world to make his love known."[31] After some years at Serampore, he moved on to Calcutta, where he worked for around five years as a native preacher and distributor of religious tracts. News of the first Hindu convert was a milestone in the history of the mission, and reports of Pal's conversion and rejection of his past ways were widely circulated to home audiences in what was to become a familiar narrative style, and an important fillip for fundraising efforts.[32] "Ye Gods of stone and clay!", reported one tract: "Did ye not tremble when, in the name of the Father, Son and Holy Spirit, one of your votaries shook you as the dust from his feet?"[33]

In early 1813, Pal and Gorachund, another native Christian, were persuaded by the Serampore missionaries to set off for the eastern region of British Bengal, which at its fullest extent stretched from the north of the Bay of Bengal, west to the Punjab, north to the border with Nepal and Bhutan, and east taking in Dacca (Dhaka), Sylhet and Chittagong.[34] Sylhet, just to the south of the Khasi Hills, had come under Islamic influence from the fourteenth century, while Dacca fell to Mughal rule from the early seventeenth century and passed to the British after the Battle of Plassey in 1765. At Dacca, Pal and Gorachund preached and distributed books, gave a Persian Bible to Muslims with whom they stayed for ten days, and then preached at Ajmeer and Baitool, before reaching Chattuck, about 35 kilometres north-west of Sylhet.

Carey had given Pal a letter of introduction to Matthew Smith, an English magistrate at Sylhet (and a friend and supporter of Carey), with whom Pal met at Chattuck and who gave him a further letter of introduction to the Judge of Sylhet.[35] They reached Sylhet on 20 March. According to Pal's account, the judge was most pleased with the books Pal had brought from Serampore, "and told me to give them to those who wanted them. I preached and distributed the tracts there."[36] The judge also encouraged Pal to take the Bible to "Khasi country", and gave him letters of introduction to the local *subadar* and *jemadar* (first and second ranked local commandants), with whom he lodged.

There is no evidence that Krishna Chandra Pal travelled to the Khasi Hills proper, but rather itinerated in the foothills for eight months, visiting the market town of Pondua (near Bholaganj), an important centre where Khasis from nearby villages and towns such as Shella and Mustoh came down to trade with Bengalis from the plains.[37] It was in this district that Pal claimed to have converted seven individuals — four sepoys, an Assamese and two Khasis named Dewankhasee (U Duwan) and Ooana-khasee (U Anna).[38] The Sylhet judge and magistrate came up to interrogate the purported converts as to their belief "in the death of Christ, that he died for sinners, and whether they wished to be baptized". Convinced that they were genuine, the British officials asked Pal to baptize the seven, using water from a silver basin:

> I told them I had never seen baptism performed in that manner. Upon their inquiring about the mode I followed, I referred to the baptism of John mentioned in the New Testament. They then said, I might do it in the way I preferred, and we went to the Dhuvuleshwuree river. There were present eight rajas, and about six hundred Khaseeyas. I read the sixth chapter of Romans, expounded and prayed, and then baptized the seven men.[39]

After Pal's departure by the end of 1813, further accounts of the "Kassai" filtered through to Serampore via Carey's Sylhet contacts:

> These mountaineers who have a constant intercourse with the people of Sylhet, have no character of their own, nor, strictly speaking, a written language. The few among them who can write use the Bengalee character. The language has a much greater affinity with the Chinese than with the Bengalee.[40]

There is no citable evidence that Pal had established a mission post at Cherrapunji during his stay in the region,[41] or indeed set up camp at Mawsmai, three miles from Cherrapunji, a first contact that is claimed by one later historian to have "exploded into a conflict which resulted in the persecution of a few converts in 1823."[42] But Pal's evangelising in 1813 — which had particularly excited the Baptist brethren, as it had pushed the mission's reach to within a week's journey of China — certainly had the effect of adding Khasi to the growing list of Bible translations running off the Serampore Mission Press.

In December 1813, after Pal's return to Serampore, Carey secured the services of a *pundit* to undertake the Khasi translation of the Gospels, believing him to be "the only one in that nation who could read and write".[43] According to some sources, a translation of the Gospel of St Matthew was circulated in 1817, and 500 copies of a New Testament translation were printed in Khasi in 1824.[44] Morris's claim that the translation was "made by a Bengali woman, who had been for some time in Cherrapoonjee as a nurse in a British Officer's family",[45] is rejected by later historians, who point to other evidence of Khasi involvement. One of Carey's Sylhet contacts had suggested in 1816 that Khasi boys could be procured from the local rajas to help in Bible translation,[46] while another account claims it was in fact the widow of a local raja who had helped Carey in the translation work.[47] Serampore College, which had opened in 1818, also admitted amongst its first intake "several Brahmins, a few Moslems, a Panjabi, a Mahratta, two Khasis, three Garos (sent by Scott, Commissioner of Cooch Behar — one of Carey's early students), two Arakanese, and the many Bengalese."[48] Hamlet Bareh suggests, too, that some Khasis were also studying at Fort William College in Calcutta in order to gain the necessary educational skills to conduct more advanced trade negotiations with the plains people.[49] While Krishna Chandra Pal himself died of malaria in 1822, there is also a suggestion in some sources that he wrote two introductory primers for elementary education among the Khasis.[50]

The original intent of the British East India Company to prevent missionary work throughout India was clearly eroded by the amendment to the Charter in 1813. Prior to this, however, the missionary activity in Bengal, inaugurated by the Serampore Baptists, had slowly but surely permeated informally throughout the province, by means of a network of converts and emissaries, and leaving a paper trail of the tracts and scriptures that continued to roll off the Mission Press. By default, and despite the East India Company's "own selfish ignorance", the appointment of Carey as language professor at Wellesley's new Fort William College was seen by mission supporters as confirmation that "the company became a principal partner in the Christianization of India and China".[51] After Pal's departure, and despite the first missionary attempts to circulate Christian scriptures in the Khasi language, the process of active evangelization the Khasi Hills went into abeyance through the 1820s. Even the texts that were circulated had little local impact as they were not only printed in Bengali characters, but used the Shella dialect which was not comprehensible to Khasis in Cherrapunji or those further upland.[52]

Pal's work had been undertaken thirty years before Thomas Jones arrived in Calcutta. The Reverend John Mack provided Thomas Jones with whatever copies of those early documents and publications that were still at hand, and he would certainly have given a verbal account of the more recent developments in the Hills through the 1830s. Mack informed some friends in England in June 1832 that the missionaries were "strongly inclined to form a Station at Cherrapoonjee, where the British Government had recently established a Sanatorium."[53] Alexander Burgh Lish, a young Anglo-Indian (Eurasian) student at Serampore, was accepted for missionary work and left for the Khasi Hills in March 1832. The eighteen-year-old Lish was ordained in Calcutta in December 1833, and a number of Khasis accompanied him to attend the service.[54] He returned to Cherrapunji in January 1834 accompanied by Joshua Rowe, an English tutor at Serampore College,[55] and a Bengali preacher named Jan.[56]

Lish worked among the Station's European residents, as well as teaching and preaching to the Khasis and "preparing reading lessons for the scholars". In the latter work he had given up on teaching English, establishing instead a class for teaching the Bengali characters in which the Khasi New Testament had been printed.[57] Lish established schools at Sohra, Mawsmai and Mawmluh, and the principal school at the British

Station at Cherrapunji was on land granted by Francis Jenkins, Commissioner of Assam. This school, located at the upper edge of the Sanitarium and in proximity to the native village at Cherrapunji, was the best attended. It was reported in mid 1837 that under Lish's instruction, the "boys of the first class" had read most of the four Gospels and some of the book of Genesis in English, had learned to read other lessons in Khasi (using Bengali script), had been schooled in translation from Khasi to English and vice versa, and were attempting long division in arithmetic.[58] Lish had revised the translation of the St Matthew's Gospel, and according to varying accounts translated the Sermon on the Mount, some of the Parables, the Acts of the Apostles, as well as setting down a Khasi vocabulary and grammar.[59] He was assisted in the schools by U Duwan Rai (one of Krishna Pal's converts), U Jungkha and U Laithat, but the thirty-six enrolments recorded in the early years ultimately fell away as little progress was made teaching in Bengali script.[60]

Lish lived and worked at Cherrapunji from 1832 until 1837, aided by Joshua Rowe, who taught at the mission school. There was a continued close association with the Serampore Baptists, not only through the visits to the recuperative climate of the hills by the Macks and the Marshmans, but also through the more extended residence there of B. W. Marshman, the son of Joshua Marshman. Tomlin observed that the work of the Serampore evangelists over their four or so years of their work in the hills, "sowing the precious seeds of God's word", was already achieving results among young Khasis in the mission schools. In September 1837, Tomlin wrote to Mr Marshman[61] from Cherrapunji, noting the fertile agricultural tracts and the industry of the Khasis:

> There is, however, room enough for other settlers, if they can be contented to eat their bread in the sweat of their brow; and to bring their wants within a narrow compass; and be more anxious to benefit the people, than to fill their pockets. Small Christian settlements or colonies, on the plan of the United Brethren, would, I think, do well in the neighbourhood of Moflong and Myrung. Thence, the gospel might be spread over the hills, east and west, and be preached in every village of the Khassias in a few years; and the joyful tidings of the gospel would doubtless soon reach the Jynteah Khassias to the east, and the Garrows on the west.[62]

In Tomlin's eyes, the Khasi Hills were ripe for mission work, free from the influences of Islam and Hinduism, and just as importantly from Catholicism, whose "emissaries are coming forth like a cloud of locusts, and settling upon every green spot that has been cultivated, by the Lord's faithful servants".[63] In March 1838 an extended account of the Khasis by Alexander Lish was published in the *Calcutta Christian Observer*.[64] It appears that by that time he had abandoned the Khasi mission, and in October 1838 he was appointed to Dacca.[65]

Conclusion

Direct missionary intervention in the Khasi Hills, sustained primarily by the

Serampore Baptists, could therefore draw a straight line from the work of Lish, Rowe and Tomlin, back to Pal's 1813 preaching tour and the ensuing period of scriptural translation, finding its source in the originating work of William Carey. As the Reverend Mack briefed Thomas Jones in Calcutta in May 1841, Jones would have realized both the opportunities and the impediments to the establishment of a successful mission in the region. The reasons for the failure of the Baptists to gain a foothold in the hills over the preceding three decades were various, and the Welsh inheritance from Serampore, though it had laid the groundwork, was erratic and at times unreliable. The inaccessibility of the terrain, the vagaries of the severe rainy season, the absence of appropriate printed language materials, and the palpable lack of progress were a stark legacy of three decades of spasmodic effort. The mission had also undergone a desta-bilising period after the Serampore missionaries had separated from the London-based Baptist Missionary Society in 1827 following disputes over the management of Serampore College and the independent finances raised at Serampore. Carey died in 1834, at a time when a drop in the value of the rupee also led to a severe financial crisis in Calcutta. The fractured mission was reunited in 1837, but in the Khasi Hills the lack of conversions and the inevitable stresses of isolation, deprivation and ill health on the young missionary families, saw their efforts relinquished by the end of the decade.[66]

Contrary to representations of Thomas Jones as the exclusive Khasi founding father, a more detailed tracking of the origins of evangelical influence in the Khasi Hills, and, in particular, the role of native preachers, complements the insights gleaned from a reading of Khasi evangelists such as U Larsing later in the century, to demonstrate a more subtle and complex picture of the nature and trajectory of intercultural exchange. Histories of missions have not always credited indigenous evangelists with agency. Krishna Chandra Pal was, of course, not himself a Khasi, but those Khasis who had come under the influence and education of Serampore missionaries prior to Thomas Jones's arrival, played an active role in negotiating and informing the process of language translation embarked on by Jones after his arrival. U Duwan Rai (one of Krishna Pal's converts) and U Jungkha had both been pupils of Lish, and, as Jones's reports demonstrate, they were key informants in his attempts to formalize Khasi in writing. It is interesting to note that Jones's reports to the mission board were them-selves the subject of translation and therefore slippage of meaning, written in English (though he was bilingual) and then translated into Welsh by John Roberts for publi-cation in the monthly Calvinistic Methodist Church newsletter *Y Drysorfa* ("The Treasury").[67] It was through this newsletter that the Welsh congregations were regu-larly kept informed not only of the general progress of the mission, but were able to read missionary reports of Khasi cultural practices, and to follow individual cases of Khasi converts.

Jones separated his own endeavours from those of Carey and Lish, regarding the latter's work as imperfect in composition and empty of edifying meaning. To the horror of those who held Carey in unassailable esteem as the progenitor of the modern mission movement, Jones was in fact highly critical of what he saw as Serampore's emphasis on quantity rather than quality:

it is hard for me to fathom why and how great men, good, learned, and wise, have contented themselves with such a superficial knowledge of the language, and have printed and published such incorrect and useless material . . . to start preaching in public after such and such a time, and to translate so many books into so many languages in such a short space of time, until they cause the world to marvel at their great talents, without considering or caring how correctly they speak, or how few people understand them; and worst of all, how many mistakes they make as they convey divine truth to the pagans.[68]

Despite these criticisms, Jones was clearly indebted to Serampore's native evangelists, and the three primary schools opened by Jones in 1842 at Mawmluh, Mawsmai and Sohra were the same that Lish had left in 1838.[69] Some of its former Khasi scholars clearly played an active role in negotiating with Jones the formalizing of various dialects and the preparation of grammars and dictionaries. That Jones used Welsh orthography, rather than the Bengali of the Serampore translators, is perhaps partly testament to his understanding of the cultural antagonisms between the hill and plains peoples. Jones's legacy is revered today by both Christian and non-Christian Khasis exactly because, as Jane Samson explains, language reduction both enforces and challenges colonial authority.

As Elizabeth Elbourne also demonstrates in this volume in relation to missionaries in South Africa at the same period, Jones's ability to be successful was premised on his success in garnering patronage within local political hierarchies. This included financial arrangements with the *Syiem* (rajah or chief) of Cherrapunji, as well as taking high status pupils into his classroom, including three heirs to the kingdom of Cherrapunji, and the nephew of the former *Syiem*. Only a few months after his arrival in the Hills, Jones was boasting that bands of up to fifty Khasis would travel great distances "to see the man who can do and teach the Kassians everything."[70] Yet the fervour with which they may have embraced him, and the expectations they placed on him, were a double-edged sword. His own motives and practices became precariously enmeshed in the machinations of Khasi social relations, and caught between the often competing, nepotistic and unpredictable alliances of the local British and Anglo-Indian military, political, commercial agents and interests. As elsewhere in other mission fields, such a complex set of indebtedness worked to the ultimate detriment of his ability to satisfy his own masters in Liverpool, who severed his connection with the Welsh Calvinistic Methodist mission in 1847.

Jones's "failure" was not necessarily interpreted as such by all of his Khasi friends. When the child of Thomas and Ann Jones died in May 1841, soon after their arrival in Calcutta, Jones had declared it the first "hostage" of the Welsh Calvinistic Methodist mission in India.[71] When Ann Jones herself died in 1845, fellow missionary William Lewis could claim that the "Lord seems to be making us at home here, for now we have a place to bury our dead!"[72] At "home" in the hills, but ostracized by his brethren, Jones went solo until his death in Calcutta in 1849. His name was for many years expunged from the lips of the mission brethren; the present-day Welsh Church, by its own admission, admits obliquely that: "history is kinder to him than were his own times."[73] But the Khasi embrace of Jones as some kind of kin is still evident in persistent stories to this day that claim he married a Khasi woman.

Thomas Jones died a sick and lonely man in Calcutta in September 1849, his son born to his second wife Emma in Cherrapoonjee in March 1850. A decade after Thomas Jones set about his linguistic work on the Khasi language, his fatherless one-and-a-half year old son sat in the garden of the stone house at Cherrapunji, chatting away in Khasi, Bengali and English.[74] Perhaps this is an appropriate symbol of the synthesis of culture and language that can yet challenge deterministic notions of cultural imperialism in mission histories.

Notes

1 Cherrapunji (and its variant spellings including Cherrapoonjee) was the former British name for the town now called Sohra.
2 Thomas Jones, Cherrapoonjee to John Roberts, Liverpool, 7 April 1842, *Y Drysorfa* 12, 139 (1842), p. 220 (Welsh original, tr. Sylvia Prys Jones. All subsequent quotations from *Y Drysorfa* are thus translated).
3 As reported by Jones in Thomas Jones, Cherrapunjee, to John Roberts, Liverpool, 8 November 1841, *Y Drysorfa* 12, 135 (1842), p. 91.
4 Thomas Jones, Cherrapoonjee, to John Roberts, Liverpool, 28 July 1841, *Y Drysorfa* 11, 131 (1841), p. 347.
5 Etherington (ed.), *Missions and Empire*.
6 Robert, "Introduction", p. 3.
7 Ghosh-Schellhorn, "Flocking to the Colonised Mission", p. 142
8 Robert, "Introduction", p. 2.
9 "KJP Assembly remembers Thomas Jones I", *Shillong Times*, 16 April 2007.
10 Ghosh-Schellhorn, "Flocking to the Colonised Mission", p. 141.
11 For a further discussion of U Larsing, see Brown-May, "Collision and Reintegration", pp. 141–61.
12 U Larsing to Kiang Katphoh, n.d. [1861], Welsh Calvinistic Methodist Archives (hereafter CMA) 27223, Papers of the Reverend William and Mary Lewis 1841–90, National Library of Wales.
13 See for example Morris, *The History of the Welsh Calvinistic Methodists' Foreign Mission*; Rees, "Jones, Thomas (1810–1849)", *Encyclopedia of Wales*, p. 433.
14 May, *Welsh Missionaries and British Imperialism in North-east India*.
15 William Carey in Carey, *William Carey*, p. 139.
16 Thomas Jones's answers to questions, 29 August 1839, Candidates Papers, London Missionary Society Archives, School of Oriental and African Studies, London.
17 John Roberts, Liverpool to Thomas Jones, Liverpool, 20 November 1840, CMA 28720, Letter Book of General Secretary, Vol. 4, 1840–3.
18 *Calcutta Christian Observer* 6, 61 (1837), p. 314.
19 Denham to Bowes, 8 August 1844, in *The Baptist Magazine for 1844*, p. 588. W. H. Denham was principal of Serampore College 1845–58.
20 Thomas Jones, Cherrapoonjee to John Roberts, Liverpool, 28 July 1841, *Y Drysorfa* 11, 131 (1841), p. 347.
21 John Roberts to Dr John Wilson, 2 December 1840, CMA 28720 Letter Book of General Secretary, Vol. 4, 1840–3.

22 Thomas Jones, Calcutta to John Roberts, Liverpool, 11 May 1841, CMA 1(F): 5898 (copy).

23 Ibid.

24 Jackson, "From Krishna Pal to Lal Behari Dey", p. 194, f. 83.

25 Thomas Jones, Calcutta to John Roberts, Liverpool, 11 May 1841, CMA 1(F): 5898 (copy).

26 Stanley, "Carey, William".

27 Carey, *An Enquiry into the Obligations of Christians*, p. 62.

28 Carey, *William Carey*, p. 67.

29 William Carey to John Ryland, 14 December 1803, in Smith, *The Life of William Carey*, p. 162.

30 See Smith, *The Life of William Carey*, Chapter 6, pp. 132–56. See also *The American Baptist Magazine and Missionary Intelligencer* New Series, 1, 2 (1817), pp. 65–7.

31 Belcher, *The First Hindoo Convert*, p. 23.

32 See for example Haggis and Allen, "Imperial Emotions".

33 Belcher, *The First Hindoo Convert*, p. 15

34 These towns are all in modern-day Bangladesh.

35 According to Morris (*The History of the Welsh Calvinistic Methodists' Foreign Mission*, p. 80), the judge was W. N. Garrett, "a nephew of Robert Raikes, the founder of the English Sunday School" Movement.

36 Belcher, *The First Hindoo Convert*, p. 34.

37 Kharakor, *Biblical Influence on Pre-Independence Khasi Literature*, p. 12.

38 'U' is the title prefixed to a man's name in Khasi, 'Ka' being the feminine equivalent.

39 Belcher, *The First Hindoo Convert*, p. 35.

40 Notes from "Periodical Accounts of the Serampore Mission" in "Memoirs of the Translations", July 1814–Jan 1815, p. 19 in CMA 27159 Correspondence (1903–24) and material relating to the Story of our Foreign Mission by John Hughes Morris.

41 As claimed, for example, in Bhattacharjee, "Social and Religious Reform Movements in Meghalaya", p. 451.

42 Mathur, *The Khasi of Meghalaya*, p. 14.

43 Carey letter, 11 December 1813, cited in Carey, *William Carey*, p. 408.

44 The British Library has a copy of the 898pp Khasi New Testament, translated by the Serampore missionaries, 1831 (*Kaju ublei bandu kattina nakababit. Kajukibriu napuna katrana u kaacara kataiya ula, etc*).

45 Morris, *The History of the Welsh Calvinistic Methodists' Foreign Mission*, p. 82.

46 Bhattacharjee, "Social and Religious Reform Movements", p. 451.

47 Bagster, *The Bible of Every Land*, p. 15.

48 Carey, *William Carey*, p. 332.

49 Bareh, *The History and Culture of the Khasi People*, p. 392.

50 Bhattacharjee, "Social and Religious Reform Movements", p. 452; Talukdar, *Khasi Cultural Resistance to Colonialism*, p. 32.

51 Smith, *The Life of William Carey*, p. 158.

52 Snaitang, *Christianity and Social Change in Northeast India*, p. 66.

53 Cited in Morris, *The History of the Welsh Calvinistic Methodists' Foreign Mission*, p. 83. See also Notes from "Periodical Accounts of the Serampore Mission", New Series, Vol. 1, January 1827 to December 1833, CMA 27159.

54 Mathur (*The Khasi of Meghalaya*, p. 14) notes perhaps over enthusiastically: "This metropolitan visit had a rousing effect upon them. They returned with their hearts aglow with enthusiasm. They became in this process the first agents of urbanization among the Khasi."

55 *Lutheran Magazine* 4, 12 (1831), p. 277.

56 Wenger, *Serampore Missionary Biographies* (Vol. IV), p. 104 cited in Jyrwa, *The Wondrous Works of God*, p. 17. See also Morris, *The History of the Welsh Calvinistic Methodists' Foreign Mission*. pp. 83–4. Morris noted that Jan was certainly back at Serampore by 1836.

57 Notes from "Periodical Accounts of the Serampore Mission", New Series, Vol. 1, January 1827 to December 1833 in CMA 27159.

58 *Friend of India*, 1 July 1837 in CMA 27159.

59 Morris, *The History of the Welsh Calvinistic Methodists' Foreign Mission*, p. 83; Dutta, *Impact of the West on the Khasis and Jaintias*, p. 195, cites "Periodical Accounts of the Serampore Mission", March 1834, No. 81.

60 Snaitang, *Christianity and Social Change*, p. 67, cites "Periodical Accounts of the Serampore Mission", 3D Series, No. 67 (January 1833), p. 2; Kharakor, *Biblical Influence on Pre-Independence Khasi Literature*, p. 13; Dutta, *Impact of the West on the Khasis and Jaintias*. p. 184, cites "Periodical Accounts of the Serampore Mission", July 1834, No. 85; September 1836, No. 140; and June 1837, No. 115.

61 Presumably Joshua Marshman at Serampore, who was to die in December of that year.

62 Tomlin, *Missionary Journals*, p. 379.

63 Tomlin, *Missionary Journals*, pp. 379–80.

64 *Calcutta Christian Observer* 7, 70 (1838), pp. 129–43.

65 *Calcutta Christian Observer* 7, 77 (1838), p. 587.

66 Bareh, *The History and Culture of the Khasi People*, p. 392; Ropmay, *Ka Centenary History Ka Balang Presbyterian* in Sten, *Khasi Poetry*, p. 45; Mathur, *The Khasi of Meghalaya*, p. 14; Bhattacharjee, "Social and Religious Reform Movements", p. 452.

67 *Y Drysorfa* was first published in 1831, and had a regular column of missionary intelligence entitled "*Hanesiaeth Cenhadol*".

68 Thomas Jones, Cherrapoonjee, to John Roberts, Liverpool, 7 April 1842, *Y Drysorfa* 12, 140 (1842), p. 254.

69 Kharakor, *Biblical Influence on Pre-Independence Khasi Literature*, p. 1. This author stretches back the origins of education in the pre-Christian era, on the back of research by Dkhar, *Primary Education in the Khasi and Jaintia Hills*.

70 Thomas Jones, Cherrapunjee, to John Roberts, Liverpool, 8 November 1841, *Y Drysorfa* 12, 135 (1842), p. 91.

71 Thomas Jones, Calcutta to John Roberts, Liverpool, 11 May 1841, CMA 1(F): 5898 (copy).

72 William Lewis to John Roberts, Liverpool, n.d. [1845] *Y Drysorfa* 15, 180 (1845), p. 376.

73 D. Ben Rees, "Jones, Thomas (1810–1849)", p. 102.

74 Emily Cattell, Cherrapoonjee to Susan Cattell, 5 January 1852, author's possession.

CHAPTER EIGHT

Translation Teams

Missionaries, Islanders, and the Reduction of Language in the Pacific

JANE SAMSON

In 1818 Cambridge was treated to the sight of the Church Missionary Society (CMS) missionary, Thomas Kendall, in company with two Maori chiefs from New Zealand, walking to and fro among the colleges to consult with specialist linguists. Hongi and Waikato also accompanied Kendall to London, although it should be noted that both chiefs, especially Hongi, were far more interested in London's armouries than in Kendall's translation work. Kendall's view, however, was that this joint visit was "for the purpose of settling the orthography and, as far as possible, of reducing the language itself of New Zealand to the rules of Grammar, with a view to the furtherance of the Mission sent out to that country".[1] Anyone researching Victorian linguistics will have noted a repeated use of the word "reduced" in connection with the introduction of literacy to oral cultures. This term seems particularly ironic when it is used in celebratory, contemporary accounts of missionary translation work. To our eyes there is inevitably something disturbing about the concept of "reduction" or "rendering" in this context, with its overtones of diminishment at the hands of some outside force. There seems no better term for linguistic colonialism.

Agreeing with Claude Lévi-Strauss's diagnosis of "organised tyranny", literary theorist Christopher Herbert has declared that missionary literacy projects in the Pacific involved "covert violence" aimed at "'reducing' the wild Polynesian libido by imposing a system of restraint upon it". According to Herbert, "the very idea of 'oral languages' in this context carries perhaps a hint of puritanical dread of bodily orifices themselves and of the brutish desires fixated upon them".[2] Teaching islanders to read and write was simply "a means of reordering the mind itself and putting it in thrall to new institutions".[3] This theory allows Herbert to contrast bigoted missionary ethnography unfavourably with the "disinterested cultural study" of modern times; for missionaries, the proper study of culture was "ruled out beyond recall" because of "the divine authority of his own religion and his own 'civilized' society".[4] Can something called "disinterested cultural study" ever be identified, let alone privileged at the expense of other forms of cross-cultural engagement? Surely modern scholars of culture are as capable as missionaries of reifying the authority of their own standpoint. Recent endorsements of Herbert's work by Pacific specialists invite a reassessment of his assumptions.[5]

96

Let us look again at Kendall's visit to England with his two Maori patrons. I say "patrons" because Kendall and the rest of the CMS mission in New Zealand were completely dependent upon support from sponsoring chiefs: so much so that they had been forced to trade firearms and ammunition for food to keep themselves and their families alive. It was not the first time that Maori chiefs had visited England. Tui and Titere had arrived two years earlier and spent some time at Cambridge with the linguist Professor Lee at the urging of the CMS Committee, which had suspicions about Kendall's translation methods.[6] Incensed, Kendall planned his own trip and brought his own Maori supporters. His modesty concerning his own knowledge of their language was striking. Writing aboard ship en route to England, Kendall informed the CMS that Maori was "a matter of such importance that I cannot allow myself to be a competent judge". He added later that he was indebted to Parkhust's Hebrew Lexicon "for much of my little knowledge of the true idiom of the New Zealand Language" because the Hebrew placement of suffixes and affixes, for example, was helpful to him, whereas his knowledge of English grammar was not.[7]

The key role of Maori themselves in the development of the first printed Maori grammar is clear, as is the influence of the language and people on Kendall himself. His biographer Judith Binney noted that Kendall based his new Maori orthography on the "Italian" open-vowel system because it was an appropriate fit with spoken Maori, while his critics believed that Maori should be forced to conform to English symbols.[8] A process of mutual conversion had taken place between Kendall and his Maori colleagues:

> The intense and constant study of words, and of ideas expressed in those words, to which Kendall had devoted himself, had created a sympathetic attitude towards the complexities and implications of a language of which understanding is gained only through knowledge of the traditions of the people.[9]

This process appears similar to that described by Vicente Rafael in his pioneering book *Contracting Colonialism* published in 1988. An early critic of theories about hegemonic colonial discourse, Rafael instead proposed that "translation and conversion produce the vernacular as that which simultaneously institutes *and* subverts colonial rule".[10] This thesis demands that we consider the complexities of European interaction with non-European cultures. Stuart Hall once declared that Christian humanitarianism was merely one of "racism's two registers," and similarly reductionist conclusions about missionary activity remain alive and well.[11] We should ask, therefore, who is "reducing" the historiography of missionary translation?

Indigenous Christians

Contemporary missionary accounts often occluded the voices and roles of non-Europeans. The most obvious example of this is simply the omission of any mention of indigenous assistance in the work of translation, especially in published accounts.

Helen Gardner's sophisticated analysis of the work of the Methodist missionary George Brown is especially helpful here. She notes that first person and past tense journal entries recorded "discomfiting differences" between indigenous interpretations (of cannibalism, in this case) and the missionary's own. Brown's published anthropology texts, however, used the third person and the present tense; this alteration "removed the action from real time, making it [cannibalism] an abstract possibility and thus eliminating his Christian responsibility to intercede in the events".[12] These important textual points about person and tense could also include analysis of the role of the passive voice in obscuring the actors involved in translation and other shared activities. How often do we read that "the gospel was translated" or "the Bible was rendered into the local language" without learning much, if anything, about the role of indigenous people in this important enterprise?

In some cases, the occlusion of Pacific Islanders' roles is more overt. Reporting on his progress in translating the New Testament into Aneiteumese (or Anejom), the Canadian Presbyterian missionary John Inglis wrote of his reliance on the Reverend T. W. Mellor, rector of Woodbridge, Suffolk. Mellor was editorial superintendent of the British and Foreign Bible Society and had somehow learned enough Aneiteumese to impress Inglis. "How he has acquired it I do not know," reported Inglis, "but that is of little consequence".[13] After praising Mellor for pages in his report, Ingis concluded with a reference to Williamu, a convert whose brief account of himself (as translated by Inglis) had been given to the mission board in Nova Scotia. Appended here to Inglis's report, it declared that Williamu had "lived here [Aneityum] a long time with Mr. and Mrs. Inglis,"[14] and according to Inglis's report he had "thrown his whole heart into the work in which we are engaged".[15] Whatever Williamu's other duties might have been in the Inglis household, Inglis himself revealed that he was a partner in the translation work. Williamu received no paeans of praise, however. Using language appropriate to that of a master writing about a servant, Inglis simply noted that he had "great satisfaction in Williamu", whose devotion to the mission persisted even after a recent epidemic had killed large numbers of his fellow Aneityumese, including family members.[16] Williamu's obviously crucial role in the translation of the Aneityumese New Testament should not have been obscured by Inglis, but neither should it be forgotten by us.

The critical importance of indigenous teachers to the spread of Christianity in the Pacific must be clearly understood. Islanders themselves undertook the most wide-spread, intensive and dangerous work of missions. Indigenous teachers, clergy and congregations made Pacific churches what they are today. Writing in 1996, Doug Munro and Andrew Thornley introduced their essay collection on indigenous ministry by "retrieving the pastors" who had been neglected: "Pacific Islanders need no such reminding of the key role of the homegrown pastors" but only recently had "Academic perception . . . finally caught up with what Pacific Islanders had known all along".[17] With refreshing candour, Helen Gardner writes that "It was more than a little discon-certing to finally admit that Islanders were not following me down a post-Christian path, or embracing a Marxist critique of Christian mission. It is now clear that Christianity is entering a new stage in its long history".[18]

Given that the Gospel could not be preached nor churches founded without indigenous participation, it should be no surprise to find the development of theological anthropologies that required missionaries to regard Pacific Christians as brethren. As I have written elsewhere, both an "othering" and a "brothering" of Islanders was required of missionaries; one cannot be reduced to the other.[19] Western-mediated knowledge is not necessarily entirely under western control, as C. A. Bayly and Tony Ballantyne have pointed out.[20] A deep ambivalence characterizes missionary translation work and ethnography; that is the main point of the inevitable inter-relationship between "othering" and "brothering". Sometimes a missionary's views changed over time, altering the balance between the two aspects. The Reverend J. E. Newell of the London Missionary Society (LMS) mission to Samoa wrote several drafts of a review of E. Schultz's *Sprichwörtliche Redensarten der Samoaner* (1906), one of which contained a commentary on the Samoan role in translation work:

> What inexhaustible patience was required in interviewing the thirty natives whose aid Dr. Schultz enlisted for his work, only those who have endeavoured to fathom the irregularities and peculiarities of this style of speech can truly estimate. Such knowledge as the author was in search of is a severe demand on the native intelligence, and implies a mental training and an appreciation of our European eagerness to know the reasons and usages of exceptional phraseology which very few (hardly any) natives possess.[21]

The colonial discourse analysis writes itself: Newell's stolid lack of reflexivity and his racist conceptions are clear. Even Newell, however, cannot help pointing the way to another reading. Later in his review he praises the "Miscellaneous" section of Schultz's book "because it gives us expressions and similes quoted from the folklore which is alas! almost a sealed book to us, notwithstanding the labours of Powell, Pratt, Dr. Kramer, Dr. Stuebel and others".[22] The fact that Samoan folklore remained a "sealed book" to outsiders, despite the alleged superiority of European intelligence and mental training, points to an alternative hermeneutic. Perhaps, despite the efforts of "the thirty natives" who did their best for Doctor Schultz, the demands on European intelligence and mental conditioning were simply too great for Schultz to grasp the meaning or significance of what they were telling him. Newell would later reflect on his own inadequacies, as we will see.

This raises the important question of European preconceptions about Pacific languages, especially during the early mission period. Christopher Herbert has claimed that "Having selected the South Seas for proselytizing largely from a belief that the 'primitive' Polynesian languages could readily be mastered in a few weeks' time by an intelligent European, the missionaries were profoundly impressed by the discovery of the complexity of these languages, which taxed their intellects nearly to the breaking point".[23] This undocumented "belief" cries out for investigation, especially when it is used to enable Herbert (and presumably his readers) to be surprised by missionary respect for the complexity of Pacific languages. "Even the bigoted George Turner exclaims over the intricate subtlety of Polynesian tongues," Herbert told us smugly, leading us to believe that missionaries went out to the Pacific for generations in a state

Jane Samson

of linguistic and philological ignorance.[24] The unexpected discovery of indigenous sophistication "seems to have altered their perception of Polynesian life in a fundamental way," Herbert concluded, remarking: "though the alteration was in good measure unconscious and never caused them to abandon the rhetoric of 'unbridled passions'".[25] The alteration was "unconscious"? Research reveals the opposite: copious evidence of immediate respect for the complexity and sophistication of Pacific languages. As the pioneering historian of Pacific missions, Niel Gunson, recognized, the primary question was not whether Pacific languages were complex, but whether they were Semitic, or Aryan, or otherwise intimately linked with the Holy Land and ultimately with Europe itself.[26]

Where did an alleged belief in a simple, easily-learned Tahitian language come from? It did not actually originate with missionaries at all. Captain William Bligh had met with the Society's leading director, Thomas Haweis, after returning to England following the *Bounty* mutiny. The two men attempted to send missionaries to Tahiti on Bligh's second voyage, but without success.[27] It was Bligh who had assured Haweis that Tahitian would be easy to learn and provided him with a wordlist that he had compiled.[28] There was no pre-existing prejudice against Tahitian; it was on Bligh's supposed authority that Haweis declared that becoming "masters of the language" would be "an attainment, I am assured, of no great difficulty".[29] As for the LMS missionaries themselves, it is clear that from the very beginning of the mission Tahitians themselves revealed the complexities of their language and culture. Recovering in New South Wales after the forced evacuation of the first mission, the semi-literate William Shelley wrote that the Tahitian language was:

> not as easily attained as is generally imagined. It is true a person may in five or six months gain such a knowledge of it as to be able to ask a question or give an answer & the natives adapting themselves to their mode of speech thay imagine thay have attained a greater knowledge of it than thay have but the farther thay advanse in knowledge the more thay see of their Ignorance. After a close application of two years & nine months I did not account myself to have half attained it.[30]

An implied criticism of Haweis and other elements of the metropolitan leadership is clear, and after the re-establishment of the mission it was repeated by John Jefferson, who made enough progress with the language to emphasize "that it a copious language, and not a barren one . . . it is sufficient to teach any Doctrine taught in the Bible".[31] There is no doubt that presumptions about European superiority and indigenous inferiority were widespread in Britain and elsewhere well into the twentieth century; popular conceptions of non-European societies were usually based on those presumptions. My point here, however, is that missionaries were *challenging* these presumptions. The early journals of Shelley and Jefferson of Tahiti echo the much later writings of Bob Love of the Presbyterian Kunmunya Mission at Port George IV in Western Australia. Clearly conscious of prejudice against "primitive" Aboriginal culture, Love praised the "amazing complexity" of the Warora language and the "beautiful regularity of the grammatical construction".[32]

100

Pacific peoples quickly impressed upon their strange visitors the sophistication of their languages. Perhaps the most eloquent description of delight comes from William Colenso, one of the early CMS missionaries to New Zealand. "The more I have seen and known of the works of the Ancient New Zealander," he wrote:

> the more I have been struck with the many indications of their superior mind, — of their fine perception of the beautiful, the regular, and symmetrical; of their desire and labour after the beautiful; of their prompt and genuine, open and fearless criticisms, — in a word, of their great Ideality. And this high faculty of theirs which they possessed in an eminent degree, will probably be better known and understood hereafter than it is at present.[33]

As evidence of this, he listed various cultural attributes including language: "its great grammatical precision, its double duals and double plurals, its euphony, its rhythm, and its brevity, and its many exquisite particles and reduplications, both singular and plural, all highly pregnant with meaning, which almost defy translation into English".[34]

For Methodist missionary Lorimer Fison, one of the most distinguished missionary anthropologists of his day, the matter came back to the imperative of "brothering". During a speech in Fiji, he defended missions from a scientific point of view, praising "They who give an alphabet to a savage tribe, who make a spoken language a written one, who ascertain its grammatical construction & the rules wh. govern its combinations", but his defence was not limited to this highly colonial discourse. He left the most important theological point to his concluding remarks, emphasizing that through their researches missionaries "add link after link to the chain of evidence, now possibly approaching completion, which form[s] the truth of that grand Bible Proposition 'God hath made of one blood all nations of man to dwell on all the face of the earth'".[35] The quest for human unity was by no means a preoccupation for scientists by the later nineteenth century, but it remained a priority for missionaries and it must be taken seriously in any analysis of their work on translation. The quotation about "one blood", taken from the Book of Acts, was at the heart of the "brothering" which missionary work demanded. This in no way forestalled prejudice, but neither was prejudice able to close the door on a biblical invitation to more respectful engagement.

Consider again the case of Newell, last seen making disparaging remarks about how difficult it was to get savages to be useful informants. This is not all that can be gleaned from the Newell papers: they also shed light on the neglected career of Timoteo, one of two Samoan mission teachers the LMS dispatched to Papua with their wives in 1884.[36] Timoteo comes to life in the Newell manuscripts, especially in a makeshift notebook titled "Timoteo's notes on Kabadi translated by Newell 1895". A letter by Newell to the Polynesian Society explained that Timoteo, "a friend and correspondent", had sent him extensive notes on the language and customs of the Kabadi people of New Guinea. "Unfortunately Pastor Timoteo does not know English and our extensive correspondence during the 12 years has been in Samoan," and Timoteo had published

Samoan-language articles on the Kabadi for *Sulu Samoa*, a periodical edited by Newell. Recognizing the anthropological value of Timoteo's work, Newell had translated portions of it into English for submission to the society's journal. He added that Pastor Timoteo had recently sent him a grammatical outline of the Kabadi language, adding that: "So far as I am aware Timoteo is the only living authority on this dialect. He is the only Native Teacher in [Rabade] who is capable of classifying his knowledge, as he is the only man possessing adequate knowledge of the dialect for philological purposes."[37]

A multiplicity of translations lie behind the subtitle "translated by Newell 1895". Newell was translating Timoteo, who had translated information from his Kabadi informants. Perhaps more intriguing, however, is the dramatic shift in Newell's opinion of the intellectual capacity and partnership of Pacific Islanders. Years earlier, he had declared Samoans inherently incapable of classification work, but by 1895 he says that a Samoan is the *only* person capable of such work because he is the only one who has conducted the appropriate linguistic research. Timoteo is a friend, correspondent, pastor and scientific "authority" to whom Newell openly defers in the context of formal scientific correspondence.[38]

Along with developing respect for the intellectual capacity of Pacific Islanders, Newell learned to reflect on his own limitations. A manuscript titled "Notes: chiefly ethnological of the Tokelau, Ellice and Some of the Gilbert or Kingsmill Islands" tells us that Newell visited these islands in 1885 and 1894 and was now writing some "brief and discursive and partial" account of the anthropological information he gathered. He added that "The writer's Samoan experience & the limits of his knowledge of other South Sea peoples & ignorance of Western Polynesia will no doubt have coloured his views as to the origin of the peoples embraced in this survey."[39] My point here is simply to show the impact of Pacific peoples on the views of outsiders like Newell, challenging preconceived notions, breaking down barriers, and provoking self-reflection.

Reflexivity can be found from the earliest mission days, as in the manuscript attributed to William Pascoe Crook, the first missionary to the Marquesas Islands. Written in 1799, the manuscript describes Crook's attempts to learn the local language. "He had met with unexpected difficulties" because:

> having no idea of any language but their own, they seemed wholly incapable of returning intelligent answers to enquiries about the meaning of their words. If asked the name of anything, they would reply "a maia havea", a thing, to be sure. Wishing to find out a term for "adrift", Mr. C. described a Canoe in that situation, & enquired how they called it. They replied, "A Canoe," & cried that they never heard of such a thing; expressing their surprise that Gods could not talk as men did.[40]

No wonder Greg Dening observed that "Crook's perceptions were changed more than Enata's".[41]

Translation Teams

One of the earliest missionary translators in Fiji, John Hunt, recorded his methodology in detail:

> 1. To read over the chapter for translating in the Greek Testament, and examine particularly any word of which I have any doubt as to its meaning. I read Bloomfield's Notes and Campbell's translation and any other books that I have to assist me to ascertain the meaning of the text. 2. After having mastered the chapters as I think, I commence translating and I use as my standards for the text the Greek and the English translations and for the translation not any man exclusively, but myself, all the Natives I can have access to, and the translations that have already been made.[42]

Hunt was more sensitive to the differences between the Fijian dialects and while at Somosomo he worked particularly closely with Noa, a convert. Noa accompanied Hunt to Viwa when the mission was relocated there. They worked together on a Viwa dialect translation of the Wesleyan catechism, but after it was printed in 1843 some of the other missionaries objected to the liberties Hunt had taken with the original English version. Hunt's greatest defender was Noa who declared that "the new catechism was using the Viwa language as it had been before missionaries came" while the older catechism was the "language of the Lotu people since the introduction of Christianity".[43]

These words of Noa's come down to us mediated by Hunt, so we must be wary of taking them entirely at face value. Nevertheless, Noa's pride in the use of a traditional Fijian language comes through clearly, as does his suggestion that the English version might be inappropriate for non-English people. There was a demonstrable focus on indigenous driven translation work at Hunt's station: he and his wife began teaching English at Viwa in order to enable Fijians to undertake their own translations of literary and scientific works in English.[44] Despite all of this, there is no doubt that later mission accounts of early pioneers like Hunt conspicuously shrink the composition of the translation team of which the missionary was only a part. Reflecting on the occasion of the centenary of the Fijian mission, Methodist superintendent J. W. Burton discussed the co-operative process of translation, but only as a collaboration between English missionaries; he made no mention of Fijian participation.[45]

George Sarawia was the first Melanesian Anglican priest, and in his autobiography he recalled how he taught the Mota language to John Coleridge Patteson (later the first Bishop of Melanesia) in 1857.[46] This was momentous: the Melanesian Mission would eventually select Mota as its primary language and it is significant that the mission's first knowledge of Mota came from the gift of a Melanesian man's time and expertise. Sarawia recalled the first visit of the mission ship and how fear and confusion wrestled with curiosity as he decided to go on board. He, Selwyn and Patteson sat down in the stern "and they asked me the name of the island, and the names of people. I told them and they wrote them down in a book, but I did not know then what a book was."[47] Nervously, Sarawia continued the lesson when "they wrote down some other words too, the words for you, he, you (plural), we two, I, all of us . . . they wrote down a few words of Mota that day, and we were astonished that they understood so quickly a little Mota and could speak it properly".[48]

This rapid progress was due in part to Patteson's astonishing linguistic ability, but also to Sarawia's willingness to teach him. Mutual teaching frequently characterized their future relationship, including catechetical sessions where Patteson imparted information about Christian beliefs while receiving first-hand testimony about the beliefs of Sarawia's people.[49] Much later, after Sarawia had returned to Vanua Lava, Patteson began teaching on the island of Mota and sometimes Sarawia visited him there. "I saw some of the things he was doing," Sarawia recalled: "He was always going round the villages, talking to the older men about some of their customs . . . "[50] The purpose of this was to admonish the islanders that some of these practices "were not good",[51] but as with the Mota language lessons years before, the ethnographical information gathered by Patteson was valued later in its own right by more anthropologically-minded members of the mission like Robert Codrington.[52]

The Anglicans also founded missions in Papua New Guinea, where the Reverend Copland King provided one of the most detailed explanations that exists of the teamwork involved in translation work. When the white staff from the up-river mission station were recalled in 1900 due to illness, most of the boarders there were sent to Dogura (at Wedau). There the young men finished school, some were baptized, and some would eventually return to teach at Dogura themselves. King recalled:

> I started one of these boys, Edmund Dudu, after he had been at Dogura for six years, and back in the district as pupil teacher for two, at translation work. He took the Wedau Gospel, and wrote it out in Binandere. As he did so, I read over his translation with him, making corrections as necessary, then typed it, made him read it over with me, and then typed it again. Several other boys, who in their turn came from Dogura, read it over with me. Every revision involved numberless discussions on the meaning of the original, the force of the words chosen, and other matters. It was my business to keep my eye on the Analytical Concordance. The boys had to tell me of anything which sounded strange or hard or wrong; then we could discuss how it could be amended.[53]

Readers at the Binandere services used drafts of the new translation in their readings, welcoming help from the congregation in clarifying meanings. Copland King was clear about his position of dependency: "I have to take the natives' opinion on trust", he declared. He was happy to do so because "they were working, not to satisfy the Missionary, but to enlighten their own people".[54] Further revisions were made after the trial run in church, and only then was a final copy typed for the printer.

In Western Australia in the 1920s the Presbyterian Kunmunya Mission had a self-described "translating team" which gathered around Bob Love to begin the translation of the Gospel of Mark, and which continued to assist him when work began on the Hebrew Scriptures. Love's partners were "Ernie (whom Bob addressed by his native name, Njimandum . . .), Albert Barunga . . . and Wondoonmoi, quite an old man now, the native who had tried twice to kill him [Love] in 1914, but who had since become his friend".[55] Every day the group met on the verandah of Love's house, sitting together around a cane table. Sharing daily life with Aboriginal people sometimes solved tricky translation problems: the great man did not simply come up with ideas and then call for indigenous responses. Love told a story about his difficulty with the word "beginning" (a serious drawback when attempting to translate the first chapter of Genesis), which plagued his team for a considerable length of time. Out pigeon hunting one day, Love and some Aboriginal friends traced a stream of water to its source in a spring:

> Next language day I told my team what we had done, in following a stream to its beginning. I sketched a map of the stream, naming the place, and following up the course to the place where it sprang from under the rock. I asked, What is this? Quick as a flash, Wondoonmoi put his finger on the source of the stream and said 'Wundjanguru'. He then ran his finger along the course of the stream till, at the place where it debouched into the sea, he said 'Umindjunguru'. A great discovery! Alpha and Omega, the beginning and the end![56]

Perhaps the greatest depth of obligation felt toward indigenous translators was expressed by the Anglican missionary Charles Elliot Fox as he recalled his work on the Arosi language of San Cristoval in the Solomon Islands. Having performed *haimarahuda* with his friend Martin Taki, they exchanged names and possessions and Fox began a new life as a member of a San Cristoval family. Living and working with his new relatives, he felt that "the main thing was to listen to them and to imitate them". Often he and the other men of the village would wake in the night to replenish their fire and there was a particular candour to these midnight conversations when "the people would speak very freely, and you could listen to what they were saying and pick up a great number of new words and phrases, writing them down later on".[57] Eventually he learned enough to create a dictionary and grammar of Arosi, and begin work on an Arosi translation of the New Testament. Fox cautioned his readers against crediting him with primary agency in this project:

> The real work of translation is done by the Melanesians, and not by the white men. We speak of Codrington translating the New Testament into Mota, but really he did the explaining of the meaning to Edward Wogale, who was a native of Mota, and Wogale did the actual phrasing of the translation in the native idiom, and this has been so in all the translations of the Mission. The Melanesians have not really got the credit that they deserved for these translations, which are spoken of as having been done by the white men.[58]

Of interest here is the difference between how missionaries like Codrington actually lived and worked and how others reported their activities. Codrington would have been the first to acknowledge his debts. Late in his life, hard at work on translating the prophetic books of the Hebrew Scriptures into Mota, he declared: "I am not altogether in favor of translating obscure passages & parts of the scripture until a fair number of natives can make something out of them", meaning that the "triumph" of completing some translation or other should take a distant second place to the needs of the audience.[59]

"Sacred Philology"?

This subsection's title comes from the work of Jaroslav Pelikan, who traces the practice of sacred philology to the Renaissance study of classical Greek and Latin texts.[60] Unlike some other religions, such as Islam, where the original language of Scripture is considered normative, Christianity endorsed the authority of its sacred texts in translation. This was not simply a question of mechanically producing a vernacular Bible. The act of translation itself was an affirmation of human unity, as understood in New Testament "one blood" terms, and it is no surprise to find that philology was one of the earliest forms of Christian ethnography. This is what Pelikan means by "sacred philology", and missionaries were among its most earnest practitioners.

A highly critical article by Sidney H. Ray, the noted linguistics specialist at Cambridge at the turn of the twentieth century, is helpful here. Ray worked closely with western Pacific missions in order to gather material, and his article on "The Study of Melanesian Languages" appeared in the Anglican *Southern Cross Log* in 1908. The article was ruthless in its condemnation of the traditional philology that so many missionaries still used to theorize about the origins and relationship of Pacific languages. "These students [of Melanesian languages] are content to take the languages, as far as they are known, and base upon comparisons various theories of origin. These theories are wrong, both in direction and method, and are also premature."[61] The method was wrong because similarities were assumed to always indicate relationship; theories were premature because relatively little was known of interior districts in Indonesia and Melanesia. The direction was wrong because various writers had argued that Melanesian languages were related, variously, to Aryan, Semitic, American Indian, Japanese, Inuit, Ural-Altaic, Dravidian, and Australian Aboriginal. "Unless all these linguistic families be regarded as related, the arguments in favour of any one of them is destroyed by the arguments in favour of the others".[62] So much for the scientific veracity of most missionary philology.

Ray, the scientist, knew that no such universal linguistic relationship existed, and, therefore, he was confident about discarding theories based on it. For missionary theorists, however, there was a wider relationship to consider. Theirs was a universalist anthropology (often enthusiastically evolutionist for that precise reason) demanded by faith. Long after metropolitan scientists had embraced modern linguistics, we find missionaries publishing theories about the "Semitic" roots of Polynesian languages, or proclaiming the discovery of Sanscrit terms among some group or other of "Aryan" Aboriginal Australians.[63] They believed that they were tracing the shape of universal human nature and destiny.

This theological priority generated a matrix of activity in which indigenous people were (and remain) full participants. Recalling the discussion of "rendering" which opened this chapter, it is useful to note that the *Oxford English Dictionary* records early uses of "to render" as meaning "To give or hand back, to restore".[64] This earlier definition is being recovered through current collaborations between indigenous leaders, academics and religious organisations in language retrieval and preservation projects. Here at the University of Alberta we celebrated the appearance of the *Alberta Elders' Cree Dictionary* in 1998 and honoured the leadership of Sister Nancy LeClaire, a Samson Cree and Roman Catholic nun, in initiating this remarkable project.[65] The introduction praises the pioneering translation work of Father Albert Lacombe, Father Rogier Vandersteene, Brother Frederick Leach and the Anglican priest, the Reverend E. A. Watkins of the CMS, among others.[66] The *Dictionary* was intended to bring the voices of ancestors (of various races) and descendants together. Another project, the complete translation of the Bible into Inukitut for Christians of the eastern Arctic, relied on the expertise of indigenous clergy, one of whom declared that the project "has given our language importance and has preserved it".[67] However meticulously theorised, any historical analysis that reduces this complex collaborative matrix down to something that is "really just" mimicry, racism or textual determinism, is unable to explain fully the historical complexities involved. Even less is it able to explain the legacy of those complexities: thriving indigenous Christianities who often construct their own orthodox identities against an immoral post-Christian west.[68]

Andrew Porter has argued that "what one might call 'cultural concessions'" were being made on all sides throughout the process of missionary translation work. The fusion of language and ideas produced a complexity of influences that is at odds with an insistence on a western "cultural imperialism".[69] R. S. Sugirtharajah noted the strange reluctance of postcolonial scholarship to engage with missionary records that "confront their own colonial and missionary administration" in order "to empower the invaded".[70] Having earlier mentioned Vicente Rafael's work on early modern Spanish translations in the Philippines, I would like to conclude with Lawrence Venuti's call to arms in his 1998 book *The Scandals of Translation: Towards an Ethics of Difference*. After dissecting the ongoing colonization of texts by English translators in today's world of globalized publishing, he observed: "Translation clearly raises ethical questions that have yet to be sorted out."[71] Indeed they do.

Notes

1 Kendall, *Language of New Zealand*, preface.
2 Herbert, *Culture and Anomie*, p. 167.
3 Herbert, *Culture and Anomie*, p. 167.
4 Herbert, *Culture and Anomie*, p. 167.
5 See Edmond, *Representing the South Pacific*; Smith, *Literary Culture and the Pacific*; and Johnston, "The Strange Career of William Ellis". Johnston's *Missionary Writing and Empire*, however, presents carefully nuanced historical research that actually belies Herbert's theory of translation-as-violence.
6 Binney, *Legacy of Guilt*, p. 50.
7 Thomas Kendall to CMS Secretary, 3 July, 1820.
8 Binney, *Legacy of Guilt*, p. 62.
9 Binney, *Legacy of Guilt*, p. 62.

10 Rafael, *Contracting Colonialism*, p. xv.

11 Cited in Hall, *Civilising Subjects*, p. 17.

12 Gardner, *Gathering for God*, p. 16.

13 J. Inglis to Reformed Presbyterian Synod, n/d, *The Home and Foreign Record* (October, 1862), p. 274.

14 "Williamu's Address," appended to J. Inglis to Reformed Presbyterian Synod, n/d, *The Home and Foreign Record* (October, 1862), p. 277.

15 "Williamu's Address," appended to J. Inglis to Reformed Presbyterian Synod, n/d, *The Home and Foreign Record* (October, 1862), p. 276.

16 "Williamu's Address," appended to J. Inglis to Reformed Presbyterian Synod, n/d, *The Home and Foreign Record* (October, 1862), p. 276.

17 Munro and Thornley, *The Covenant Makers*, pp. 1, 3.

18 Gardner, *Gathering for God*, p. 12.

19 For more on this see Samson, "Ethnology and Theology" and *Race and Redemption*.

20 For more on this see Bayly, *Empire and Information* and Ballantyne, *Orientalism and Race*.

21 "Dr. Schultz on Samoan proverbial sayings and figures of speech: A criticism and an appreciation by the Rev. J. E. Newell, London Missionary Society," J.E. Newell Papers, Box 9 "Anthropological", South Seas Personal — Special, CWM Archives (SOAS, London). Schultz's book was originally published in Apia in 1906; the first English edition appeared as *Proverbial Expressions of the Samoans* (Wellington: The Polynesian Society, 1953).

22 "Dr. Schultz on Samoan proverbial sayings and figures of speech: A criticism and an appreciation by the Rev. J. E. Newell, London Missionary Society," J.E. Newell Papers, Box 9 "Anthropological", South Seas Personal - Special, CWM Archives, School of Oriental and African Studies, London, hereafter SOAS.

23 Herbert, *Culture and Anomie*, p. 185.

24 Colley, *Captives;* Michaud, "French Missionary Expansion"; Coombes *Reinventing Africa*, especially p. 162.

25 Herbert, *Culture and Anomie*, p. 185.

26 Gunson, *Messengers of Grace*, p. 207.

27 The plan was thwarted by the missionaries themselves when they demanded (and were refused) ordination before departure; Newbury, *The Tahitian Mission*, p. xxviii.

28 Newbury, *The Tahitian Mission*, xxix confuses the source of the quotation. Haweis, "The Very Probable Success" is actually found in 3:7 (July) of the 1795 *Evangelical Magazine*.

29 Haweis, "The Very Probable Success", p. 266.

30 William Shelley to "Rev. Fathers", 30 April, 1800; M1/SSJ, Box 1; CWM Archives, SOAS. Also see Newbury, *The Tahitian Mission*, p. xliv (where the date is given erroneously as 10 April 1779).

31 Cited in Gunson, *Messengers of Grace*, p. 255.

32 McKenzie, *Road to Mowanjum*, p. 48. This was James "Bob" Love who arrived in 1914 to allow the founders of the mission, Frances and Robert Wilson, to go on furlough.

33 Colenso, "Better Knowledge of the Maori Race", p. 80.

34 Colenso, "Better Knowledge of the Maori Race", p. 82.

35 Lorimer Fison, "Press copy book: Sermons, articles and letters, 1867–1873"; ML B591 (CY Reel 1360), ff. 365–6.

36 Latukefu and Sinclair, "Pacific Islanders as International Missionaries", p. 2.

37 "Timoteo's notes on Kabadi translated by Newell 1895", J.E. Newell Papers, Box 9 "Anthropological", folder 2, South Seas Personal — Special, Council for World Mission (hereafter CWM) Archives, School of Oriental and African Studies (hereafter SOAS), London.

38 The notes were duly published as Newell, "Notes on the Kabadi Dialect".

39 "Notes: chiefly ethnological of the Tokelau, Ellice and Some of the Gilbert or Kingsmill Islands", J.E. Newell Papers, Box 9 "Anthropological", folder 2, South Seas Personal — Special, CWM Archives (SOAS, London) published as Newell, "Notes: chiefly ethnological".

40 [William Pascoe Crook], "Account of Marquesas Islands, 1799", ML CY Reel 329, ff 165–6.

41 Dening, *Islands and Beaches*, p. 142.

42 Quoted in Birtwhistle, *In His Armour*, pp. 92–3.

43 Quoted in Thornley, *Inheritance of Hope*, 4. Hunt's views of Fijian dialects was not unproblematic however; he was the main advocate for Bauan as a lingua franca, claiming (probably wrongly) that most Fijians understood Bauan as well as their own local dialect. He himself disputed this claim later on. (Thornley, *Inheritance of Hope*, pp. 250, 266).

44 Thornley, *Inheritance of Hope*, p. 232.

45 Burton, *A Hundred Years in Fiji*, p. 63.

46 George Sarawia, *They Came to My Island*, p. ii. See also Gardner in this volume.

47 Sarawia, *They Came to My Island*, p. 2.

48 Sarawia, *They Came to My Island*, p. 2.

49 Sarawia, *They Came to My Island*, p. 10.

50 Sarawia, *They Came to My Island*, p. 17.

51 Sarawia, *They Came to My Island*, p. 17.

52 Codrington, *The Melanesians*, pp. v–vi.

53 King, *A.B.M. Review*, pp. 187–8.

54 King, *A.B.M. Review*, p. 188.

55 McKenzie, *Road to Mowanjum*, p. 89.

56 McKenzie, *Road to Mowanjum*, p. 90.

57 Fox, "A Missionary in Melanesia".

58 Fox, "A Missionary in Melanesia".

59 Cited in Davidson, *International Bulletin of Missionary Research*, p. 174.

60 Pelikan, *Jesus Through the Centuries*, p. 152.

61 Ray, "The Study of Melanesian Languages", pp. 176–8.

62 Ray, "The Study of Melanesian Languages", p. 177.

63 Possibly the most persistent of these sacred philologists was Daniel Macdonald of the Presbyterian New Hebrides Mission; he published dozens of articles into the early twentieth century and even found a leading publisher for his lengthy book on "Semitic" Polynesian languages: see *The Oceanic Languages*.

64 *Oxford English Dictionary Online*.

65 LeClaire and Cardinal, *Alberta Elders' Cree Dictionary*.

66 LeClaire and Cardinal, *Alberta Elders' Cree Dictionary*, pp. xii, xiv.

67 Solange de Santis, "Team Translates Bible Into Inukitut"

68 For more on race, colonialism and theology see Kidd, *The Forging of Races* and Carter, *Race: A Theological Account*.

69 Porter, *Religion Versus Empire*, p. 328.

70 Sugirtharajah, *The Bible and Empire*, p. 5.

71 Venuti, *The Scandals of Translation*, p. 6.

CHAPTER NINE

Practising Christianity, Writing Anthropology
Missionary Anthropologists and their Informants

HELEN BETHEA GARDNER

Throughout the nineteenth century the anthropological theorists of Europe sought missionary accounts of indigenous societies.[1] During the 1860s and 1870s, as debates raged in the new anthropological journals on the nature and measurement of human difference and the best means of defining distinctions between human populations, missionaries in Oceania read and critiqued the iconic anthropological texts of the period, particularly Sir John Lubbock's *The Origin of Civilzation* (1870) in which he repeated Maine's call for the gathering of data from those "trained to habits of method-ological observation".[2] Missionaries became actively involved in the analyses of the nascent discipline, often in response to questionnaires or schedules from the metropole. While theorists presumed that objective data and details could be simply garnered from mission fields, residents were aware that they were deeply entangled in the knowledge being gathered. Missionaries used local beliefs and cosmology as a source of analogy for Christian translations but often found themselves implicated as knowledge holders in forms of power that they struggled to understand: for example medical ability might be read as an expression of sorcery according to the foreign etiologies of their neigh-bours. Nascent Christians/informants negotiated a difficult path between the demands of the new deity and their own societies, particularly their kin to whom they owned allegiance and specific cultural responses. Further, in many parts of Melanesia and Australia knowledge was closely guarded by elders who owed their status and power to their store of magic and other cultural information, which was carefully and ritually released.[3]

One of the earliest and most extensively distributed questionnaires in the islands of the South Pacific and the colonies of Australasia was the schedule on kinship terms sent around the world by American lawyer, Lewis Henry Morgan. Just prior to the publication of *Systems of Consanguinity and Affinity* (1871), in which he argued for the evolutionist development of kinship systems from primitive promiscuity to the civi-lized patriarchal family, Morgan received data on Fijian and Tongan relationships from Lorimer Fison, Methodist missionary to the large island of Viti Levu in the Fiji group.[4] Fison was intrigued by the broader questions of human origin, development and dispersion related to the kinship studies of the period and was determined to collect schedules from all the language groups of Oceania. He established a large network of missionary collaborators and posted versions of Morgan's kinship schedule around the Australian colonies and the southern Pacific islands.[5] Among the many with whom he corresponded were fellow Methodist George Brown, missionary to Samoa and pioneer of the New Britain field off the large island of New Guinea, 1860–80; George Taplin, Congregational minister to the Ngarrindjeri of South Australia, 1859–79; and Robert Codrington, teacher and headmaster of the Anglican Melanesian Mission, 1861–86. Despite denominational differences and some disquiet on Morgan's materialism — the belief that humankind had progressed through natural rather than deistic forces — all were eager recruits to this new investigation. All recognized the theological value of an inquiry that sought to prove the common origin of humankind against a background of fierce debate on the issue and all were keen to formally extend their previously casual studies of the cultures of their congregations. In their engagement with the new discipline, missionaries were very dependent on their early converts.

George Brown, Paula Kaplen and Peni Lelei

Methodist George Brown was one of the first to receive Fison's handwritten kinship schedule copied from the Morgan pamphlet in early 1870.[6] Five years later, the two men shared the Sydney/Fiji leg of the pioneer voyage to establish the mission on the Duke of York Islands in the straits between the large islands of New Britain and New Ireland off the coast of New Guinea.[7] Fison was returning to the Fiji mission after a prolonged furlough spent largely in Melbourne in the southern Australian colony of Victoria, where he collected the data for the analysis of Aboriginal and south Pacific kinship *Kamilaroi and Kurnai* (1880), co-written with magistrate, explorer and geologist, Alfred Howitt. Trained by Fison in the study of kinship, Brown added this skill to his knowledge of geology, flora and fauna and became a keen student of culture. His first published anthropological paper — "Notes on the Duke of York Group, New Britain and New Ireland", *Journal of the Royal Geographical Society* (1877) — proposed that the principal difference between the peoples of the east and west Pacific could be found in their kinship systems rather than in physical distinctions (such as the curl of the hair, the colour of the skin or the size or shape of the skull) which had previously dominated analyses of any division.[8]

Brown had two primary informants on the customs of the villagers of the Duke of York islands where the pioneer mission was established in 1875. Kaplen was a resident of the village of Kinawanua and a nephew of the big men, Waruwarum and To Pulu, who had grown wealthy through their control of the victualling trade with vessels plying between the Australian colonies and China.[9] He became Brown's companion during frequent journeys around the coastal villages of New Britain, New Ireland and the Duke of York Islands and was the mediator between the mission party and his uncles, who allowed Brown to establish the mission in the villages under their control.[10] Kaplen soothed the tensions caused by Brown's attempts to escape the strictures of his uncles' trading alliances and he negotiated settlements using shell money when the big men and Brown clashed on points of principle, such as the rescuing of one of Waruwarum's wives following a severe beating.[11] Less powerful in the Duke of York Islands but perhaps more significant as cultural informant was Lelei from the neighbouring village of Molot, who first appeared in Brown's journal in 1878 in a record of his prayer in Duke of York language during a polyglot prayer-meeting held in Fijian, Samoan and English as well as Duke of York and New Ireland languages.[12] Probably in his early twenties when the mission was established, Lelei was converted by the celebrated Fijian minister Amino Beledrokadroka, who was one of the pioneer teachers to New Britain and was stationed in the Duke of York Islands for seventeen years.[13] Kaplen and Lelei were among the first five baptized in December 1878, taking the Christian names Paula (Paul) and Penijimani or Peni (Benjamin) respectively.[14] In 1880 Peni Lelei was appointed as one of the first three local preachers and assessed by Brown as a "steady friend ever since we began the mission . . . a very intelligent young man. He was my best pundit, and gave me great help in the work of translation."[15] For his latter skills he was chosen to accompany the Brown family back to Sydney to assist with the development of a Duke of York dictionary and the translation of the Gospel of Mark.[16]

Along with the missionaries and colonial administrators, German and British, who followed him to the region, Brown was both intrigued by and entangled in the shell money economy that was used throughout the islands to purchase goods as well as spells, knowledge, rituals and brides.[17] As this currency mediated nearly all transactions between islanders, Brown became adept in its use to avoid trouble and to pay for "frights", "insults" and even deaths that were the result of the presence of the mission.[18] He also deployed shell money in discussions with metropolitan theorists, for whom the presence of a currency analogous to European money represented a technological marker of human development within the evolutionist paradigm. During Lelei's residency in Sydney, Brown extended the anthropological investigations he had begun in the islands and established contact with British theorist Edward B. Tylor, who had edited the first edition of *Notes and Queries on Anthropology for the use of travellers and residents in uncivilised lands* (1874) and was later appointed to Oxford.[19] Brown's introductory letter to Tylor included a specimen of shell money and a copy of the newly translated Gospel of Mark. Tylor was excited by the "curious specimens" of money, noting that they contrasted "remarkably with the general rude condition of these islanders", and suggested that Malay traders might solve this anomaly.[20] Brown turned to Lelei and responded that there was no evidence of Malay trading in the region and described the extensive economic vocabulary of the Duke of York language, which contained words for "depreciation" and "to sell at a sacrifice".[21] His subsequent investigations into the distinctions between the peoples of the east and west Pacific provided further details on the shell money that — along with other aspects of material culture found in Melanesia but absent from Polynesia such as the bow and arrow and pottery — was a challenge to the evolutionist hierarchy of Polynesia over Melanesia.

While Lelei and Kaplen were Brown's primary informants, they were not named in his anthropological texts. The anthropological genre called for descriptions of normative behaviour in the third person and the past tense; therefore proper nouns and individual experiences were eschewed as unscientific. Informants appeared under general identifiers such as "New Britain native" or third person pronouns, principally "they". In the introduction to *Melanesians and Polynesians*, Brown wrote that during his residence in New Britain, he "secured from time to time the services of intelligent natives" to answer the questions of *Anthropological Notes and Queries*, "and wrote down at the time the answers which were given me."[22] Amongst these notes is a single reference to Peni Lelei's response on shell money, history and the population of the Duke of York Islands:

> They believe that they were much fewer formerly and much more peaceable than now. They say that villages which now are always fighting formerly dwelt in peace; that diwara [shell money] was very scarce formerly, now it is much more plentiful. Peni thinks it originates thus: — formerly there were few now there are many, formerly they had little money, now plenty, because formerly they had no good canoes. But now with improved tools they have larger ones and can go further and get more money. Then money (the root of all evil) makes them fight a man who has money and wishes to use it.[23]

In the passage from *Melanesians and Polynesians* corresponding to the details described above, the direct reference to Lelei was dropped and he was identified simply as "my informant".[24] Therefore, despite Lelei's contribution to Brown's understanding of shell money, and other cultural practices, and Kaplen's assistance, mediation and knowledge, neither was named in *Melanesians and Polynesians*. The only names that appeared were those of Brown's fellow missionary observers who helped compile the data. Therefore the text is littered with references to missionaries and their fields: Bromilow on the Trobriand Islands; Danks on New Britain; Powell on Samoa and Fison on Fiji.

George Taplin and James Ngunaitponi

George Taplin began his mission a year before George Brown in 1859, when he established the Congregational station on Ngarrindjeri[25] country at Raukkan on the shores of Lake Alexandrina in South Australia. Immediately drawn to the culture of his neighbours, Taplin's early journal was thick with discussions on custom and included the names of his interlocutors, though such entries tailed off during the 1860s. As with Brown, Taplin was influenced by Fison's kinship investigations though his first anthropological publication which appeared in the first volume of the *Journal of the Anthropological Institute of Great Britain and Ireland* in 1872 was a comparison of common words in twenty-four Aboriginal languages and predated his acquaintance with the Methodist.[26] But he was eager to extend his investigations and was delighted to receive Fison's circular and covering letter which noted Taplin's growing reputation in "all Australian Aboriginal lore" and called him to the new science of ethnology, chiefly to add "link after link to the chain of evidence which proves the truth of that great Bible proposition, 'God hath made of one blood all manner of men.'"[27] Yet while Taplin was able to answer the questions on the forms of marriage, inheritance, nomenclature and heredity in the questionnaire, he was defeated by the complexity of the printed schedule of 220 questions on kinship and provided instead a truncated list of Ngarrindjeri relationships.[28] The completed schedule was sent the following month accompanied by Taplin's note that "I have got most of my information about the relationships from our native teacher and Deacon James Unaipon.[29] He is an intelligent Christian of 10 years standing."[30]

By 1872 Taplin and Ngunaitponi had been working together on the Raukkan mission for six years. Through a combination of Taplin's anthropological and mission details Ngunaitponi can be identified as a Piltindjeri man — one of the eighteen *lakalinyerar*[31] or tribes identified by Taplin that made up the Ngarrindjeri nation.[32] (Subsequent details identify his birthplace as Piwingang, his clan as the Wunyalkundi and his language group as Potawolin).[33] Born in the 1830s, Ngunaitponi was raised in the country adjacent to the township of Wellington on the Murray River in the headwaters of Lake Alexandrina, during a rare period of relative harmony between settlers and Aborigines as the gold rush in neighbouring Victoria lured agricultural workers from the new farms and Ngarrindjeri were employed in their stead.[34] Ngunaitponi came to Raukkan following the drowning of his missionary mentor, James Reid.[35] Recognizing his skill as a preacher and translator of the new religion, Taplin trained Ngunaitponi as a teacher.[36] Only a few years younger than the missionary, Ngunaitponi was both a baptized Christian and an adult initiated man. As a result he was a force to be reckoned with, both in the Raukkan community and more widely amongst the Ngarrindjeri peoples with whom he worked as an itinerant preacher, from the Coorong in the south east to Cape Jervis in the west and Wellington and Murray Bridge at the northern extremities of the boundaries of the country described by Taplin as the Ngarrindjeri nation.[37] Ngunaitponi gathered a group of Christian seekers around him and together they began to oppose some of the Ngarrindjeri practices that they believed to be against the wishes of the Christian God, in particular the long funerary rites which involved the identification of the sorcerer who had caused the death, then the slow drying of the corpse first over a fire then within the *wurleys*[38] in which the old people lived.[39] In May 1871, Ngunaitponi was inducted into the office of deacon, though he was never ordained.[40]

In the years between his first correspondence with Fison and his death in 1879, Taplin completed two monographs on the customs, cultures and history of the Ngarrindjeri and other Aboriginal groups of South Australia. *The Narrinyeri* was published in 1873 and then revised for inclusion in a collection edited by journalist J. D. Woods *The Native Tribes of South Australia* (1879) with only a few additions. Anxious to "salvage" information they feared would be lost with the relentless drive of settlers onto Aboriginal land, the colonial governments of Victoria, South Australia and Western Australia, authorized and commissioned the collection and publication of anthropological data. Taplin was commissioned to draw up a circular on Aboriginal manners, customs and folklore to be sent to missionaries, settlers and police throughout South Australia and the Northern Territory, following a similar exercise in South Africa.[41] The answers in relation to approximately twenty groups were published verbatim in *The Folklore, Manners, Customs and Languages of the South Australian Aborigines* (1879). Taplin's publications dedicated to the Ngarrindjeri contain six short anthropological chapters covering marriage, initiation, funeral rites, sorcery, governance, games, weapons, and mythology and conclude with a long chapter titled "The history of the mission at Point Macleay", made up of selections of Taplin's journal entries linked by explanatory notes and describing the Ngarrindjeri encounter with Christianity. In marked contrast to the anthropological chapters, the history chapter is filled with named individuals whose lives are described principally in relation to their missionary. For example, there are frequent references to Taplin's first friend Teenminne, whom he described as "a truly excellent woman — kind hearted, intelligent, faithful, courageous, devout", and whose death in 1869 he narrated with a clear grief.[42] Ngunaitponi also appears here in the selection of journal entries and as a key figure in the early formation of the Christian society; in the first entry he is described as a "steady Christian adult native, who would always take the side of truth and righteousness. He became also a nucleus around which those who were impressed by divine truth could rally."[43]

While Ngunaitponi was the principal informant for Taplin's anthropological chapters, he shared the same fate as his New Britain counterparts, Peni Lelei and Paula Kaplen, and was rarely acknowledged within them. As with Brown, Taplin was corralled by the directives of the anthropological genre, which shrouded the informant. Ngunaitponi's contribution can, however, be directly identified in Taplin's journal, particularly in 1873 and 1874. Frequent entries during these years refer to "long conversations" with Ngunaitponi and include a depiction of the great Ngarrindjeri creator spirit *Nurundere*, the songs of *corroborees*, the wrestling with spirits, and, in the midst of a series of entries in April and May that simply note "read with James" an account of the *tandi*, the Ngarrindjeri council, described as a "judgement council" consisting of the tribal elders of each of the *lakalinyerar* that made up the Ngarrindjeri nation.[44] It is telling that Taplin had neither encountered nor been aware of this important institution that appeared in the second version the "The Narrinyeri" in Woods (ed.), *The Native Tribes of South Australia*, but not in his 1873 publication *The Narrinyeri*.[45]

While Taplin's anthropological and historical chapters were clearly delineated in his 1873 and 1879 publications, they often depicted the same category of action though in very different voices. One example was the description of the custom of *kalduke*, in which the umbilical cord of the child of one family was given to the father of the children of another clan. This act established strict avoidance rules between the children. On reaching adulthood such children became the conduits through which the clans would negotiate the exchange of goods. Thus, noted Taplin, any collusion between the agents would be avoided as they were forbidden to speak or go near each other. In his anthropological description the activities were depicted as standard and normative practices:

> When a man has a child born to him he preserves its umbilical cord by tying it up
> in the middle of a bunch of feathers. This is called a kalduke. He then gives this to

the father of a child or children belonging to another tribe, and those children are thenceforth ngia-ngiampe to the child from whom the kalduke was procured, and that child is ngia-ngiampe to them . . . When two individuals who are in this position with regard to each other have arrived at adult age, they become the agents through which their respective tribes carry on barter.[46]

While Taplin first encountered this custom prior to the arrival of James Ngunaitponi,[47] it was Ngunaitponi's rejection of the practice that gave him the greatest insight into both the custom and the regard in which it was held by Ngarrindjeri. The account was given in the chapter "The History of the Mission to the Aborigines at Point McLeay", and was introduced as "illustration of the power of Christianity":

> I have several times mentioned the name of Baalpulare in the course of this narrative. The people bearing this name were a large and influential but extremely superstitious and heathen family of the Point Macleay tribe . . . Now this family was by native law ngia-ngiampe to James Unaipon, consequently they were forbidden to have the slightest intercourse with him, or he with them. One day James came to me and brought a kalduke which he said had been sent to him by Minora Baalpulare upon the birth of his child to show that he wished the same custom to be kept up between their children. James felt that he could not agree to this as he was a Christian; but it would have been risking a quarrel if he had gone and spoken to Minora about it, so he asked me what he had better do. I told him that I would carry back the kalduke and settle the matter. Consequently I went to Minora . . . and I gave him back the plume. The Baalpulares were very much scandalised, and very ill friends with James for a long time after this occurred.[48]

Important to the distinctions between the voices was Taplin's shift in moral tone from one to the other text. In the anthropological syntax he described the custom then provided an interpretation of its function within Ngarrindjeri society: "It gives security to the tribes that there will be no collusion between their agents for their own private advantage, and also compels the two always to conduct the business through third parties."[49] Yet the description of Ngunaitponi's refusal to continue the practice was told in the historical chapter in terms of Christian triumph; any inherent value of the custom was lost in the depiction of the individual's struggle with those aspects of culture that were believed to be against the dictates of Christianity. Set into a narrative, the conclusion provided the moral significance: two members of the Baalpulare family became distressed at the thought of their sins and sought out Ngunaitponi as the first step to admission and baptism in the church. In this mode the tale became "an instance of the power of Christianity to break down native customs; these men cast aside all thoughts of ngia-ngiampe, and under pressure of religious concern, sought counsel from the very man whom native law forbade them to speak to. And to this time they are the most intimate friends of James Unaipon."[50]

As an adult initiated man, Ngunaitponi's understanding of Ngarrindjeri society would have been extensive, but constrained by directives on the dissemination of information and he would have been permanently excluded from some types of knowledge, in particular, that held and practised by women.[51] It is not possible to identify which elements of knowledge he was prepared to share with Taplin or, indeed, whether Taplin was seeking prescribed knowledge, such as the words to specific spells or song cycles, or simply broader cultural information that was not subject to ownership or restrictions. It is probable that Taplin sought the latter as his anthropology was largely a description of the external manifestations of Ngarrindjeri culture. There was an inherent tension between the missionary's interest in culture and his efforts to change it; indeed, much of the cultural information he gathered was gained through his efforts to challenge particular aspects of Ngarrindjeri life. For example, his description of the directives against the cutting or combing of the hair of the young boys from the age of ten until the first rites of initiation, was followed by a discussion of his attempts to persuade a young (unnamed) boy to ignore these directives, offering new clothes as inducement. The reluctant boy did as his missionary requested until he fell ill, the result, Taplin believed, of "a superstitious fear of the result of having his hair cut".[52]

Robert Codrington and George Sarawia

Taplin's complex relationship to the anthropological details of those whose lives he sought to change was experienced by all missionary/anthropologists. Anglican missionary Robert Codrington's knowledge of the men's societies that characterized the lives of the people of northern Vanuatu (then New Hebrides) and the islands of the southern Solomons was also fraught. Virtually all men in each village were members and gradually rose through the grades by killing pigs and raising money. In the Banks Islands of northern Vanuatu, the public society was known as the *sukwe*. The secret societies of the *tamate*, which were housed in the *salagoro* was more exclusive and many remained separate. Payment of shell money was required for entry upon which the members were taught to make the masks worn in public.[53] While Codrington recognized the importance of these institutions in village life, he was ambivalent about their influence particularly on his friend, George Sarawia, his chief anthropological informant and the first Melanesian priest of the Melanesian Mission.

A former fellow at Wadham College, Oxford, Codrington began his mission at the Auckland school of Kohimarama in 1860 and was headmaster of the Melanesian Mission School on Norfolk Island from 1867, a position he held, with some long furloughs, for 20 years. Initiated into kinship studies by Fison in 1871, Codrington brought his considerable linguistic and analytic skills to the new science. His first anthropological articles, "Religious beliefs and practices in Melanesia" and "Notes on the customs of Mota, Banks Islands", were published in 1881, the latter with lengthy annotations by Fison. In "Religious beliefs and practices in Melanesia", Codrington considered the complications for the missionary/anthropologist, particularly in his case as he was reliant on the younger members of the societies he was studying. His students on Norfolk Island had little initiation into the details of local beliefs and practices and the situation was further complicated by the reluctance of their elders to "share their sacred *wisdom* with Christian converts", for whom the spirits of their community were now a source of unease.[54] Throughout the 1880s and 1890s, and particularly during a furlough back at Oxford, when he attended British anthropologist Edward B. Tylor's first lectures in anthropology, Codrington continued his publication of anthropological articles; his influential *The Melanesians, Studies in Their Anthropology and Folklore* (1891), appeared following his retirement from the field. In the preface he acknowledged a number of his informants but in particular the "very valuable assistance of a native who was a grown youth before his people had been at all affected by intercourse with Europeans or had heard any Christian teaching — the Rev. George Sarawia".[55]

Sarawia was born in approximately 1841 in the Banks Islands in northern Vanuatu on the finger of land on Vanua Lava that came to be called Port Patteson after the father of the first Bishop of Melanesia, John Coleridge Patteson, who encountered the sixteen-year-old Sarawia in 1857 when he was seeking scholars for the mission. Sarawia began his training for the church at Lifu on the Loyalty Islands, then moved to the mission school of Kohimarama in Auckland where he taught Mota to Patteson and helped entrench the language as the lingua franca of the mission before being baptised in 1863.[56] While in Auckland, Sarawia came under the tuition of Codrington and the two men moved to the new mission site at Norfolk Island in 1867. Two years later, Sarawia returned to the Banks Islands to establish a new Christian village on Mota, for while the language of this island was used by staff and students of the mission, the people had not proved receptive to the new deity. Within three years a dozen houses surrounded the lime church of the Christian village of Kohimarama. The school taught 150 people for an hour every morning and evening and one quarter of the population on the island attended Sunday school.[57] In 1873, on the voyage that was to take Sarawia to Auckland for his ordination, his neighbours and congregations were tested by Codrington, on whether he was "diligent in teaching, in visiting the sick, in composing quarrels, and that his life was blameless".[58] It seemed that Sarawia's Christian village was a success, and an important breakthrough on the very slow rate of conversion for the Melanesian Mission in comparison to those missions with an ongoing missionary presence, either Polynesian or European.

As with Taplin, Codrington had also been alert to cultural issues from the origins of his work in Melanesia for theological, linguistic and eventually anthropological reasons. He also spent time with those who were not interested in the new faith: a journal record of his visit to Mota in 1869 described time spent in the men's houses or *gamal*, and the debates and discussions on the spirit world of the *tamates*, or ghosts, of Mota who maintained a constant presence on the island.[59] These details were supplemented by later inquiries, and published in the article "Religious beliefs and practices in Melanesia" (1881); his monograph, *The Melanesians: Studies in their Anthropology and Folklore*, and his dictionary, which gives no less than twenty words derived from *tamate*.[60] In the preface to his monograph, Codrington described how twice during his recurrent visits to the islands he conducted a "systematic enquiry into the religious beliefs and practices of the Melanesians and the social regulations and conditions prevailing among them". His principal informant on the first occasion was George Sarawia.[61]

The Melanesian Mission maintained an uneasy relationship with the spirits and ghosts of Mota as well as the men's societies in which they were discussed and debated. The mission aimed for the gradual introduction of Christianity and, as Codrington noted in one of his footnotes, Bishop Patteson made an early decision not to "interfere in an arbitrary manner with the institutions of the people".[62] Throughout the first fifty years of the mission, the church struggled to develop a coherent position on the societies.[63] Early pupils, including Sarawia, debated the question of whether membership of the *sukwe* and *tamate* societies was incompatible with a Christian life. The Bishop asked them to consider "the real character of the societies; did they offer worship and prayer to ghosts or spirits; were they required to take part in anything indecent or atrocious; did membership involve any profession of belief or practice of superstition peculiar to the members". The young men reported that apart from the association with ghosts, which was already losing ground among the people, they could find nothing wrong in the societies and the Bishop decided he would "not condemn" them. Codrington, however, perhaps because of his greater knowledge of their influence, was ambivalent about them and concluded his footnote with the comment that "in the Banks Islands they continue to exist, and indeed to flourish more that it is at all desirable that they should".[64] In the text, he noted that "the social power of these societies was too great to be readily dissolved" and he attributed their continuation to the absence of any "strong political organization" in the islands.

Codrington's knowledge of the societies had come through a number of his pupils, but it was his relationship to Sarawia and the latter's involvement in the institutions that brought him both the greatest information and unease regarding their continuing influence in the islands. In early 1883 Sarawia wrote to Codrington, now on furlough in England attending Tylor's lectures in Oxford, with some disturbing news. Sickness, which had devastated the island while Sarawia was being ordained in Auckland and had killed many in the Christian village including his wife, was continuing to overwhelm the converts and he himself was frequently ill. The point of Sarawia's letter, however, was to head off some gossip that he feared might reach Codrington from "people who are trying to tell false witness about us". Sarawia had joined a *tamate*. Fearful that these tales might reach Codrington via the European missionary Palmer, Sarawia attempted to explain his actions. He did not deny his membership but insisted: "It does not mean praying to the *tamate*, no we cannot pray to that *tamate*. It is true that the ceremony of making men become members of the *tamate* is still continuing." If Codrington was ambivalent about the first Melanesian priest's membership of a society that mediated the temporal and spiritual worlds, he may well have been soothed by the words that followed regarding the most important and public of the men's societies: "Concerning the suqe, they seem to be forgetting about it. It is not as before, some of its customs also we are not practising".[65] While Sarawia may well have been accurately reporting the state of the *sukwe* in 1883 the situation clearly changed over the next twenty years. For by the time of his death in 1901 both the *tamate* and the *sukwe* were flourishing in Mota. The churches had fallen into disrepair and attendance was feeble.

Sunday was not observed and to the horror of his European peers, in the final years of Sarawia's life rumours abounded that the first Melanesian priest was also the highest ranked member of the *sukwe* on the island.[66]

Concluding Comments

Missionary anthropologists disentangled themselves from the realities of their day-to-day lives through the third person, present tense descriptions of culture that characterized anthropological texts. Yet their relationship to the information they sought was often deeply fraught and their responses to these details ranged from acceptance of some practices to an uneasy accommodation of others to outright rejection in a few cases. Despite missionary rhetoric and the expectations of home congregations who were fed a steady diet of conversion narratives and uplifting examples of the success of the Christian message, all residents of the mission field were aware that the situation on the ground was thick with ambiguities and complexities. Armchair anthropological theorists in the northern hemisphere shared with evangelical congregations a belief in the transformative power of the European presence. Believing that custom would evaporate on contact with Europeans, theorists were desperate to salvage "pure" data, convinced such information could position each culture or language group on the evolutionist ladder of progress. Yet most of the detailed information came from converted informants whose relationship to their societies was profoundly complicated by their engagement with the new faith. For reasons principally related to the demands of the anthropological genre, these informants are difficult to identify in the texts and their presence must be winnowed from accompanying evidence.

Notes

1 Gunson, "British Missionaries and their Contribution to Science in the Pacific Islands" pp. 283–317.
2 Lubbock, *The Origin of Civilization*, pp. 3–5.
3 This does not presume straightforward similarities in knowledge systems and holdings across the vast range of cultures and languages in Australia and Melanesia, though recent work suggests that some comparisons can be drawn. See for example Wassmann, "The Politics of Religious Secrecy", pp. 43–71. For a discussion of the holding and exchanging of information in mid to late 20th century Melanesia, see Lindstrom, "Doctor, Lawyer, Wiseman, Priest", pp. 291–9.
4 Gardner, "The Origin of Kinship in Oceania", p. 142.
5 Fison, "Circular Letter with Accompanying Schedule", 6 March 1871.
6 Fison to Brown, 1 January 1870, Letterbook 2; Gardner "The Origin of Kinship in Oceania", p. 143.
7 Gardner, *Gathering for God*, pp. 110–11.
8 Brown, "Notes on the Duke of York Group, New Britain and New Ireland", pp. 137–50.
9 For an analysis of the importance of the kinship links between Kaplen and his uncles, see Schütte, "To Pulu and his Brothers", pp. 53–68.

10 See for example, Brown Journal, 30 November 1875, 18 January 1876; Brown, *George Brown*, pp. 135, 145.

11 Gardner, *Gathering for God*, pp. 56–63, 139.

12 Brown, Journal, 31 October 1878; Brown, *George Brown*, p. 231.

13 Gardner, *Gathering for God*, p. 54.

14 Brown, *George Brown*, p. 289.

15 Brown, *George Brown*, p. 378; see also Brown to Reed, 28 May 1880.

16 Gardner, *Gathering for God*, p. 85.

17 For a discussion of the considerable literature on shell money see Errington and Gewertz, *Articulating Change*, pp. 54–6.

18 See for example, Brown's use of shell money during his retaliatory raid on villages accused of killing and consuming four Fijian teachers, Gardner, *Gathering for God*, pp. 65–84.

19 Stocking, *Victorian Anthropology*, p. 264.

20 Tylor to Brown, 23 September 1881, Brown, Scientific and Ethnological papers.

21 Brown to Tylor, 28 April 1882, The Papers of Sir E. B. Tylor.

22 Brown, *Melanesians and Polynesians*, p. vi.

23 Brown, Scientific and Ethnological papers.

24 Brown, *Melanesians and Polynesians*, p. 353.

25 Known at the time as Narrinyeri.

26 Taplin, "Notes on a Comparative Table of Australian Languages", pp. 84–8.

27 Fison to Taplin, 13 August 1872, Fison, Letterbook 3.

28 Taplin to Fison 5 September 1872, Fison Correspondence TIP70/10/24.

29 Other spellings for Ngunaitponi include Ngunaipon and Unaipon. Taplin experimented with a number of spellings then settled for Unaipon, which has become the popular spelling both for James and his more famous son David.

30 Taplin to Fison 16 October 1872, Fison Correspondence TIP70/10/24.

31 On the language groups see Berndt and Berndt, *A World That Was*, pp. 2–3.

32 Subsequent anthropologists Berndt and Berndt, working largely in the 1940s and 1950s, challenged Taplin's theory of the Ngarrindjeri nation, *A World that Was*, p. 19.

33 Jones, "Unaipon, James *c.* 1835–1907", p. 389.

34 Linn, *A Diverse Land*, p. 43.

35 Jenkins, *Conquest of the Ngarrindjeri*, pp. 104–5, 117.

36 Taplin, Journal, 20 February 1865; Jenkins, *Conquest of the Ngarrindjeri*, pp. 142–3.

37 Taplin, *The Folklore, Manners, Customs and Languages of the South Australian Aborigines*, p. 34; see Jenkins, *Conquest of the Ngarrindjeri*, map, p. 23.

38 This word was the common term for an Aboriginal dwelling in South Australia from the Adelaide people. The Narrindjeri term is *mante*. Taplin, "The Narrinyeri", p. 12.

39 The accounts of the opposition to this practice appear frequently in the Taplin Journals, see for example 19 March 1865.

40 Taplin, Journal 29 May 1871.

41 Taplin (ed.), *The Folklore, Manners, Customs and Languages of the South Australian Aborigines*, p. 1.

42 Taplin, "The Narrinyeri", pp. 88, 90, 94, 97, 98, 109, 110,114.

43 Taplin, " The Narrinyeri", p. 101.

44 Taplin, Journal, 5 November 1872; 6 January 1873; 5, 6, 25, 26 April 1874; 8, 9, 15, 16 June 1874; 21 July 1874.

45 Taplin, "The Narrinyeri", p. xliii.

46 Taplin, "The Narrinyeri", p. 33.
47 Taplin, Journal, 7 March 1861.
48 Taplin, "The Narrinyeri", p. 116.
49 Taplin, "The Narrinyeri", p. 33.
50 Taplin, "The Narrinyeri", p. 116.
51 For a discussion on gendered knowledge, particularly in relation to contemporary events in South Australia, see Bell, *Ngarrindjeri Wurruwarrin*, pp. 385–92.
52 Taplin, "The Narrinyeri", p. 16.
53 Codrington, *The Melanesians*, pp. 287–8.
54 Codrington, "Religious beliefs and practices in Melanesia", p. 262.
55 Codrington, *The Melanesians*, pp. v–vi.
56 Sarawia, *They Came to My Island*, pp. 10–23.
57 Hilliard, *God's Gentlemen*, p. 60
58 Codrington, Melanesian Mission *Annual Reports 1873*, p. 139.
59 Codrington, Journal 11, 16 Sept 1869, 1 June, 1871, *The Mission Field*.
60 Codrington, "Religious beliefs and practices in Melanesia", pp. 231–316, *The Melanesians*, pp. 150–72, with J. Palmer, *A Dictionary of the Language of Mota*.
61 Codrington, *The Melanesians*, p. v. In 1874, following his introduction to kinship studies, Codrington spent some weeks on Mota during the annual mission visit to the field, and presumably conducted his investigations into religious beliefs and practices during this time. *Melanesian Mission Annual Reports: The First Voyage of the New Southern Cross*, 1874, pp. 4–8.
62 Codrington, *The Melanesians, Their Anthropology and Folklore*, p. 74.
63 Durrad, "The Attitude of the Church to the Suqe".
64 Codrington, *The Melanesians*, p. 74.
65 Sarawia to Codrington, Codrington Correspondence 1866–1922. This letter was translated by Selwyn Wotlimaru, Mota.
66 Hilliard, *God's Gentleman*, pp. 200–1.

CHAPTER TEN

Missionaries, Africans and the State in the Development of Education in Colonial Natal, 1836–1910

NORMAN ETHERINGTON

Because of the huge role played by missions in providing education in colonial sub-Saharan Africa, the evangelist is virtually synonymous with the teacher in popular culture. The opening sequence of the motion picture, *The African Queen*, presents the stereotype: Katherine Hepburn and her ineffectual missionary brother vainly struggle to impose musical order on a crowd of children in the suffocating heat of a corrugated iron church that doubles as a school house. This image obscures the messy and complicated process by which many different approaches to Christian education gradually gave way to routines of schooling that varied only slightly from denomination to denomination. Natal is a good place to study that process because it was one of the first regions in Africa to receive the concentrated attention of many different missionary societies. From the United States of America, Scotland, Norway, France, Germany, England, Sweden and Austria they came, beginning in the 1830s, bringing with them many different notions about the relationship between evangelization and education.[1]

Although there has been renewed scholarly attention to missionaries as agents of cultural imperialism in recent decades,[2] other studies emphasize the role of indigenous people in shaping Christianity to their own needs. Chiefs and commoners, males and females, parents and children — all had different and often competing ideas about the education their communities required.[3] A further complication noted in several investigations is the role of the state as a regulator and contributor to mission education; missions that defied or ignored official requirements could lose funding or even the right to continue.[4] When white settlers had a voice in government, missions were likely to be even more tightly regulated as settlers commonly sought to direct them towards the production of the kind of compliant and useful servants they desired, and away from the production of skilled farmers, scholars and tradesmen who might operate as economic competitors and make inconvenient demands for political equality.

The development of missionary education in Natal and Zululand from the advent of the first missionaries up to the inauguration of the Union of South Africa in 1910 displayed all of these conflicting interests. Missions founded schools and set educational goals in accordance with their theological beliefs and missiological theories. Africans embraced some of the educational goods offered to them while rejecting others, depending on their status, gender and economic position. Early colonial governors looked to missions to relieve them of some of the burden of providing education to the African population. Later, as white settler voices became more influential, governments demanded that subsidized missions bend their educational efforts toward the production of a subservient workforce largely composed of domestic servants and unskilled labourers.

Meeting African Requirements

In the early decades, when it was not yet clear that Britain would acquire all of Natal and Zululand, it was not taken for granted that missionaries would be the partners of the colonial state.[5] The first plans for education emphasized involving African authorities in promoting and financing education. Missionary authorities in Europe or the United States constantly reiterated the importance of this task. The evangelization of the world could not be accomplished by philanthropy alone. In the cant phrase of the early nineteenth century, missions should be self-governing, self-supporting and self-propagating.[6] The search for self-support made the first missionaries eager to supply the learning African rulers requested. During this brief period, a simple transplantation of the schooling characteristic of industrializing Europe was out of the question. Instead a many-sided conversation about education flourished.

Voices from home insisted that conversion was the first, possibly the only objective; what people called "civilization" would follow as an inevitable consequence. For most Protestant missions, the one educational prerequisite to conversion was literacy. People must be able to read the Bible. American missionaries new to Natal in 1837 plunged directly into the work of translation:

> *A Printer here we do need most imperiously* . . . The gospels of Matthew and Mark have been translated and need a thorough revision only to be ready. These we need very much as text books in preaching to the people and reading books in the schools. They are much interested in hearing, *"the book speak news"*.[7]

Initially they seemed to get the response they hoped for. "Dingan [the Zulu king] . . . sent from his own place to be taught in reading, writing, and work, four boys, and seven girls, some of whom are bright children, and are getting on perhaps as well as could be expected without books."[8] The passage of time showed, however, that the educational goods most prized by African rulers were technology transfers. To some extent, missionaries responded by supplying wagons, nails, medicines, dental services and alternative techniques of agriculture. Henry Callaway, an Anglican missionary who was also a doctor, took a broad view of education, arguing that there could be no greater mistake "than to imagine that the missionary has nothing to do but to consider . . . abstract spiritual needs. His attention must be directed to raise them, to get them [Africans] to build better houses, to be better herdsmen and shepherds, and more skilful cultivators of the land."[9] Callaway's bishop agreed: Africans should be taught "a better kind of agriculture than that which they at present practice".[10]

Insofar as these endeavours were designed to open the way for conversion of chiefs, the missionaries did not succeed. No important chief read the Bible or embraced Christianity in nineteenth-century Natal.[11] Missionaries built wagons and houses for the Zulu royal house in return for promises of royal children to educate, but the children never came.[12] The children that King Dingane sent were not his own. Mpande promised royal children on many occasions, but the only part of his brood who fell into missionary hands were refugees who fled into Natal following the civil war of 1856–7.[13] Later King Cetshwayo promised children for the Anglican missionary Robert Robertson to educate, but they never came. On the eve of the Anglo-Zulu war, Bishop J. W. Colenso was claiming that friendly relations "might have been promoted by getting Cetshwayo and his Indunas to send down children for education, as they were quite disposed to do when Magema spoke with them".[14] Nonetheless, Zululand continued to be barren territory for missionaries both in education and conversion until after the civil war of the 1880s. All the noteworthy transformations occurred in Natal.

Without an accession of chiefly converts, the idea that the Bible could be sold as an educational commodity had to be abandoned. Missionaries were much more successful in promoting the idea that, without elementary education, the African people could never face white settlers on an equal footing. When Colenso asked the "powerful chief Langalibalele" in 1855 whether he wished his children to be taught, the reply he received was "*We* are the children; we wish to be taught. We came here to save our lives from our enemy, and now we wish to know what our protectors know."[15] Of course, it was beyond the means of any mission to take up adult education on such a scale, but similar practical arguments were used to promote schooling of children as an investment in the future. By the end of the 1870s they were getting some response from petty chiefs in Natal. A Methodist missionary reported from York in 1871 that he had "visited some of the chiefs" in the district and "some of them . . . expressed a strong desire to have their children educated, and are willing to assist in the erection of a school, but they wish to know how much money they would have to pay for the Teacher".[16] Given the limited resources available to rural people still on the margins of the cash economy, the most that could conceivably be supported was "an intelligent devoted native evangelist".

Very few schools in nineteenth-century Natal were sustained by people in such impoverished circumstances. On the other hand, abundant evidence shows that individuals who had significant sources of income from cash-cropping, small business or wage labour could and did pay fees for their children's education. At one end of the scale were descendants of the alliances with African women formed by the early white traders at Port Natal, especially Fynns and Ogles. These took leading roles in some congregations where, as one missionary put it: "they have a great influence among the natives and are very anxious to have them civilized and Christianized". Frankly racially aspirant, one of them entered the American boarding school for young women at Umzumbe, saying she wished to be taught to "do housework as the white people do".[17] At the other end of the scale were people whose cash income barely exceeded the money required to pay the annual government Hut Tax, such as the man who left his son at the mission school with the injunction that "if you learn and get on well . . . you will be the great people of the Land, and we your inferiors, your servants".[18] Some place in between were the partners in the sugar-growing co-operative at Umvoti who by 1863 were managing to pay the whole £75 per annum needed to employ a white day-school teacher.[19] Less than twenty years later, private entrepreneurs were locating schools near major centres of employment that could aspire to thrive on black contributions alone.[20]

Missionaries, who subscribed to the self-supporting, self-propagating ideal, perpetually hoped that as children progressed through elementary and secondary schools they would form an ever-expanding pool of black teachers. However, the same economic forces that increased the ability of some congregations to pay teachers were simultaneously opening alternative employment opportunities for educated black youth. These young people would not work for low salaries, but communities could not afford to pay them higher ones. If missionaries raised their salaries to levels commanded by white teachers, the goal of self-support remained as distant as ever. "It is painful", William Ireland lamented in 1877, "to observe that there is a growing unwillingness on the part of these young men to teach, except at the more eligible and desirable posts, or unless they can receive considerably larger salaries, than it has been hitherto thought wise, or indeed practicable to allow them".[21]

Such financial considerations forced missions to pay close attention to what communities wanted from education. A curriculum that consisted solely of instruction in holiness and Scripture would attract few, if any, paying customers. African Christians proved to be knowledgeable consumers of mission education. Parents showed their dissatisfaction with the standard of education provided by their own missions by moving their children to schools run by rivals. At the higher levels of education quality counted for much more than denominational loyalty, as Methodist missionary H. M. Cameron found in 1879 when he "tried to press the claims of Edendale" against those of the American Congregational high school, Adams College.[22] The American missionaries, in turn, found their more affluent converts sending children to Church of England schools in Cape Town.[23]

Poorer families were equally particular about the education they required for their children. They wanted practical education in the rudiments of literacy and arithmetic. The literacy they craved was in English, not in Zulu, a demand that ran directly contrary to the aim of several of the missions to produce a Zulu version of the Scriptures that could supply a self-propagating African church. Many African families were quite willing to pay, so far as their slender resources permitted, for what they perceived as their direct educational needs. Surveying the educational scene in Pietermaritzburg at the end of 1867, Walter Baugh reported that Africans:

> are most anxious to acquire a knowledge of reading and writing; and they shew it by actually paying Europeans from 2/6 to 5/ per month for instructing them. I spoke to a store-keeper only 2 days ago who informed me that he had then 21 such pupils . . . They paid him 2/6 per month — he himself not knowing a word of Kafir. He was

teaching them to read English. Some of the Natives I find prefer paying more (5/ per month) and attending a European Evening School. One teacher told me that he had 4 such pupils at one time, and that some of them got as far as to do sums in the first four rules of arithmetic.[24]

A major quarrel over curriculum developed in 1876 between Wilhelm Illing and the parents of children at his station near Ladysmith. By birth and training Illing was Prussian. When he transferred his allegiance from the Berlin Missionary Society to the Church of England, he took Prussian ideas of education with him. Children were instructed in English, German, Latin, Greek and Hebrew, as well as four-part harmony, geography and European history.[25] Parents, on the other hand, were mainly interested in elementary English literacy and mathematics. Illing was disgusted that they regarded "Bok wagon arithmetic" as the chief of all the sciences because they perceived it as the key to success in small-scale trade. When he and his wife refused to bend to their demands, the station people threatened to withdraw their children and to hire their own teacher.[26]

Theological education also languished so long as its material rewards fell short of those available to African Christians who pursued secular careers. Before the missions faced up to the realities of settler capitalism, they had imagined that, in converted territories, the Christian ministry would command the same respect and authority it did in Europe or America. After forty years of American evangelism the head of the Amanzimtoti Theological School admitted: "it is a discouraging feature in our missionary work, that comparatively few of our best-minded and best-educated young men are studying for the ministry. Were it not for the fact that God often makes use of weak things to confound the mighty, we might almost despair."[27] Another American missionary feared they had "erred in admitting boys too young to appreciate the advantages of the Seminary and allowing those to enter who only cared to secure a knowledge of English that they might the better compete with the white colonists in making money".[28] It was such boys who virtually brought theological education to a halt in 1877 by a concerted rebellion against institutional food.[29]

Apart from the offspring of the fledgling black middle class, it was difficult for missionaries to take rural children very far beyond the elementary branches of learning. Parents struggled to pay fees for the simpler forms of education they required. Young boys were needed for herding or watching crops.[30] In certain areas planters employed African child labour.[31] When girls married, they left school, never to return.[32] Under these circumstances, curriculum development was a perpetual challenge. Missionaries were tugged in conflicting directions. Their supporting authorities in Europe and America constantly emphasized that religious instruction should take precedence over secular instruction. "As to common schools," wrote the secretary of the American Board of Commissioners for Foreign Missions:

> I have only this to say at present, that we shall have to reduce the proportional expense
> of that department in the India missions considerably, partly because we cannot bear
> the expense of such an amount of instrumentalities merely auxiliary to the preaching

of the gospel, and partly because so extensive a system of education is found really to interfere, in practice, with the <u>progress</u> of the gospel![33]

Many mission authorities also pushed the aim of instruction in Zulu, which they believed would speed the establishment of a self-propagating African church. Missionaries had constantly to reply that local factors pushed them in a contrary direction. Black parents regarded the teaching of English as one of the "chief attractions" of mission schools.[34] White settlers condemned teaching in Zulu as "contributing only to confirm and perpetuate the barbarous tongue of a barbarous people".[35]

When missionaries attempted to implement models of schooling unsuited to local conditions, they usually failed. Bishop Colenso initially hoped to make the school at his own station "a Public School", where the sons of chiefs would conduct themselves "as any young nobleman would at Eton or Harrow".[36] They would, he observed in 1856, "make excellent Cricketeers (sic), and even now pitch and catch a light ball, as if they had been used to it all their lives".[37] Boys who stuck tongues out at their teachers were flogged by the bishop, regardless of their rank or parentage.[38] Within only five or six years of its foundation, however, Colenso's Ekukanyeni had grown into a quite different sort of institution. Manual work, which had at first been an adjunct to the main educational endeavour, assumed an overriding importance. When elder boys had completed their basic education they were apprenticed "to different Tradesmen in Town", including "carpentry, waggon building, smithy work, tailoring, shoemaking, printing and bookbinding".[39] By 1863, the educational routine at the boarding school had settled into a mundane pattern far different from Colenso's original vision:

> The children are instructed in household and other work, and, together with such children as can be collected daily from the natives . . . are taught reading (in Zulu and English) writing, arithmetic, sewing etc. The youths are employed in printing.[40]

A similar scaling down of ideals occurred with the American female boarding school. On behalf of the mission, H. M. Bridgman wrote to Boston in 1864 that: "we absolutely need <u>now</u> a girls' Seminary, modelled after Mt. Holyoke Seminary [a famous American school] as much as the case will admit."[41] Within a few years of the school being established at Inanda, the headmistress had lowered her sights to the production of first-class servants for white settlers. "Christian Kaffirs," she wrote in 1857, "don't make such servants as the English like, and money expended for any other purpose is worse than thrown away. I try to teach the girls that labor is honorable, and that one who is truly a Christian will work."[42] In primary schools the gap between aspiration and achievement loomed less large, only because less was expected of them to begin with.

Mid-Victorian Educational Routines

Some examples will evoke the flavour of the mid-Victorian curriculum in a range of schools. The foundation of primary education in rural areas was a one-room school taught by the missionary or his wife. American missionaries gave these establishments the apt name, "family schools". They were composed in the early years of children whom they paid a small wage for attendance and work on the mission station — "persons we can of course teach when and what we please".[43] Occasionally the meagre offerings of such operations were supplemented by special lecturers, such as when Hyman Wilder lectured at Umvoti on the principles of astronomy with the aid of a magic lantern.[44] At outstations in vicinity of their mission centres, African teachers ran junior schools. Natal's superintendent of education in 1869 visited the Esingomonkulu outstation where Africans had for the last three years maintained "their own school with their own teacher", a youth of eighteen. The superintendent "found them to be very well taught, particularly in arithmetic, where they compared favorably with Europeans . . . The children . . . fell into their places with military precision" and demonstrated their ability to read "in English, spell and sing, also answer questions from the First Wesleyan Catechism".[45]

Offerings in the towns were more diverse. Sunday Schools were very much *schools* on Sunday, not the religious child-minding services of the twentieth century. For example the Methodists of Pietermaritzburg in the late 1840s ran one:

Sunday School in the Native Chapel which is well conducted and is attended by English, the children of emancipated slaves, and Kaffirs . . . Three languages are used from necessity, English, Dutch and Kaffir, but we are happy in having at present competent teachers in all those languages. Several adult Natives are now beginning to read the Word of God . . . [46]

In the same village, the Anglican day school by 1872 had:

30 children attending. One new and good feature connected with it is the taking in of boarders by Mr. and Mrs. Markham. They have now 7 little boys and girls under their charge, and most of them are paid for by their parents. These children are dressed in uniform garments of blue serge and their appearance together going to and coming from school is attracting attention to our school. The little girls will, I think, find a loving helper and Teacher in Mrs. Markham. She knows something of the Kafir language and also of Dutch, and she very heartily takes them in hand and teaches them sewing and domestic work.[47]

Secondary education, available at a very few centres, provided an advanced curriculum comparable to that given to white students of the same ages. The American girls' seminary at Inanda offered in the first class, "geography and reading the 'Science Primer' on Astronomy of the series edited by Prof. Huxley and others". The second class reading studies comprised "Line upon Line" in English, "Sweet Story of Old" in Zulu.[48] A valuable description of Amanzimtoti School for Boys, also run by American Congregationalists, was set out by its headmaster, William Ireland in 1867:

Each desk is designed to accommodate two boys. They are arranged in three rows with an aisle or passage on each side so that each boy can leave his seat without disturbing his neighbor. Altogether the room is a cheerful and pleasant one . . . The year now under review has been divided into three terms making in the aggregate thirty-seven weeks of term time, which is some two or three weeks less than will ordinarily be the case. The year commenced with fifteen scholars, the middle term this number was increased to eighteen and the last term we have had twenty. The boys who have been in the school for the past two years, have made good progress in Arithmetic as also in reading, writing and spelling. The first class numbering six have performed hundreds of examples in almost all the Rules, with the exception of Square and Cube root. In order to shew the rapidity with which this class can perform plain work, I may say that they have repeatedly worked out a dozen examples in Compound Multiplication and Division in which more than half of the multipliers and divisors contained three or four figures in less than half an hour. Several in the same class will answer a series of nearly one hundred and fifty question on the Map of the World, with but little faltering or hesitation. About two thirds of the school have spent a quarter of an hour a day in writing from dictation in which exercise it is thought they have done surprisingly well. About five hours of daylight have been devoted each day to the above and such like studies, five evenings each week not including the Sabbath have been . . . devoted to the study of the Gospels, taking the Chronological order of events . . . my experience is leading me to the same conclusion that I find is entertained by attentive observers in reference to the Freedmen in our late slave states — via, that up to a given point they manifest an equal capacity for acquiring knowledge with the white races. That in reading, writing, spelling, Geography & Arithmetic, vocal Music and in committing to memory, they cannot be outdone by English boys who have enjoyed like advantages.[49]

Wilhelm Illing, the German previously mentioned as instructing Africans in Hebrew, Greek, Latin and German, concurred. In his opinion "the Kafir nation . . . have obtained by the Lord God a fair share of intellectual powers".[50]

Entanglements with the Colonial State

Whether missionaries developed those powers did not depend on themselves alone. Even more powerful than African demands for curricula relevant to their immediate needs were the pressures exerted by government officials and white settler politicians. All the major missionary societies depended to some extent on government support. Those societies lucky enough to have arrived before 1860 received substantial grants of land.[51] Natal's Charter dictated that £5000 per annum must be spent on African welfare. In 1865 nearly 40 percent of this Reserve Fund went to mission schools.[52] For organizations perpetually short of cash and under instructions to make themselves self-supporting, this money was a godsend. When the Society for the Propagation of the Gospel cut off funds to Bishop Colenso because of his "heretical" teachings, he fell back on government grants to support the clergy who remained loyal to him.[53]

Government grants covered most of the American mission's education program. From the beginning there was a recognized danger that financial dependence could lead to government control. On behalf of the American mission, Daniel Lindley in 1866 tried to explain why they applied for grants that required the teaching of English:

> we do not propose to teach English, in any measure, because of the pecuniary aid offered to us, but because we think it would be wise to do . . . the money offered to us, is raised by a direct tax on native huts, and <u>must</u> be appropriated, in someway, for the improvement of the natives . . . we have no connection with the Government System of Education, properly so called, which is a creature of the Colonial Legislature. With this body we have as little to do, as with the American Congress . . . The trustees of the "Native Reserve Fund" offer us aid without condition . . . [54]

Nonetheless, dependence and control did come, little by little over the decades. Through the power to give or withhold grants, the state subtly wielded influence.[55] Also important were the powers it had to direct refugees as "apprentices" to missionaries.[56] Governors had a good deal of personal influence on educational policy in the early days of the colony. Under Governors Pine and Scott, a range of different kinds of mission schools was supported. Sir George Grey as High Commissioner for South Africa in the later 1850s strongly supported both Bishop Colenso's "school for chiefs' sons" and "practical" industrial training.[57] Later governors tended to put more and more emphasis on industrial schools. Dr Mann's Report on Industrial Training and Education for 1864 listed six industrial schools, all run by missionaries, where instruction included such crafts as wagon making, carpentry, brick making, cabinet making, sewing, stone masonry and ploughing.[58] Responding to an opportunity, missionaries rushed into industrial schemes which would attract grants, even when they were dubious about their educational value.[59]

Whenever there was a change of governor, missionaries did what they could to shift the emphasis away from mechanical training to a general scheme of education. Many of them believed that training Africans as skilled workers was a waste of time so long as white colonists feared their competition and refused to take them on as apprentices.[60] Just before Scott was replaced by Keate as Governor, Colenso tried to interest the Colonial Office in a general scheme of education supported by the £5000 Reserve Fund. He was, he said, willing to resign his embattled bishopric in order to assume the oversight of the programme.[61] The Methodist Synod likewise sent a deputation to the new governor, asking that: "grants to the Industrial Schools might be transferred to the carrying out of a scheme for general education".[62] Unfortunately, Keate was even less inclined to favour grand schemes. He wanted fewer industrial schools run at a higher standard of efficiency.[63] After his departure, missionaries revived their pleas for a general system of compulsory education for African children.[64] Lt. Governor Bulwer in 1879 indicated his support for change. Industrial schools had, he said, proved too expensive for the meagre results they had so far achieved. What was wanted was general education of "a certain elementary standard", a standard that "should be as simple as possible". Anything beyond that "will probably be confined to a small number of the population . . . and may perhaps, for some years to come, be left for the most part to the voluntary efforts of associations and individuals".[65]

Thus, just as Africans were beginning in significant numbers to seek secondary and higher education, pressures from settlers and government combined to force the publicly funded institutions into narrow and more stultifying channels. Not all missionaries were moved to resist the trend; racial "science" made inroads on their consciousness in the latter part of the century.[66] Ambitions sank. Bishop Macrorie of the Church of the Province of South Africa gave school prizes away in 1873 for "the longest period of service in one place".[67] The annual report of the American Zulu Mission for 1889 remarked that: "missionaries are looking with more and more favor upon the industrial training of natives as a valuable feature of missionary work. Idleness and ignorance are great obstacles to the advancement of the people, and to the proper development of Christian manhood".[68] Adams College acquired its first industrial department in 1887, just as the Natal General Inspector of Education announced that *no* school for Africans would be assisted unless it could prove that industrial training was provided.[69]

Catholic missionaries of the Trappist monastic order put the state industrial education policy to the test in the 1880s. Here was a mission virtually tailored to suit the demands of white settlers. Their foundation settlement at Marianhill dispensed industrial education on a grand scale. Stone masons, "carpenters, cabinet makers, blacksmiths, wheelwrights, wagon-makers, plumbers, tinsmiths, tanners, bootmakers, harness-makers, tailors, printers, and even professional photographers" — here was a veritable marvel of practical training.[70] The monks had even taken vows of silence, thus they offered no prospect of "over-educating" Africans.[71] The Abbott of Marianhill was equally promising on female education: "it is neither good nor necessary that the girls make such an extensive study of book subjects as boys. To form and train up useful girls and honest wives is the aim."[72] Nonetheless, when the Trappists applied for large government grants, they met strong opposition from colonists who insisted they wanted "to make the natives good labourers, but not farmers or skilled artisans".[73]

The Menace of White Settler Control

The achievement of responsible government in 1893 set the stage for a head-on confrontation between missionary educational aspirations and the white colonists' insistence on the lowest possible standards. The story of this contest has been told by several scholars drawn to the key issues of reserve lands and Ethiopian churches.[74] Less notice has been taken of education as an issue.[75] Although the actions of the colonial state affected every mission in Natal, the American Zulu Mission was singled out for special attention. Their large landholdings and their Congregational goal of raising up self-governing African churches made them an object of suspicion in an era when the first "Ethiopian churches" had alarmed authorities. By 1907 the American mission comprised 59 primary schools, three boarding schools and a theological college — 3964 pupils in all.[76] Since the middle of the last century, the government had supported schools from the £5000 Reserve Fund. Under new legislation, all mission reserves were required to collect rents from African residents, part of which was to be spent on education and other welfare services. This not only served the old settler objective of driving Africans out to wage labour, but also gave the Natal Government leverage over mission schools. Once again the principal demand was that schools provide basic education in agricultural and mechanical skills. Once again the missions, beholden to the government for land, buckled under.

The colonial state could not, however, secure the total victory on the educational front that it won in relation to land and civil rights. So long as there were Africans willing to pay for higher education and foreign missions willing to support elite schools, a small coterie was able to achieve equality in qualifications, if not in social status. The first African university graduate returned to Natal in 1876 with a degree from America's Howard University. Others followed: doctors, lawyers, teachers. From that group emerged such notable future political leaders as John L. Dube, H. S. Msimang, A. W. G. Champion, Saul Msane and Albert Luthuli. Significant as these achievements were, they were a far cry from both the diverse aspirations of the nineteenth-century missionary pioneers and the insistence of African communities on education for equality and freedom. The situation grew steadily worse after Natal was absorbed into the Union of South Africa in 1910. So-called adaptationist doctrines of education stemming from the United States were widely adopted, based on the premise that education for Africans should be adapted to their special (inferior) capacities.[77] Government regulation encroached more and more on the freedom of mission societies to run their schools as they wished, culminating in the Bantu Education Act enacted by the *apartheid* regime of 1953, which resulted in eventual transference of most mission schools to government control.

Conclusion

Taken together, the Natal experience demonstrates that the history of mission education cannot be reduced to simple formulae. Missionary intentions mattered a great deal in the early years and there was great diversity in the approaches taken by representatives of different denominations. Soon, however, the institutional practices of all missions began to accommodate themselves in important ways to the needs and wants of indigenous populations. Government assistance was welcomed at first but proved to be something of a poisoned chalice, as the paymasters tugged the mission schools toward vocational education. With the advent of white settler control of the levers of power both missions and African people found their options for schooling severely limited.[78]

Notes

1   Before the exigencies of local circumstances modified their practices many missionary societies expounded complex educational strategies based on their theological stance and evangelical theory. See, for example, Savage, "Missionaries and the Development of a

Colonial Ideology of Female Education in India", pp. 201–21, and Erlank, "Raising up the Degraded Daughters of Africa", pp. 24–38.

2 Although complaints against missionaries as cultural imperialists can be traced back to the early twentieth century, the most influential restatement of that position was made by Comaroff, *Of Revelation and Revolution*. Clifton Crais has described the South African mission stations as "a colonialist institution *par excellence*", in *White Supremacy and Black Resistance in Pre-industrial South Africa* p. 104. For a broad critical perspective on subsequent debates, see Elbourne, "Word made Flesh", pp. 435–59.

3 Established elites were most active in resisting missions where entrenched religious interests were involved such as Islam; see, for example, Yahya, "The Christian Missions and Western Education in Ilorin, Nigeria", pp. 149–54. In India, Hindu resistance was muted after missions agreed to establish schools which provided useful education without religious indoctrination: Frykenberg, "Christian Missions and the Raj", pp. 126–8. A number of studies have called attention to the gendered nature of indigenous responses to missions. Some women saw missions as an escape route from patriarchal control, as detailed in Summers, "If You can Educate the Native Woman", p. 452. Others took a leading role in opposition to missionary interference with the structure of family life; see Fitzgerald, "Jumping the Fences", pp. 175–92; Porterfield, "The Impact of Early New England Missionaries on Women's Role in Zulu Culture", pp. 72–5.

4 For a nuanced treatment of different colonial government discourses on education and the way these were modified in practice see Madeira, "Portuguese, French and British Discourse on Colonial Education", pp. 31–60.

5 When the first missionaries arrived Natal was ruled by Africans recognizing the suzerainty of the Zulu King, Dingane. An invasion of white Afrikaners in 1837 led to war with the Zulu kingdom and the splitting of the territory into the white-ruled Republic of Natalia and the independent kingdom of Zululand to the east. A British invasion established a new government in 1843 but the Zulu kingdom remained formally independent until 1887. The combined territories today constitute the single province of KwaZulu-Natal within the Republic of South Africa.

6 Walls, "British Missions", p. 162.

7 Champion to Hill, 1 June 1837, Volume 1, series 15.4, Archives of the American Board of Commissioners for Foreign Missions, Houghton Library, Harvard University (hereafter ABC).

8 Champion to Hill, 1 June 1837.

9 Callaway, Journal, July to September 1860, folio E7, Archives of the United Society for the Propagation of the Gospel in Foreign Parts, Rhodes House, Oxford University (hereafter, SPG).

10 Colenso, unaddressed letter, 9 November 1855, D8, SPG.

11 Missionaries fell on their knees before small mercies such as an Mpondo chief who sent children to be educated in 1872: Milward to Boyce, 10 June 1872, Natal District papers, Archives of the Wesleyan Methodist Missionary Society, University of London (hereafter WES).

12 R. Robertson to Colenso, 6 December 1861, E9, SPG.

13 The first of these was Mkhungu kaMpande whom Bishop Colenso hoped in the late 1850s to raise up as a future Christian king of Zululand. The child soon drifted away from both Christianity and the ambitious Bishop.

14 Colenso to Chesson, 1 January 1879, folio Z, Colenso Papers, Killie Campbell Africana

Library of the University of KwaZulu-Natal, Durban (hereafter Colenso Papers). The Magema referred to here is Magema M. Fuze, Colenso's long-time associate.

15 Colenso, *Church Missions Among the Heathen in the Diocese of Natal*, p. 8; my italics. The reference to "our enemy" refers to Mpande and the Zulu kingdom.

16 Harmon to Boyce, 9 September 1871, WES.

17 Myron Pinkerton to Clark, 6 January 1873, Mary Pinkerton to the Mission Rooms, 18 June 1877; ABC 15.4, v. 8.

18 Tönnesen report, 30 September 1861, E9, SPG.

19 Aldin Grout to Treat, 27 Nov. 1863, ABC 15.4, v. 6.

20 However, no schools of this type managed to stay in existence for very long. A good example was Adamshurst, founded by William Adams on his own farm with money supplied by Africans exempted from Native Law. That he soon was applying to the government for support indicates the precarious nature of his enterprise. "Correspondence re Adamshurst School, 2 July 1877 to 23 May 1878", listed African contributions towards buildings and furniture of £70, 12 shillings. Twenty pounds of the white teacher's annual salary of £50 was paid by fees, the remaining £30 from "other contributions".

21 Annual Report of Amanzimtote Seminary , 22 May 1877.

22 H. M. Cameron to Mason, 29 March 1879, WES.

23 Bridgman to Shepstone, 20 October 1864, Secretary for Native Affairs , 1/1/14, KwaZulu-Natal Archives, (hereafter SNA).

24 Baugh, quarterly report, 31 December 1867, E20, SPG. The evening schools he spoke of were Methodist, Presbyterian and Anglican. Reports in this vein are too numerous to cite in a short paper. One worth noting is an Anglican missionary's comment in 1877 that in twenty-seven years' residence in Natal he had never seen anything to match the "spirit of enquiry" then manifested by Africans of all classes; Walton, quarterly report for Pinetown, 31 December 1877, E32, SPG.

25 Illing, 3 March 1869, quarterly report for 30 June 1879, D37 and E34, SPG.

26 Illing, quarterly reports, 30 June 1876 and 31 March 1877, E31 and E32, SPG. Eventually a compromise was patched up because the people could see the disadvantages of losing the government grant that supported Illing's school. He continued education in the higher branches of learning, while a young African teacher took elementary education for boys, supported by parental fees at a salary of £3 per month.

27 E. Robbins, Report of the Amanzimtoti Theological School for the year ended June 1875, ABC15.4, v. 8.

28 S. Pixel, Report of Amanzimtoti Seminary, Normal Department for term ended 16 May 1876, ABC 15.4, v. 8.

29 No doubt food rebellions are an eternal feature of boarding school life. This one was noteworthy in indicating the degree to which even students for the ministry refused to be passive consumers of missionary fare, theological or material. For some indication of the many troubles of the American theological training program see: Ireland to Rood and Abraham, 16 October 1877; Ireland to Clark, 11 February 1878, Abraham to Clark, 6 December 1877; and Robbins, Report of Adams Theological School for the year ending May, 1878; all in ABC 15.4, v. 8.

30 C. Roberts, Report of Zwartkops Schools, Synod Minutes, 1877 and Watkins to Kilner, 15 September 1879, WES.

31 A. Tönnesen to Trustees of Umnini's Estate, Report for 1875, SNA 1/1/26.

32 S. Stone to Anderson, 6 February 1852, ABC 15.4, v. 5; K. Lloyd , unaddressed letter, July 1867, ABC 15.4, v. 7.

33 Anderson to Brethren of the South African Mission 10 April 1848, ABC 2.1.1, v. 10. See also: Anderson to South African Mission 6 March 1852, ABC 2.1., v. 16 and Clark to Ireland, 31 October 1866, ABC 2.1.1, v. 32.

34 Ireland to Anderson, 11 Nov. 1865, ABC 15.4, v. 7. The tug of war between Boston and Natal over this issue was a permanent feature of the nineteenth-century American mission. See, for example, K. L. Lindley to Clark, 8 July, 1872, ABC 15.4, v. 8, and J. Bryant to Anderson, 10 May 1849, ABC 15.4, v. 4 .

35 *Natal Witness*, 12 November 1869.

36 Colenso, unaddressed, 8 August 1857, D8, SPG.

37 Colenso to Hawkins, 5 February 1856, D8, SPG.

38 Alice Mackenzie, diary for 1859, typescript in Colenso Papers. Ekukanyeni school, like Amanimtote Seminary, also had its food riots; see Grubb to Hawkins, 9 May 1859, E5, SPG.

39 W. Baugh to Hawkins, 1 October 1859, E5, SPG.

40 Grubb to Hawkins, 26 June 1863, D 25, SPG. The emphasis on printing resulted from the indefatigable bishop's flood of work on biblical criticism.

41 Bridgman to Anderson, 18 January 1864, ABC 15.4, vol. 6.

42 Edwards to Clark, 27 September 1877, ABC 15.4, vol. 8.

43 General Letter from the Zulu Mission to R. Anderson, 12 September 1849, ABC 15.4, v. 4.

44 A. Grout, Report Umvoti station, June 1851, ABC 15.4, v. 4.

45 J. R. Cameron to Boyce, 13 April 1869, WES.

46 Pietermaritzburg Circuit Report for 1846, Synod Minutes, WES.

47 Baugh to Bullock, 20 March 1872, D37, SPG.

48 C. Kilbon to Clark, 26 February 1876, ABC 15.4, v. 8.

49 Second Annual Report of the Amanzimtote High School (later Adams College), ABC 15.4, v. 6.

50 Illing to the Secretaries, 3 March 1869, D37, SPG.

51 See Etherington: "Christianity and African Society", pp. 294–5; and *Preachers, Peasants and Politics in Southeast Africa, 1835–1880*, p. 23. For an insight into the technicalities of land granting to missionaries see Pilcher to the Secretaries of the Wesleyan Methodist Missionary Society, 6 September 1862, WES.

52 *Natal Blue Book*, 1865.

53 Colenso also used his position as one of the three trustees for land belonging to Chief Mnini to generate support for his clergy; Colenso to Domville, 29 June 1867, folio B. Colenso Papers.

54 Lindley to Anderson, 1 June 1866, ABC 15.4, vol. 7. It had been, however, the American missionaries who took the initiative in seeking schools for English; see Wilder to Shepstone, 6 May 1863, SNA 1/1/13.

55 Minutes by Shepstone and Scott on J. Allison to Scott, December 1863, SNA 1/1/13; Colenso to Secretaries, 10 October 1860, D25, SPG.

56 F. Ferreira, unaddressed letter from St. Michael's Mission, 7 April 1860, D25 SPG.

57 Colenso to Allnutt, 12 November 1855, folio E. Colenso Papers, and unaddressed letter, 9 Nov. 1855, D8, SPG; Pearse to Jenkins, 8 May 1857, 3/1/2, Methodist Missionary Papers, KwaZulu-Natal Archives (henceforth MNA). Grey also had plans for something like the concentrated village settlements he favoured for the Eastern Cape, each of which would have its own industrial training centre; see Fynn to the Colonial Sec., 31 Aug. 1857, SNA 1/3/6.

58 Mann to Shepstone, 25 July 1864, First Annual Report on Industrial Training, SNA 1/1/14. Subsequent reports were sporadic 1/1/14. A report by Governor Bulwer to the Legislative Council in 1879 found reports extant for 1864–65, 1868 and 1877; LC No. 15, 2nd Session, 1879–80.

59 For only a handful of scores of examples, see: W. Campbell to Shepstone, 28 March 1860, SNA 1/1/10; W. Mellen to Shepstone, 25 October 1859, SNA 1/1/9; A. Tönnesen to Secretaries, 31 March 1862, E9, SPG.

60 Grubb to the Secretaries, 3 January 1859, E4 SPG; Boyce to Cameron, 9 April 1866, MNA 2/1; W. Adams, letter to the *Witness*, 28 September 1878.

61 Colenso to T. Shepstone, 9 March 1865, folio N, Colenso Papers.

62 Cameron to Boyce, 20 December 1869, WES.

63 Colenso to Domville, 29 June 1867, folio B, Colenso Papers; Erskine to Jas. Cameron, 9 September 1869, MNA 2/2; T. W. Brooke to Shepstone 28 February 1868, SNA 1/1/18.

64 *Witness*, 10 June 1873; Pastor Hohls address , *Proceedings of the Natal Missionary Conference, 1877* (Pietermaritzburg, 1877).

65 Bulwer, Minute on Native Education, 10 December 1879, transmitted to the Legislative Council as LC No. 15, 2nd session, 1879–80. The result of this review was Bill No. 27, 1879 "For the Promotion of Elementary Education among the Children of the Native Population."

66 Etherington, *Preachers, Peasants and Politics*, pp. 28, 32, 43–6.

67 Macrorie to Bullock, 1 January 1873, D37, SPG.

68 Annual letter of the mission, over the signature of S. Pixel, 26 June 1889, ABC 15.4, vol. 9.

69 Annual letter, over the signature of J. Tyler, 15 June 1887, ABC 15.4, vol. 9.

70 Brain, *Catholics in Natal*, pp. 135–6.

71 Though many dispensations were granted to make lessons possible.

72 Brain, *Catholics in Natal*, 142.

73 *Witness*, 12 June 1889, quoted in Brain, *Catholics in Natal*, p. 144.

74 Marks, *Reluctant Rebellion*; Norman, "Responsible Government in Natal and the American Zulu Mission: 1893–1907"; McKeough, "Reluctant Defender".

75 A notable exception is Bloemen, "The Impact of the American Zulu Mission", pp. 39–49.

76 Bloemen, "The Impact of the American Zulu Mission", p. 39.

77 Krige, "Trustees and Agents of the State", pp. 74–94, and "Segregation, Science and Commissions of Enquiry", pp. 491–506.

CHAPTER ELEVEN

Colonial Agents

German Moravian Missionaries in the English-Speaking World

FELICITY JENSZ

Christian missions throughout the colonial period stood as complex sites of cultural exchange, not only between missionaries and the indigenous peoples amongst whom they toiled, but also between missionaries and the colonial governments under whom they worked. There is no simple formula for the history of missions. Despite the common aim of missionary organizations to follow the instruction of Mark 16:15 or Matthew 28:19–20, which states: "And he said unto them, Go ye into all the world, and preach the gospel to every creature", the manner in which this was undertaken, and the situations in which missionaries from various organizations found themselves, differed in complex ways. Within this chapter, the experiences of German-speaking evangelical Moravian missionaries within British colonies and ex-colonies in the nineteenth century are examined to demonstrate that missionaries from the same institution reacted differently to particular cultural and political situations, despite having similar backgrounds and instructions. Moreover, such actions had wide-ranging effects on the indigenous people amongst whom they worked. By following the activities of one Moravian missionary in the British colony of Victoria, Brother Friedrich August Hagenauer, the tensions between missionaries, local governments, mission supporters, local settlers, missionary administrative bodies, and indigenous people are made apparent, demonstrating the historical specificities of these cultural exchanges.

Throughout the world, relationships between colonialism and Christian missionaries were complex. Jane Samson has taken this into account when she cautioned historians of missions not to "marginalize human spirituality and the role of religious belief in influencing attitudes and actions".[1] By contemplating how the belief systems of missionaries impacted upon their work within colonial frameworks, the relationship between missionaries and the state can begin to be clarified. Within the nineteenth-century colonial period there were differences not only between missionaries and the state, but also between colonial officers, traders, settlers and missionaries and the differences between these groups cannot be unambiguously elided. Andrew Porter has noted that missionaries often "saw themselves much of the times as 'anti-imperialist', and their relationship with empire as deeply ambiguous at best".[2] Relationships between imperialism, colonialism, and the Christian missionary outreach were just as complex as those between the different groups within the colonial world mentioned above. In spite of the intricate nexus between imperialism and Christianity, there were common aims of both government and missionaries, such as those of "civilization" and control of the so-called "native". The rationales behind these aims, however, were often different. Thus, to understand the motives for missionaries entering into indigenous affairs, their cultural heritage, relationships with government, and above all, their faith, must be considered. There were also differences between various missionary organizations in terms of spiritual, cultural and intellectual heritage. The historian Timothy Keegan has argued that a fundamental difference existed between British and German missionaries in the nineteenth century, with British missionaries more likely to mirror the contemporary discourses of imperialism in matters such as race, whereas German Moravian missionaries, somewhat more distanced from imperialism, were more inclined to relegate decisions to providence.[3] For example, Keegan has argued that British missionaries were more likely to ascribe social Darwinian aspects to ethnographic descriptions of heathen people who had failed to convert to Christianity, whereas Moravian missionaries were more inclined to ascribe events to providence, such as that it was not yet God's will.[4]

Such differences between missionary organizations are steeped in the histories and self-perceptions of the churches. The Moravian Church saw itself as a missionary church, and was intent on sending out missionaries to heathen people around the world, especially those judged to be "the lowest of the low", as one Moravian Brother described the Australian Aborigines in 1896.[5] Over decades the Moravians gained a reputation for being successful missionaries through their substantial missionary activity, with many heathen people converting to the Christian faith and many Christian communities formed. The church was not afraid, according to the mission historian Stephen Neill, to send out missionaries to the "most remote, unfavourable, and neglected parts of the surface of the earth", including mission fields where other denominations had failed to convert a single heathen to Christianity.[6] Yet in order to do so, the church relied on the involvement of all members to support its large mission field, as they needed both financial support and personnel to sustain the missions. A large minority of the church's membership worked as missionaries — one in sixty, compared to one in 5,000 for the rest of the Protestant world — and almost everyone within the church contributed in some way to the missionary movement.[7]

From the early eighteenth into the early twentieth century German-speaking Moravian missionaries spread across the new world to all inhabited continents, taking with them their religious fervour and desire to convert the heathen people to their Protestant beliefs, which had been shaped by the Pietist tradition of deep personal devotion. They had begun their missionary work in 1732 amongst the African slaves of the Danish West Indies and by the end of the nineteenth century there were over ninety Moravian mission stations in fifteen mission districts around the globe.[8] As evangelical missionaries, the Moravians had a great impact on the English evangelical revival of the eighteenth century, affecting missionary work beyond their own society.[9] From the eighteenth and into the nineteenth century the age of imperial Britain was at its height. British flags were raised in foreign lands all over the globe, with non-British missionaries, including many German-speaking Moravians, aiding the British colonizers by civilizing and Christianizing the so-called native heathen in the British domains.

As interlopers in a foreign environment, with foreign languages, laws and customs to navigate — both those of the colonizer and the colonized — the writings of non-British missionaries such as the Moravians provide unique insights into the frameworks of the colonial governments amongst whom they worked.[10] Furthermore, as their mission was global, these writings provide material for comparative analyses of common issues they faced in various locations, as well as providing points of divergence. The Moravian mission was indeed varied with stations in British colonies, including those of North America, Africa, Australia, and Tibet; as well as stations in areas controlled by the Danish, Russian, American, and Dutch colonial systems, such as those found in Africa, the Americas, Europe, and Asia. The present analysis focuses upon the writings of German Moravian missionaries in British colonies and ex-colonies. Through these it can be quickly ascertained that the situations in which missionaries found themselves were complex; that personalities often dominated proceedings; and that missionaries had to respond not only to government demands, but also those from their Board at home, as well as local settlers, and the needs and wants of the Indigenous people amongst whom they worked.

Directions for Development of Mission Fields

During the eighteenth and nineteenth centuries, the general direction of the church came from its headquarters in Germany. This was also the seat of the *Missionsdepartement*, the committee in charge of the missionary activities of the church.[11] With so many missionaries scattered across the globe, the Moravian administration kept abreast of developments through prolific communications sent to and from the mission fields, adding many tomes to the extensive missionary writings that had been compiled by missionary organizations over the centuries.[12] The Moravian administration also guided the relationships of its missionaries through various instructions, including booklets of instructions to be used by missionaries in the field, booklets of general regulations with regard to the temporal position of the missionaries and booklets of instructions for congregational members in different lands.

It took some fifty years after the initial missionaries were sent out for the first missionary instructions to be compiled and published. In 1782 a German-language edition appeared, with a second and updated German version printed in 1837. English-language versions (*Instructions for the Members of the Unitas Fratrum, who Minister in the Gospel among the Heathen*) appeared in 1784 and 1840 respectively. The booklet was a template for how missions should be established and conducted across the globe, with the generic instructions devised to apply to all situations and people. Such was the applicability of the Moravian *Instructions* that the Lutheran *Berliner Missionsgesellschaft* incorporated some of them into their own instruction booklet.[13] Despite the apparent flexibility of the *Instructions*, it was obviously unrealistic to expect that they would be universally followed, given the multitude of different people with different religious and cultural heritages amongst whom the missionaries worked and also the various political regimes under which they lived.

The *Instructions* consisted of advice including: preparation in becoming a missionary (§9); establishing schools for the heathen children (§39); how to behave amongst heathen people of the opposite sex (§41); writing detailed accounts of the mission station for the missionary board (§54); and why not to tempt converts away from other missionary societies (§59). It also advised the missionaries on how to interact with the government:

> [§61] The Brethren [. . .] demean themselves as loyal and obedient subjects, and strive to act in such a manner, under the difficult relations in which they are often placed, as may evince, that they have no desire to intermeddle with the politics of the country in which they labour, but are solely intent on the fulfilment of their official duties.[14]

This was a particularly important instruction, for, as the Moravian historian J. C. S. Manson argued, the Moravian Church's development during the latter part of the eighteenth century was "highly dependent on the attitude of governments and officials who needed to be satisfied that Moravians were neither sectarian at home nor seditious overseas".[15] Mason further argued that: in order to be as amenable to local situations as possible, the Moravians stated their objectives in inter-confessional terms, and their members were taught to hold the laws of whatever land they were in profound respect.[16]

However, sometimes the local governments did not hold the Moravians, or any other missionary society, in great respect. In 1823 Governor Cass of Ohio in the United States reclaimed land that the Moravians had been granted for missionary purposes in Tuscarawas country, desiring to give primacy to commercial farming over mission stations, through his intent to sell the "valuable" land on which the missions were located.[17] Five years later in the State of Georgia a similar situation arose, demonstrating the governing body's unfavourable stance towards the use of land for missionary purposes and more broadly the political conditions in North America towards indigenous people. Until 1829 the Georgian Government had tolerated missionary attempts amongst the Cherokee, after which Andrew Jackson was elected the seventh President of the United States of America. The Federal Government however actively tried to dissuade such work, due in part to the European settlers' coveting Cherokee land that was previously protected by federal treaties. Regarded by Jackson as "savages" not "able to meet the standards required for equal citizenship", the Cherokee were effectively turned into second-class citizens as laws were passed in the Georgian legislature that took away all native title, abolished their tribal government, and denied them their right to testify in court.[18] The Moravians, as well as other missionaries, had difficulty in responding to these laws. In analysing the situation, the historian Andrew McLoughlin has suggested that "the missionaries felt trapped. If they spoke out against removal, whites would accuse them of meddling in politics. If they did not at least let the Cherokees know where they stood, they would lose all respect and influence among them."[19] The Moravians, although allowed to criticize the government rulings, were instructed not to meddle in state politics.[20] They turned for advice to their governing body, which told them to vacate the mission field if they could not pursue missionary labours peacefully. They complied, leaving the Cherokee to their own devices.[21]

Methodists also worked amongst the Cherokee at this time and for them a similar key article in their Discipline stated that it was the missionary's duty to abide by the laws of the land in which they resided, and to keep the laws of state and church separated.[22] Although the Methodists risked their personal freedom to support the Cherokee and stay on as missionaries, McLoughlin concluded that the Methodists ultimately failed the Cherokee Nation on "the critical issues of dignity and patriotism".[23] Yet, as other historians have noted, the Georgian Government was also to blame for hindering the mission stations.[24] Combined with the active interference of the Federal Government, the result was a relatively small and ineffectual mission to the southeastern Native Americans.[25]

Conversely, where governments did support Moravian mission fields, Moravians were often considered successful in terms of the spiritual and material longevity of mission. This was evident in the British Government's support of the Moravian southeastern mission to the Inuit, which resulted in effective and successful missions in both far North America and Greenland. In Labrador, moreover, the Moravian success was seen to be due to the British Government's support for the mission, which was partly given as a way to secure the land mass for the British Crown; the inhospitable landscape also deterred any competing interests for the land.[26] The success of the Labrador mission stations was aided by the fact that they had exclusive, Crown-granted trading rights on the lands surrounding their mission stations.[27] Another example of the symbiotic relationship between Moravian missions and colonial governments was the South African field, where the Cape Colony Government invited the Moravians to establish a mission in the 1820s. As they were well aware of their "status as aliens on sufferance in a British colony", they acted in a deferential and politically conservative way, winning them the support of the government in the early nineteenth century to expand their missionary activity.[28]

Moravian Perceptions of the Australian Government

In the Australian mission field the Moravians had responded to a request in 1841 to send missionaries to colonial Victoria, which had come through the secretary of the British arm of the church, Brother Peter La Trobe, who himself was the brother of the first Lieutenant Governor of the Colony of Victoria, Charles Joseph La Trobe.[29] Peter La Trobe put forward three reasons as to why a mission field should be established in Australia. The first was that it was the church's desire to bring the word of God to what he described as "poor, despised creatures, who are on the lowest level". The second reason was that current opinion amongst the English, and even of the Archbishop of

Dublin, was that *only* the Moravian Church could be successful amongst the "degraded" Aborigines. The third reason was that:

> So many favourable conditions for the Mission concern come together and that is; that the Colonial government in England and besides from that, 3 of the 4 Colonial Governors of [Australia] are completely interested and they are using their influence.[30]

Thus, the three reasons related to internal perceptions, external perceptions and perceived material and government support. After much discussion and time, two Moravian missionaries arrived in Australia to establish a station that they named Lake Boga in 1850, almost ten years after La Trobe's initial suggestion. The mission closed in 1856 without converting a single Aborigine to Christianity and with the failure blamed, by both the missionaries and their supporters in Australia, on the government's lack of support.[31]

The critical stance towards the government in this particular case was also broadly levelled towards British colonial policy in later situations. For example, in an 1882 history of the Moravian Church in Australia, the German Moravian historian H. G. Schneider wrote critically of English colonial rule:

> England came into the possession of the continent of Australia in a very cheap way. Cook travelled there and declared it property of the English crown; with that it belonged to the same. That he did not ask the male Papus [Aborigines] their opinion, or their agreement, one will not find astonishing. In any case, no other country would have considered to do the same if they were in possession of the power which England had. One is also not allowed to trust in any of our modern states, such [. . .] charity, that he for the sake of the unhappy, heathen Aborigines wishes to take on the colonisation of strange lands, and it is indeed the civilisation and order, which a Christian state carries along, is a blessing for heathen tribes, which tear each other to pieces and eat each other. We want, however, to keep it a little in mind, that the Papus were the actual masters and owners of New Holland, and that the land was taken from them by the white strangers, and not bought, as happened to the Indians of America from the first settlers.[32]

Schneider viewed British acts of colonization as more devastating than those of other colonial powers. This was despite many other atrocities that European powers committed towards indienous people across the globe — the Spanish in Mexico being one bloody example — and despite the fact that Germany's own oppressive colonial history had not yet been fully played out.[33] Schneider also deemed indienous people in need of Christianization, and assumed their own spiritual beliefs to be inferior to European Christian beliefs. Furthermore, he stated that Australian Aborigines were treated worse than other indienous people, such as indigenous Native Americans, notwithstanding the Moravian's own negative experiences within that country. The American experience was defined through an horrific event in which American militia slaughtered ninety-six Christian Moravian Indians at Gnadenhutten, Ohio on 8 March 1782 during the American Revolutionary War. These innocent people were killed as they were supposedly colluding with the enemy.[34] Yet in spite of such horrendous violence levelled towards Christian Native Americans, the Australian Aborigines were deemed to be in a worse position than other indienous people as they had been force-fully dispossessed of their land and had not been given the opportunity to engage in commercial transactions over it — regardless of how unscrupulous these transactions may have been. Criticism toward the British Government's treatment of indigenous inhabitants was, it seems, permissible by the Moravian Church as long as it did not involve the missionaries contravening their instructions not to "intermeddle" in the politics of the country in which they worked.

After the Lake Boga failure, the Moravians returned to Australia in 1859 to estab-lish the Ebenezer Mission in the north-west of Victoria. Although the Moravian Church and its missionaries had lost confidence in the colonial government, they nevertheless needed to work within the confines of government regulations. This, however, did not stop the missionaries criticizing the government in letters sent back to Germany.

Some of the first criticisms of the government were sent less than a year after the Ebenezer Mission was established. The missionaries' expectations of support had clearly not been met, with the young Brother Friedrich August Hagenauer writing back to headquarters:

> The Government – As we came to Melbourne in the year [18]58, everything seemed to go smoothly, however, experience has taught us differently . . . We still have [after a 14 month waiting period] no land! And when will we receive it? . . . We don't know what will happen, if the government won't give [us support]. This support is not always certain, in that, as far as I know, the Church Mission on the Murray received nothing last year. A tribe at the Goulbourne [River] applied for agricultural imple-ments etc. but didn't receive any.[35]

Similar to missionaries in other parts of the globe, the Moravian missionaries in Victoria preferred to fund their mission stations through outside bodies rather than rely on their church. However, as the above quote indicates, government funding for missions of any denomination could not be relied upon in Victoria. Moreover, even if government funding was free-flowing it was often at the expense of missionary freedom, for, as Norman Etherington's chapter in this volume argues, although government assistance was initially welcomed by missions in South Africa, it was often "a poisoned chalice" as it made missionaries beholden to the state's wants.

An alternative source of funding for missions, including for the Moravians in Victoria, was the Christian public. As the Moravians saw themselves as the "handmaid of the other larger Churches",[36] they actively sought donations from members of other Protestant churches. The missionaries had hoped that the mission would be able to be self-supporting, or at least not be a burden to the homeland, yet the Christian public in Victoria was initially unwilling to provide this much needed financial support.[37] Thus, caught between an unsupportive government and an unwilling public, the

Moravian missionaries struggled economically. Furthermore, the difficulties of the early days of the mission were accentuated by the lack of Aboriginal engagement. By the 1870s, however, a number of Indigenous people had converted to Christianity for reasons that included economic necessity, family obligations, beliefs, or strengthening relationships between Indigenous people and the mission. This success, which was showing signs of promise from the early 1860s, was applauded by the Christian public, with the Presbyterian Church offering to support the establishment of a mission in the east of the colony if the Moravians supplied the missionaries. The Moravians agreed to this "experiment" and in 1862 the Ramahyuck Mission in Gippsland was established.[38]

In spite of the growing success of the missions in converting Aborigines and providing schooling opportunities, the missionaries still complained about the amount of administrative interference in Indigenous affairs in Victoria. Hagenauer, at this point the manager of the Ramahyuck Mission, was particularly vocal in his displeasure with committees, when he wrote to the *Missionsdepartement* of the Moravian Church in Germany: "You dear Brothers . . . are probably thinking, 'there was no end to committees in Australia, and that they grow like mushrooms' [emphasis in the original]".[39] He thus indicated his frustration at the multitude of administrative obstacles that he had to navigate in the running of a mission. Furthermore, the Moravian missionaries complained not only about the amount of secular administration, but also about the state's interference in the spiritual side of the mission, and what they perceived to be the un-Christian stance of the government in relation to Aboriginal affairs. This became more apparent in the later years of the mission stations, when the Moravian missionaries compared Christian work and success in converting Aborigines to Christianity on the colony's three mission stations with the work in the cultivation of souls on the three main secular government reserves. In the eyes of the Moravian missionaries, and in particular Hagenauer, the government reserves were inadequate for teaching the Christian word. He argued that "there should be only Mission Stations in the colony" as they "had been far better managed than the Government Station, and had cost nothing to the state". Christianity, he claimed, served Aborigines better than the government.[40] Strictly, however, this was problematic as the mission relied on land grants from the government and government supplies to support the mission residents.

Furthermore, Hagenauer's own religious affiliations were malleable when he saw it to be politically advantageous. In 1869 he became an employee of the Presbyterian Church, which conferred on him "the full status of a minister of [their] Church", which allowed him to be drawn into the politics of other Christian denominations in Victoria.[41] In accepting the appointment, however, he made it clear to the Moravian administration that he did so only to further his missionary work, and that "he wanted only to belong to the Moravian Church, and not to leave them", reiterating his strong commitment to the Moravian faith.[42] His association with the Presbyterian Church was congruent with the Moravian Church's view of themselves as the "handmaid of the other larger Churches".[43] This supports Porter's notion that "missionaries viewed their world first of all with the eyes of faith and then through theological lenses".[44] In 1871 the Church of England honoured Hagenauer when it appointed him superintendent of its Aboriginal mission station at Lake Tyers, just a short distance from the Ramahyuck Mission. This appointment allowed him to participate in administrative duties pertaining to the Church of England's mission. He commented to the *Missionsdepartement* that this was "proof of the appreciation and love that the Church of England has towards the dear Moravian Church". He thus deflected recognition on his own behalf, as well as any need to justify his political or religious positioning to his own church body.[45] Through these positions Hagenauer became responsible to the administrative bodies of both the Presbyterian Church and the Church of England, as well as to the government through the Board for the Protection of the Aborigines (BPA), which was ultimately responsible for the administration of Aboriginal mission stations and reserves within the colony. Through all this, however, he remained beholden to the Moravian Church's administrative bodies, and, through his fervent beliefs, ultimately to God.

The "Double-Position" of Victorian Moravians

The Victorian mission field was an exception for the Moravian Church. The missionaries had a "double-position" as both missionaries and government officials responsible for distributing rations to Aborigines. According to Adolf Schulze, the author of an early twentieth-century Moravian official history, the missionaries in Victoria were "rather dependent on the Government".[46] Thus, they needed to fulfil both their secular and religious functions by working closely with the government. This situation differed from that of the Moravian missionaries in North America, where from the mid eighteenth century the Moravians had undertaken mission work amongst the Delaware Indians. Due to both social and political pressures, the missionary congregations were relocated numerous times across Ohio, Pennsylvania and New York, moving when physically in danger or when unable to continue the mission due to political interference.[47] Finally in 1782 a more permanent mission station for the Delaware was established in Upper Canada (present day Ontario, Canada) as the Canadian Government offered better protection than that available in the United States.[48] The political climate of eighteenth-century North America was different from nineteenth-century Victoria. Indeed, there were no international borders for the Moravians in Victoria to cross to continue their mission under a more supportive government, nor was colonial Victoria the war zone that eighteenth-century America was. However, the Moravian experience amongst the Delaware, and their subsequent desertion of the mission field to the Cherokee in Georgia in the nineteenth century, clearly demonstrated that other options were available to the Moravian missionaries, which did not include such close connections with government bodies and active engagement within the colonial system as Victoria.

Within the Victoria colonial environment, Hagenauer became an agent of the state above and beyond his position as a public servant handing out government supplies and rations, to the extent that he became a member of the Board for the Protection of the Aborigines (BPA). The BPA, established in 1869 through an Act of parliament, was responsible for the "management and control" of Victoria's Indigenous inhabitants.[49] In 1889 Hagenauer was offered the role as general inspector for the BPA; his responsibilities for the Board increased the following year with his appointment as its secretary. In the years leading up to his appointment he had worked closely with this secular committee, particularly in relation to its discussion over options for the future of the mission stations. By the 1880s the number of "full-blood" Aborigines, to use the terminology of the day, on the mission stations was falling, with many mixed descent Aborigines living "civilized" and Christian lives on the missions. This caused political unrest, as funding to Aboriginal mission stations and reserves was limited. Some public discontent was levelled at maintaining mission stations and reserves for "half-castes", as they were deemed capable of earning their own living. The BPA asked Hagenauer to submit a plan for "how these people would be dealt with justly and kindly", in response to which he submitted a proposal "like one used before in South America", which, he claimed, "was adopted by the Board with very few omissions".[50] The resulting piece of legislation was the so-called "Half-Caste Act" of 1886, which bore the full name of *An Act to amend an Act intituled 'An Act to provide for the Protection and Management of the Aboriginal Natives of Victoria'* (No. DCCCCXII). As a consequence of this Act, Aboriginal people were classified in racial terms. Those of mixed decent under the age of 35 were ejected from mission and government stations, and their access to rations was curtailed over a seven-year period, after which rations were completely stopped. These actions broke up families and forced many into abject poverty.[51]

Hagenauer approached the "Half-Caste Act" with predominantly spiritual outcomes in mind. His role on government boards contradicted the *Instructions* but it also reflected his desire that a religious voice be heard in relation to Indigenous affairs. He was a Christian blinkered to the racial discrimination rife around him, believing that, because Victoria was a Christian land, with its churches and schools everywhere, the former mission residents would be well catered for in the sphere of religion, and that a benevolent society would not discriminate against his "flock".[52] He conceded to headquarters, however, when writing about the beginning of the end of the Victorian mission stations, that "to speak about it in human terms, it almost seems as God does whatever pleases him".[53] Moreover, when informing his administration in Germany about the Act, he diminished his own input into it by deferring responsibility to God: if God pleased, God would do the best for the "poor people".[54] He thus underscored his belief in providence above all else, further dismissing his contravention of the *Instructions*. He thereby deflected attention from his own agency in shaping a draconian and destructive piece of legislation by attributing it to God, whose attested omnipotence rendered redundant the powers of mortal believers. Hagenauer saw himself as nothing other than an instrument of God; he therefore could not conceive of the destructive consequences of his actions for the people affected by the 1886 Act. Once the Act had been approved he lamented that, although he had done his best for the "half-castes", he was sceptical of the government's ability to deal with the question and thought it "would probably be put to the side".[55] It was not, and with the Act enshrined in law, the number of Indigenous people on the missions fell further. The result was the slow fading to closure of the Moravian missions in Victoria within a couple of decades, and the continued struggle for Indigenous people to survive in the harsh social environment of colonial Victoria.

In reflecting on the history of the Moravian mission in Victoria in the context of the Moravian Church's bicentenary of mission work, the Moravian historian Adolf Schulz wrote:

> The mission-work in southern Australia, whose short history we have just had an overview of, was, and stayed, from the very beginnings only a small twig on the world-wide mission tree. It could never show off with large numbers [of converts]. But one should nevertheless award it a mission history of no small importance. For it had supplied through deeds the irresistible proof of the efficacy of Evangelism, which was able to raise also the most deeply sunken people in both their external living standards as well as in their ability to be spiritually cultivated, and above all to raise them in their religious lives.[56]

Schulz's comments aptly describe the Moravians' experiences of southern Australia: compared to the global Moravian mission enterprise the Australian endeavour was small, yet it followed the "civilizing and Christianizing" paradigm of all Moravian stations, despite the belief that the Australian Aborigines were the most "deeply sunken" people, both materially and spiritually. Overall, the text demonstrated the Moravian notion that each of the mission sites across the globe were but one part of a broader enterprise of spreading the Christian word to the farthest reaches of the earth, including to the many inhabitants of the British colonies. As we have read, however, every single "twig on the world-wide mission tree" had its own peculiarities, despite the common goal of the Church.

Moravian missionaries around the globe faced many difficulties in their quest to convert the heathens. As men and women of devout faith and strong attachment to their church, they subscribed to the church's grand narrative of how a mission should be established and how missionaries should behave. Yet, once in the field, the missionaries had to grapple with situations that lay beyond the realms of Moravian experience, and, thus, could not be shaped through generic *Instructions* from home. Specific directions from Germany could also be discounted if found unpalatable by missionaries, with the missionaries blaming the tyranny of distance for their otherwise apparent insubordination.[57] Yet despite occasional lapses, Moravian missionaries generally identified strongly with the aims of their church. Hagenauer's own attachment to the Moravian Church profoundly shaped his work in colonial politics, and thereby influenced Aboriginal secular affairs. However, above and beyond the complexities of local politics, Hagenauer's belief in divine providence reigned supreme and it was through this lens that he viewed the colonial government. As a confidante and subsequent employee of the government, Hagenauer, unlike his North American colleagues, paradoxically could make decisions in his secular capacity that would impact on his missionary work. And, despite Schulz's characterization of Australia as being a "small twig", the secular work in which Hagenauer was involved was of no small consequence for the lives of Indigenous people far beyond the borders of the missions. Thus, although the abiding global aim of the Moravian Church was to save the souls of heathens across the globe, the manner in which this was undertaken and the outcomes for Indigenous people were crucially dependent upon the situations in which the missionaries found themselves. There is no singular historical narrative of the Moravian Mission in the British world. Rather, what becomes evident through a comparative analysis of missionary endeavours is that a complex understanding of broad historical and contemporary positions is essential to understanding significant interactions upon multiple sites of cultural exchange.

Notes

1 Samson, "Landscapes of Faith", p. 93.
2 Porter, *Religion Versus Empire?*, p. 13.
3 Keegan, *Moravians in the Eastern Cape*, pp. xxii–iii.
4 Keegan, *Moravians in the Eastern Cape*, pp. xxii–iii.
5 La Trobe, *The Moravian Missions*, p. 42.
6 Neill, *A History of Christian Missions*, p. 237.
7 Hassé, *Women's Work*, p. 3.
8 Libbey, *The Missionary Character*, pp. 12 & 14–15.
9 Bebbington, *Evangelicalism in Modern Britain*, p. 40; Mason, *The Moravian Church*, p. 89.
10 This theme is explored in relation to the Colony of Victoria, Australia in: Jensz, *Influential Strangers*. Note that in reference to Aborigines current usage is to capitalize 'Indigenous'.
11 Hamilton, *The Moravian Manual*, pp. 69–70.
12 Etherington, "The Missionary Writing Machine", pp. 37–50.
13 The *Berlin Missionsgesellschaft* provided a book of instructions for their missionaries in South Africa modelled on Spangenberg's Instructions. See: Richter, *Geschichte der Berliner Missionsgesellschaft*, p. 128 and pp. 131–2.
14 Spangenberg, *Instructions for Missionaries*, p. 68.
15 Mason, *The Moravian Church*, p. 8.
16 Mason, *The Moravian Church*, p. 8.
17 *National Advocate*, Monday August 25, 1823, col F. [no page number].
18 McLoughlin, "Cherokees and Methodists", p. 51.
19 McLoughlin, "Cherokees and Methodists", p. 51.
20 Spangenberg, *Unterricht für die Brüder und Schwestern*, §61, pp. 85–7.
21 McLoughlin, "Cherokees and Methodists", p. 58.
22 McLoughlin, "Cherokees and Methodists", p. 45.
23 McLoughlin, "Cherokees and Methodists", p. 63.
24 Stock, "A Resume of Christian Missions", pp. 368–85.
25 See for example: Graham, *Medicine Man to Missionary*; Wallace, "They Knew the Indian".
26 Whitely, "The Moravian Missionaries", pp. 76–92.
27 Richling, "'Very Serious Reflections'", pp. 148–69.
28 Keegan, *Moravians in the Eastern Cape*, pp. xix–xx.
29 Mason and Torode, *Three Generations of the La Trobe Family*, p. 26.
30 Protocoll des UAC [PUAC], 1841, 23 February, #5, p. 176, Unitäts-Archiv [UA] Herrnhut, Germany.
31 Jensz, "Writing the Lake Boga Failure", pp. 147–61.
32 Schneider, Missionsarbeit, pp. 50–1.
33 For an overview of German colonial history see: Timm, *Deutsche Kolonien*.

34 For an overview of the influence of the massacre at Gnadenhutten for further missions in North America see: Westmeier, "Becoming All Things to All People", pp. 172–6.
35 Hagenauer to Th. Reichel, 11 November 1860, Papers of the Moravian Missions in Australia, Microfilm [MF] 177, AIATSIS.
36 Libbey, *The Missionary Character*, p. 7.
37 Hagenauer to Th. Reichel, 11 November 1860, MF 177, Australian Institute of Aboriginal and Torres Strait Islander Studies.
38 Badham to Th. Reichel, 1860, 10 October, R.15.V.I.b.6.a (1860), UA.
39 Hagenauer to Th. Reichel, 1866, 24 May, Manuscript [MS] 3343, National Library of Australia (hereafter NLA), p. 62.
40 Hagenauer to Morris, 1875, 29 December, MS 3343, NLA, pp. 109–11.
41 Hagenaur to Th. Reichel, 1869, 2 December, MS 3343, NLA, p. 370.
42 Protocoll der Missionsdepartement, 1870, 9 March, #7, UA, p. 111.
43 Libbey, *The Missionary Character*, p. 7.
44 Porter, *Religion Versus Empire?*, p. 13.
45 Hagenauer to Th. Reichel, 1871, 23 March, MS 3343, NLA, p. 422; Hagenauer to W. E. Morris Esq., 1871, 3 April, MS 3343, NLA, p. 422.
46 Schulze, *200 Jahre Brüdermission*, p. 573.
47 See: Römer, *Die Indianer und ihr Freund David Zeisberger*; Wellenreuther and Wessels, *The Moravian Mission Diaries of David Zeisberger*.
48 Bowes, "The Gnadenhutten Effect", pp. 107–17.
49 *First Report*, p. 11. See also: Chesterman and Galligan, *Citizens without Rights*, p. 17.
50 Hagenauer does not clarify where or when this plan was implemented. Hagenauer to Hardie, 1885, 19 January, MS 3343, NLA, p. 597.
51 See for example: Wilkinson, "Fractured Families".
52 Hagenauer to Connor, 1884, 9 June, MS 3343, NLA, pp 583–9.
53 Hagenauer to Connor, 1882, 3 June, MS 3343, NLA, p. 537.
54 Hagenauer to Connor, 1884, 24 March, MS 3343, NLA, p. 581.
55 Hagenauer to Connor, 1884, 24 March, MS 3343, NLA, p. 581.
56 Schulze, *200 Jahre Brüdermission*, p. 575.
57 See PUAC, 1861, 9 April, #16, p. 38, UA; PUAC, 1862, 10 May, #17, p. 149.

CHAPTER TWELVE

"A Matter of No Small Importance to the Colony"

Moravian Missionaries on Cape York Peninsula, Queensland, 1891–1919[1]

JOANNA CRUICKSHANK AND PATRICIA GRIMSHAW

In the late English summer of 1891 three Moravian missionaries, James and Matilda Ward and Nicholas Hey, set sail from Portsmouth bound for the colony of Queensland in northern Australia to found a mission among Aborigines on the Cape York Peninsula. James and Matilda Ward were from the British branch of the Moravians; Hey was German born and trained. In November the missionaries arrived at Thursday Island, off the northern tip of Cape York, where the official Queensland Resident had his headquarters. The two men wasted no time in setting out on an exploratory trip to evaluate prospective mission sites. Much to their surprise, an armed police escort accompanied them. James Ward wrote to Benjamin La Trobe, Secretary of the English Moravian Brotherhood:

> Moravian Missionaries under police protection! I don't know if others have ever been in like predicament, but I must confess or own to a sense of degradation as we landed under an escort armed with revolvers and rifle . . . In this, as in other matters, we have had nothing to say . . . The Government, knowing better than we do the condition of things, gave the Resident of Thursday Island instructions concerning our safety in a matter of no small importance to the Colony if successful.[2]

Still under police protection, they chose a site at the mouth of the Batavia River, on the western coast of the Cape York Peninsular, that they named Mapoon.

The story of Mapoon and the subsequent Moravian stations of Weipa and Arukun offers insight into the fraught path of the humanitarian project in Queensland and the forces of settler colonialism that shaped it. The missionaries were members of a church that dated its heritage from the German Reformation, that was known in the British imperial world for painstaking mission outreach to difficult environments and for their strict injunction that missionaries should strive to separate their spiritual quest from local politics.[3] Ward and Hey were uncomfortable with the local authorities' extreme effort on their behalf, but they appreciated this act of governmental patronage. These missionaries, and the fellow Moravians who joined them over the next two decades, sought to convert Cape York Aborigines to Christianity and to nurture their faith through a western education and the creation of Christian families. They would find themselves called upon to negotiate complex relationships to fulfil this aspiration. Remote though Cape York was from the main city, Brisbane, and the halls of colonial power, the mission faced not only the expectations of their church sponsors but the demands of traders, pastoralists, officials and politicians bent on promoting the colony's unfettered economic development. Within this context the missionaries would find themselves grafting traditional Moravian ideals of Christian outreach to practices that sorely compromised their integrity and the human rights of their Indigenous converts and their communities.

This chapter begins with a brief outline of the background of the foundation of the Moravian mission and the initial years of Mapoon. It then examines the missionaries' development of strategies to protect their attempts to persuade Indigenous people to embrace Christianity and aspects of western society amidst an increasing reliance on an authoritarian power that the state legislation bestowed upon them. It concludes with the Moravians' departure in the wake of the discouragements they faced during the First World War, at once defensive, cautiously hopeful and ultimately unreflective about the consequences of their interventions in the lives of Cape York Indigenous people.

Overseas Recruits for a Late Nineteenth-Century Mission

There had been sporadic earlier efforts to establish missions in Queensland but, given a raw frontier and the absence of government interest, they had quickly faltered. German Lutherans and Italian Passionist Catholic missionaries had run short-lived missions and a few individuals — a Primitive Methodist lay preacher, two Anglican clergymen, a Catholic priest, and Daniel Matthews, founder of Maloga in New South Wales, had made attempts that similarly failed.[4] The settler invasion of Indigenous lands in Queensland had intensified from the 1850s, provoking resistance that was put down with the ruthless use of guns.[5] As with the other colonies on the island continent, the British government recognized no land rights and entered into no treaties; furthermore, when the British handed over internal self-government swiftly after the colony received a constitution in 1859, control of native affairs lay with the settler government.[6] British humanitarian voices thus became muted as successive British governments declared any anomalies no longer within their jurisdiction, while local humanitarians faced fierce hostility. Aborigines suffered drastic reduction of numbers, severe social dislocation and compromised health as invaders bent on the exploitation of the land and coastal resources threatened their hunter/gatherer economy. By the 1880s, when pockets of Aboriginal resistance remained only in remote areas, politicians were prepared to respond to humanitarian calls for reserves and missions to offer survivors a place in the new order. The Lutherans established missions in North Queensland, at Mari Yamba and Cape Bedford (later Hopevale) in 1886, and at the

Bloomfield River Reserve in 1887.[7] The Presbyterians turned for help to the Moravian church.

Nicholas Hey had good reason for his confidence in 1891 that the Moravians' mission initiative would prove significant for Queensland: Presbyterians had solicited their services with unusual zeal. The Presbyterian Church's contribution to missions had been slim in relation to the desperate plight of so many Aborigines and the wealth they gained from Aboriginal dispossession. They had to turn to Moravians from overseas at this crucial juncture. Settler Christians for the most part shared prevalent derogatory attitudes to Aborigines, while the missionaries in the southern colonies had failed to prepare enough Indigenous evangelists to fill the gap. When colonial Presbyterians met in Sydney in 1882, a Melbourne clergyman, the Reverend M. Macdonald, delivered a rousing speech castigating colonial Christians. They owed Aborigines reparation, he declared, since they had "deprived the Aborigines of their heritage". At the very least white Christians should endeavour to "make them heirs of the inheritance that faded not away".[8] As evidence of the value of mission work among Aboriginal people, Macdonald pointed to the only existing Presbyterian work of this kind. This was the Presbyterian-sponsored mission station of Ramahyuck in Gippsland, Victoria, which Macdonald described as "good, earnest and fairly successful work". The superintendent of this mission for over twenty years was the Moravian missionary, Friedrich Hagenauer, whom Macdonald praised as a model missionary, "thoroughly qualified to train others".[9]

Presbyterian concern moved slowly. Suitable local recruits among the colonial faithful failed to surface and donations to Aboriginal causes were miserly. It took four more years before the Presbyterian Foreign Missions Committee (Mission Committee) sponsored Hagenauer on an exploratory tour. He produced a graphic report intended to jolt them into action about the condition of Cape York "wild blacks":

> [When] you are surrounded by one or two or three hundred of such poor and degraded human beings who had not a sign of clothing about them, with no hope nor prospect in themselves for the better, but to live and die in misery like the beasts of the field, what Christian heart will not be filled with the intense pity and compassion for these our fellow-men . . . but alas! How little is done.[10]

In Hagenauer's outburst it was hard to disentangle where customary European abhorrence of Indigenous culture ended and recognition of the ill-health and impoverishment induced by colonization began. His urgent tone was, however, unmistakeable. It was another four years again before the church acted: Queensland Presbyterians, busy establishing a mission among Pacific Islander sugar industry contract workers, were reluctant to commit to a further missionary effort.[11] The Presbyterian Church in Victoria thus took the lead in furthering plans for a Queensland mission, consulting Hagenauer for his practical advice. In Victoria, Hagenauer had developed an unusually close relationship with the colonial administration, eventually accepting the significant position of secretary of the Board for the Protection of Aborigines (BPA).[12] In their initial negotiations with the Queensland Government, the Mission Committee was offered a grant of land and some initial funding, on the expectation that the mission would then become self-supporting. Hagenauer strongly advised the committee against accepting this arrangement, arguing "nothing could be done for the Aboriginal people without donations of supplies by the government".[13] Hagenauer's attitude won out and contributed to the development of a close relationship between the mission and the colonial government. In 1890 the Queensland Government agreed to provide ongoing support for a Presbyterian mission in North Queensland, an offer that the Mission Committee accepted.[14] Cape York was a particularly fraught area because the coastal traders in pearl fishing were openly exploiting the services of Indigenous men and women.

The Queensland Government's motives for supporting missions were predominantly self-serving. Aboriginal resistance having abated, politicians could afford a grudging response to twinges of conscience about the desperate plight of so many Aborigines, which had the capacity to embarrass them. There was a particular issue on Cape York, where an expanding pearl-shelling industry was utilising Indigenous labour in clearly exploitative ways. In 1890, with governmental support for the proposed mission secured, the Presbyterian Foreign Missions Committee wrote to the Moravian Church to appeal for the provision of missionaries. The Moravians had previously sent a number of missionaries to the Aborigines in Victoria. The Presbyterian request made it clear how important positive relations with settler governments and churches were considered for the missionary task. The committee asked the Moravians to provide "men . . . with university training, able to appear before our General Assemblies and Governments, and plead the cause of the aborigines . . . while others might be men with practical training in farm and industrial work".[15] To negotiate with Australian administrations, the Moravians decided an Englishman was necessary, and selected James Ward, who was pastor at a church in Ballinderry, Ireland. Nicholas Hey, their second selection, had experience as a farmer. James had recently married an Irishwoman named Matilda Barnes. Before departing for Australia, Nicholas joined the Wards in Ballinderry, where he became engaged to Matilda's sister, Minnie. She would join the party at Mapoon in 1892.

Settler Colonialism and Mission Strategies

In the first four years after their arrival at the mission site under police protection, the missionaries concentrated on making contact with the local Aboriginal people and encouraging them to settle on or around the mission where they could be Christianized and "civilized". Reports published by the Moravian Mission Board described how labour was divided. James Ward, who was in charge of the mission, acted as preacher, evangelist and teacher for the older children in the mission school. He also acted as assistant to Nicholas Hey in the task of building a physical infrastructure for the mission, which by the end of 1892 included a mission house and a small church/school, several acres of fenced land and a wide variety of crops.[16] A letter from Matilda Ward, published in early 1893, explained that she was teaching the smaller children among the 25 "boys, girls and young women" attending the mission school.[17] She also had responsibility for the heavy domestic duties of cooking, washing and cleaning. From early 1893 she was assisted in the latter tasks by her sister, Minnie, who was now married to Nicholas Hey. Aborigines living on or near the land that the mission had appropriated assisted the missionaries in their physical labour. By 1894 the missionaries reported that around 260 Aboriginal people were associated with the mission, with about sixty of these children attending the school.[18] For the missionaries, however, mere numerical growth would not produce the goals of personal and cultural transformation for which they aimed.

The Moravians' attitudes towards Aboriginal participation in the trade became, more than any other reason, the basis of their subsequent collusion in the Queensland Government's stringent control of Aborigines from the late 1890s. By 1894 James Ward complained of a number of factors that were frustrating the missionaries' efforts by unsettling the mission. Two of these — runaway matches" and the "arrival of boats" — were connected to the pearl-fishing industry.[19] This was the period of greatest growth for the pearl-shelling industry: between 1890 and 1900 the amount of shell collected grew from 630 to 1212 tonnes, doubling the value of the industry.[20] Aboriginal labour was thus in great demand, and ostensibly might have provided incomes and access to marketable skills. Absence on pearl-fishing boats — by the men as labourers or by the women "for immoral purposes" — separated people who were married or promised in marriage. As a result of this separation, Ward claimed, men and women were making "runaway matches" with new partners. He recounted multiple instances in which violence was the result.

In addition, pearl-fishing boats were sailing down to Mapoon and landing near the mission. This led to repeated instances of conflict between local Aboriginal people and those involved in pearl-fishing, sparked in many cases by the kidnapping of Aboriginal men and boys for labour or Aboriginal women for sexual purposes. The growth of the pearl-fishing industry also had disastrous effects on Aboriginal health, with syphilis along with tuberculosis the major causes of death within the local Aboriginal community.[21] The Government Resident at Thursday Island, John Douglas, had thus proposed that a Presbyterian mission be established at a site on the north-west coast of the Cape York Peninsula, with the aim of protecting Aboriginal people from the incursions of pearl-fishers and enabling the pearl shelling industry to grow without fear of Aboriginal discord.[22]

Ward lamented the labour trade in a style that intertwined horror at non-Christian sexual practices with these multiple adverse social and health outcomes:

> In all cases there was a large amount of immoral connexion twixt the crews & our native women. The people will do almost anything for tobacco & the temptation to obtain tobacco so cheaply is too strong for many of the men. So they just place their women at the disposal of white & coloured alike – regardless of our warnings.'[23]

Though Ward alleged that this practice had occurred in previous years, he reported that the women had advanced "from a state of nervous dread to a state of brazen-faced impudence". In addition to the upheavals caused by the pearl-fishing society, Ward also complained of the treatment of Aboriginal women by Aboriginal men. He alleged that men were habitually violent to their wives and would "chuck" them when they got old: an allegation that was, of course, a staple of missionary discourse.

James Ward's anxieties about "runaway matches", unregulated female sexuality and violence against women demonstrate the missionaries' broad concern with establishing marriages that conformed to their understanding of the Christian ideal: monogamous, non-violent, with clearly established gender roles and a commitment to passing on the Christian gospel from parent to child. Such a concern was, of course, commonplace among nineteenth-century missionaries in Australia. While missionaries' most important aim was always individual conversions, the establishment of Christian marriages and families was seen as both an important outcome of such conversions and the main way in which Christianity could become permanently entrenched within Aboriginal communities.[24] For the missionaries in North Queensland, however, the creation of Christian Aboriginal families posed particular opportunities and challenges. In the ten years after Ward wrote his letter, these challenges and opportunities would come into stark focus, as the missionaries engaged with local settlers, settler governments and Aboriginal people themselves.

In December 1894, shortly after writing this letter, James Ward fell seriously ill and, after several days of delirium, died. Grief-stricken, ill, exhausted and with serious storms threatening, the missionaries decided to retreat to Thursday Island. From here the Heys were sent for recuperation to Brisbane and Matilda Ward to Melbourne.[25] The Heys came back to Mapoon in June 1895, followed three months later by Matilda Ward.

The return of the three missionaries marked a new phase in the mission. With James Ward's death there was internal reorganisation of the division of labour. Nicholas Hey was now in charge of the mission, responsible for corresponding with church and state officials as well as his practical duties. Matilda Ward took charge of the entire school, assisted by her sister Minnie Hey, whose energies were also taken up by her own four children. Ward, whose return to the mission as a widow had earned her significant status among mission supporters, was now employed as an agent of the newly formed Presbyterian Women's Missionary Union (PWMU).[26] Her independent status was a notable elevation of her authority.

Mission Models for Aboriginal Christians

From 1897 the missionaries were empowered to exert authority over the employment of Aborigines but conversely faced novel external challenges, as parliament brought down new legislation that enshrined wide-ranging management of Aborigines in which missions would play a part. In response to mounting humanitarian pressure, on the one hand, and racist anxieties about the presence of Aboriginal people within the ever-growing settler population, on the other, the government passed that year the hugely influential *Aborigines Protection and Restriction of the Sale of Opium Act*. Archibald

Meston, journalist and self-appointed expert on Aboriginal culture, had been important in its genesis. Three years previously the government had commissioned Meston
to report on ways to improve the condition of Aboriginal people and he subsequently
recommended that the only "prospect of any satisfactory or permanent good is the
creation of suitable reserves . . . and absolute isolation from contact with whites".[27]
Among other provisions, the Act created a number of reserves for the "protection" of
Aboriginal people and appointed Protectors of Aborigines who had enormous power
over Aboriginal people, including the authority to transfer people to reserves. Existing
missions, including Mapoon, were given the status of reserves. A Northern Protector
of Aborigines, Walter Roth, was appointed with oversight of these reserves. Local
Protectors — usually policemen or magistrates — were also appointed.

In effect, Aborigines faced stringent state control because settler authorities could
not curtail the bad actions of settlers towards them. These developments, in effect,
provided significant state support for the existing missionary policy of isolating
Aborigines from settler society.[28] As in James Ward's letter of 1894, the missionaries
had repeatedly complained of the negative results they saw arising from contact
between Aborigines and what Hey called "so-called civilisation".[29] "Complete isolation
and detachment from the outside world" was necessary, Hey contended, or "the extinc-
tion of the race" would inevitably result. From 1899, when Hey was appointed the
official superintendent of Mapoon, anyone seeking to employ an Aboriginal person
from the territory covered by the mission was officially required to get his permission.
While, in reality, many Aboriginal people continued to move on and off the mission
and to take employment on pearl shelling boats when they chose, Hey did exercise his
new powers whenever possible.[30]

The missionaries operated from a fraught basis. They desired to isolate Aboriginal
mission residents from contact with white society, but also from their traditional
culture. This was virtually impossible among adult Aborigines: significant numbers of
Aboriginal men from Mapoon, for example, still worked on the pearl-fishing boats.
And so, as on other missions, the missionaries at Mapoon focused on converting and
training the children. Having established a school in which children could receive religious and secular instruction, the missionaries very quickly moved to establishing
dormitories to extend their influence over the children. Hey reported to the
Presbyterian Foreign Missions Committee that Ward not only had charge of the school
"but also takes care of the children in the boys' and girls' house so as to keep them away
from the bad influence of camp life".[31]

In the early years of the mission, the children appear to have been primarily
"boarders" whose parents lived either in the Aboriginal camps on or around the mission.
The missionaries had no power, at that time, to compel parents to place their children
in the dormitories and the presence of parents nearby undermined missionary influence.[32] The passing of the 1897 Act, however, gave Protectors greater power to forcibly
remove children or adults from other parts of Queensland. Along with the Church of
England mission Yarrabah on the south-eastern side of the Peninsula, Mapoon became
a favourite location for removed children to be sent. In 1901, Mapoon was appointed
an "Industrial School and Reformatory", which allowed the Protectors to send children

there under the provisions of the Act. Walter Roth, the Northern Protector, wrote in 1902: "Experience continues to teach me that we are working on correct lines in dealing with the transfer of half-caste and full-blood children from the hands of private employers to the various mission stations and reformatories."[33] Roth argued that where children were employed by "responsible and reputable people . . . in a civilised and settled district where the dangers besetting them are minimised", the children should not be removed. In less "civilized" districts, however, children should be removed "at once to the Missions, etc. where their future welfare and happiness are assured from the day they enter till the day they die".[34]

Roth's account of child removal contained no mention of the parents of the removed children. However, the lists of children and young adults sent to Yarrabah and Mapoon make it clear that not all were orphans. In 1901 Roth wrote that he had sent a "Chinese-Aboriginal half-caste" named Nellie to Mapoon, noting she was the daughter of "Lizzie" from Gregory Downs. Seven other girls and women were sent by the Protectors to Mapoon, including "Georgina Lee, a half-caste girl with baby", and a ten-year-old named Lucy who was suffering from syphilis.[35] By 1905, Hey recorded that 22 "half-caste" children had been "sentenced" to the Mapoon Reformatory.[36] As "half-caste" girls were considered to be doomed to prostitution if left without what the Protector considered proper supervision, the majority of those sent to the mission appear to have been girls. These children made up a substantial minority of those in the Mapoon school and dormitories.

The children who boarded at the mission — either with their parents' consent, or involuntarily — became the core of the growing Christian community at Mapoon. In 1898 Hey noted: "The boarding system has proved a valuable help to the Mission work, as is shown by the fact that out of seven converts four were inmates of the girls' dormitory".[37] In 1905 Ward made the same point, writing about ten baptisms that had been performed:

> Our converts are principally those who have passed through the school. It's difficult for the older people with their darkened minds to grasp the Simplicity of God's love. They are so very superstitious! Many of our girls have asked to be baptized, but we always wait to see if they show the change in their lives.[38]

The relationship between Ward's work among the children and the task of establishing Christian families was also made explicit. Hey claimed that as a result of her work "much good among the girls has followed, as is shown by the small percentage of unnatural marriages and the healthier condition of the children born".[39]

As Walter Roth had made clear, the extended powers granted by the 1897 Act meant that the Queensland Government was able to place those children they removed under the control of the missionaries for life. This power allowed the missionaries to develop their aims of establishing a settled community of Christian Aboriginal families, isolated from contact with wider society. Where southern Australian missions such as the Presbyterian-Moravian mission at Ramahyuck had attempted to develop communities of Christian families within the immediate confines of the main mission, the expanse of land granted to North Queensland missions like Mapoon presented alternative possibilities. Following the example of Ernest Gribble, the Anglican missionary at the North Queensland mission of Yarrabah, in 1904 the Mapoon missionaries established a "model farm" or "out-station" four miles from the main mission house.[40] From here, Hey wrote patronisingly in 1909, "a number of little homesteads have sprung up, where young married couples enjoy the novel sensation of home".[41]

The original couples that moved to the outstation were drawn from the local people who had settled on the mission. As the "half-caste" girls in the dormitories grew older, however, the missionaries were facing the question of their long-term future, given that neither marriage to "full-blooded blacks, who . . . are not able to provide for them" nor domestic service outside the mission were considered acceptable options.[42] In 1909 Hey wrote that the only solution to the problem of "what shall become of the half-caste Aboriginals" seemed to be found "in the settling of young couples upon the land removed from outside influences & placed under Christian supervision".[43]

The women who grew up in the mission dormitories were soon in great demand as wives, with the missionaries noting that "applications" to marry Mapoon women had been received from both "the islanders under the care of the London Missionary Society [LMS]" — South Sea Islanders from the LMS missions in the central Pacific had been recruited to help establish new missions in the Torres Strait from 1871 — and "even . . . Europeans".[44] Though these women were adults, the missionaries had the power to decide whether or not these applications would be granted. While it is not clear whether any Mapoon women married Europeans, marriages to Christian South Sea Islanders were seen favourably, particularly as such relationships could contribute to the missionaries' aims. By 1910 Hey noted that "four South Sea Islanders married to Aboriginals have been appointed and are stationed at the Mapoon Outstation . . . it is expected that their influence and example should further the cause of Christ".[45] One of these four men, Dick Kemp, was supervising the outstation.[46]

In the context of the Cape York Peninsula, therefore, specific factors, including expansion of the largely unregulated pearl shelling industry, the extension of state control over Aboriginal people through Protectors, the missionary belief that Aboriginal people must be isolated from wider society for their own survival, the missionary commitment to promoting "Christian marriages" and the proximity to LMS missions, combined to produce a model of mission somewhat different from that developed on southern missions. The Aboriginal outstation, established at a distance from the main mission, represented an attempt to create a long-term, sustainable, semi-autonomous alternative to Aboriginal engagement in settler society. Hey wrote that he hoped it would "foster self-reliance, energy and self-help".[47] The involvement of Islander Christians as supervisors of this community was seen as a step towards an increasing degree of autonomy.

Christian marriages and families were crucial to this project because they were integral to missionaries' vision of Christian character and community and also because they provided an incentive for Aboriginal converts, both those from local communities and those who had been removed from distant locations, to stay on the mission for the long term. The extent to which this project became central to the missionaries' understanding of the Christianization of Aboriginal people at Mapoon is seen in a comment Hey made in 1909 when he noted of the work of the school: "The higher and real aim has been the training of their hearts and the conversion of their souls — we want homes and our young people must make them."[48]

During this same period, encouraged by the apparent success of the missionaries at Mapoon, the Presbyterian Foreign Missions Committee (from 1901 the Board of Missions) supported the establishment of other missions on the Cape York Peninsula, to the south of Mapoon. In 1898 an English Moravian couple, Edwin and Thekla Brown, established a mission named Weipa. In late 1899, the pair was joined by Thekla's sister, Laura Schick, who like Matilda Ward was employed by of the PWMU. In 1904 German Moravians, Arthur and Mary Richter, went further south on the Peninsula to form the Aurukun Mission. Each of these missions followed the same basic strategy as Mapoon, starting a school and building dormitories, while attempting to also establish "outstations" for young married couples.[49]

Towards the Exercise of Excessive Power

The more power the state invested in the missionaries' hands, the more authoritarian they could afford to become. Aborigines resisted mission domination but the combination of missionary ideology and state policy had the effect of promoting increasing mission control over residents. In practice, this control was limited by a range of factors. Many local Aboriginal people chose to remain off the mission, or visited only for short periods; some remained in the "camp" outside the central mission buildings. These choices were more problematic for those with children to provide for. While Aboriginal people who were "removed" to Mapoon had no choice but to join the mission, all those who came into contact with the missionaries made choices about how to respond to the message and values they promoted. Matilda Ward's diaries contained repeated references to mission residents who had in her perception rejected missionary understandings of ideal familial behaviour by engaging in pre- or extra-marital sexual relations, behaving violently towards a marriage partner, changing partners or — so she suspected — committing infanticide.[50]

Other Aboriginal people accepted the missionaries' values and became involved in the task of promoting them on the mission. By 1912, for example, when two couples on the mission were found to have engaged in extra-marital relations, Ward reported that the Mission Council, made up of mission residents, had been convened by Johnny Georgina, its elected leader. The council, with a missionary in attendance, decided "the women should weed gardens for a week, the men make a fence". One of the men so sentenced challenged the missionary, "Show me laws by Gov. on paper then I'll do it." "You and your countrymen made these laws", replied the missionary.[51] While such accounts are filtered through missionary assumptions, they provide clear evidence of Aboriginal agency in engaging with and negotiating with missionary values and power. They also demonstrate that in North Queensland, as elsewhere, Aboriginal people were quickly aware of the potential for negotiation that derived from the complicated and often tense relationship between missionary attempts to assume control and the authority of the state.

Varying relationships between missionaries and the state could also result in different outcomes for Aboriginal people. Weipa and Aurukun were not state reformatories, and so the Aboriginal children living at these missions were largely from local communities and the missionaries relied on the cooperation of the parents.[52] At Weipa, while the Browns and Laura Schick certainly shared the Mapoon missionaries' belief that Aboriginal children were best raised on the mission, they appear to have had much stronger qualms about children being denied access to their parents. Edwin Brown conducted a fierce argument with Walter Roth, the Chief Protector, when the latter ordered the removal of a young man from Weipa to Mapoon. Brown defended the right of Aboriginal people to stay within their own "country" and within reach of their families.[53] But there are indications of harsh treatment at Aurukun. In 1907 all the girls in the dormitories at Aurukun ran away, after (according to Arthur Richter) they heard a rumour that "the Protector of Aboriginals would take these girls away and marry them to South Sea Islanders".[54] Robert Wilson, a young Presbyterian missionary who worked for a time at Aurukun, wrote in his diary in 1911 that he was horrified to discover that the Richters were regularly and severely beating the girls in the dormitory.[55] He had previously lived at Mapoon but made no such reports of the missionaries there.

More severe tensions involving the Mapoon missionaries occurred after a new Chief Protector, Richard Howard, was appointed in 1906. Howard was unsympathetic to the religious aims of the missionaries and saw missions as a potential source of valuable labour. He was thus unwilling to support the missionary (and official state) policy of isolation of Aboriginal people from the wider community. A conflict developed between Howard and the missionaries in 1907, when Howard approved the illegal recruitment of Mapoon residents by pearl shelling boats. When the Local Protector refused to respond to Hey's complaints about this decision, the Presbyterian Board of Missions and the Home Secretary were brought into the fray, with the Home Secretary eventually rebuking Howard for his actions.[56] Nonetheless, the incident marked a significant change in the relationship between the Mapoon missionaries and the Protectors. Under ongoing pressure from the Protectors to allow mission residents to take paid employment off the mission, the missionaries eventually agreed to allow a number of older girls to work as domestic servants on Thursday Island.

But tensions heightened further after Michael Baltzer, a former assistant to Nicholas Hey, accused the Mapoon missionaries of a variety of misdemeanours and Howard instituted a formal inquiry. Most allegations were dismissed, but one claim, that Hey had ordered Baltzer to beat Ethel, one of the older girls on the mission, was found to have substance. Ethel, a state ward, gave evidence herself of the harsh beating, though she said she had previously only been treated kindly at the mission. The missionaries freely admitted that Ethel had been beaten and then tied up for two days after hitting her teacher, Minnie Hey, but denied that their response represented serious wrongdoing.[57] To them, the girl's misdemeanour seemed so shocking it called for drastic action. As the beating of Ethel showed, the Mapoon missionaries by this stage were willing to countenance the use of extreme violence against a defenceless girl as a means of achieving their aims. The Moravians had once had other hopes of their means to persuade their protégés.

Concluding Comments

The outbreak of World War I in 1914 brought significant change to the western Cape York missions. The German nationality of some of the missionaries had significant implications. The Richters, on furlough in Germany, were unable to return to Australia. Arthur Richter was drafted into the German army and the Presbyterian Board of Missions terminated his employment. Nicholas Hey, whose eldest son was serving overseas with the Australian Imperial Forces, was, nonetheless, a figure of some suspicion. In 1917 the Australian army raided Mapoon after reports spread that the missionaries were arming the Aborigines. The Browns, whose relationship with the Presbyterian Board of Missions had always been problematic, resigned and left the mission in 1916. And in 1917 Matilda Ward resigned from the mission because of ill health. When the Heys finally retired in 1919, a new generation of Presbytarian missionaries drawn from the Australian church were placed in charge of Mapoon, Aurukun, Weipa and a newly opened mission on Mornington Island.

The departing missionaries clung to hopes that their aims had borne some good fruit. In a pamphlet, "A Visit to Mapoon", published by the Presbyterian Women's Association of New South Wales to raise support for the mission, Nicholas Hey attempted to summarise the mission's achievements.[58] Though he commented negatively on those "hard cases" who resisted Christianization, he outlined an overall hopeful sketch of the Aboriginal village the missionaries had founded. [59] Men were in leadership positions but he lauded female skills. The women, with few exceptions, kept the cottages clean and neat, "no doubt the outcome of the training the young wives received as girls in the dormitories".[60] Two men, an Aboriginal "Counsellor", elected by the village residents, and a "native pastor" from the Solomon Islands supervised the village. Both men had Aboriginal wives whom Hey evaluated comparatively. The Counsellor's wife did not seem to be a great help to him: born on one of the many islands off the mainland, she had not passed through the Mapoon school and dormitories.[61] By contrast, the pastor's wife, trained in Mapoon, proved an exemplary wife and mother. A meticulous housekeeper, her domestic skills extended to making her own and her children's clothes. She was better educated than her husband and as a result, she kept the church books: Hey commented that it would not have been surprising if she also prepared his sermons.[62]

Matilda Ward had gratifying evidence of her influence. In October 1917 she received a letter of farewell from a young woman named Rhyda, one of a number of previous students who wrote in this vein. Describing Ward as "our dear Mother, teacher, adviser and Missionary", Rhyda asked her to accept the letter as coming from both her and her husband Gibson, who "will try and meet you if not on earth in Heaven above and we also will bring our little boy".[63] She signed the letter affectionately: "Your son and daughter in Christ, Gibson and Rhyda". Martha Ward must have welcomed the letters of Rhyda and her friends with their expressions of gratitude and piety: she preserved them among her personal papers. As a young Christian Aboriginal couple, bringing up their child to share their religious values, Rhyda and Gibson represented everything the missionaries had laboured to achieve.

But overall the Moravians knew, as did their protégés, that the mission enterprise had been far more problematic. Numerous Aborigines had embraced their interpretations of spirituality and values but the missionaries had afforded them poor protection from the increasing state regime of surveillance and control: indeed the missionaries had colluded with the state if policies coincided with mission goals. The missionaries felt perpetually embattled by the settler community that surrounded the mission, which offered little spiritual sustenance for new Christians. The Moravians' urgent desire to bring Aborigines within a Christian community, in conjunction with the degree of authority granted the missionaries by settler administrations, led them to give rein to their own authoritarian tendencies. They had embarked on their task with customary Moravian expectations of separation from state involvement, but became, in effect, an arm of state policy. The Moravian Christian humanitarian mission had proved indeed to be "a matter of no small importance", but the life chances of new Christians were compromised. The new Christian communities of the western Cape would continue to sustain their Indigenous heritage alongside Christian spirituality for decades to come, a testimony to their agency, courage and resilience.[64]

Notes

1 The authors would like to thank Claire McLisky and Fiona Davis, who read drafts of this chapter and provided helpful suggestions.
2 J. G. Ward to Benjamin La Trobe, 15 December 1891. MF 186. Australian Institute of Aboriginal and Torres Strait Islander Studies, hereafter AIATSIS.
3 See Felicity Jensz in this volume.
4 See the Queensland State Library website: 'Footprints Before Me'. <http://www.slq.qld.gov.au/info/ind/footprints/community/missions>.
5 Loos, *Invasion and Resistance: Aboriginal-European Relations on the North Queensland Frontier, 1861–1897*; Kidd, *'The Way We Civilise': Aboriginal Affairs — The Untold Story*; Evans, *A History of Queensland*; Reid, *'That Unhappy Race'*, pp. 99–116; O'Brien, "Saving the Empty North".
6 See Evans et al., *Equal Subjects, Unequal Rights: Indigenous Peoples in British Settler Colonies*.
7 Harris, *One Blood*, p. 484.
8 Macdonald, "Missions to the Australian Aborigines", p. 36.
9 Macdonald, "Missions to the Australian Aborigines", p. 36.
10 From the account of "Rev. F. A. Hagenauer's Tour of Queensland", pp. 517–18.
11 Harrison, "Missions, Fisheries and Government", pp. 7–11.
12 Hagenauer became Secretary of the BPA in 1889. Blake, 'Hagenauer, Friedrich August (1829–1909)', pp. 314–15.
13 *Minutes of Proceedings of the Federal Assembly of the Presbyterian Churches of Australia and Tasmania, September 1887*, pp. 32–3.
14 Reid, *"That Unhappy Race"*, pp. 161–2.
15 Harrison, "Missions, Fisheries and Government", pp. 72–3.
16 *Extracts of the Periodical Accounts* (March 1892), pp. 494–8; (March 1893), pp. 34–6.

17 *Extracts of the Periodical Accounts, Missions of the Church of the United Brethren Among the Heathen* (March 1893), 34–5.

18 "Report of Committee on Foreign Missions" (September 1894), p. ii.

19 J. G. Ward to Br. O'Connor, 11 September 1894. MF 187. AIATSIS.

20 Statistics collected by the Torres Strait Pearlshellers Association, quoted in Harrison, "Missions, Fisheries and Government", p. 19.

21 Harrison, "Missions, Fisheries and Government", 37–43.

22 Reid, *"That Unhappy Race"*, pp. 129–30.

23 J. G. Ward to Br. O'Connor, 11 September 1894. MF 187. AIATSIS.

24 For discussions of this theme in other Aboriginal missions, see Joanna Cruickshank, "To exercise a beneficial influence over a man"; Broome, *Aboriginal Australians*, pp. 112–15.

25 *Extracts of the Periodical Accounts* (June 1895), pp. 474–5; (December 1895), p. 624.

26 Campbell, *After Fifty Years*, p. 9.

27 Archibald Meston, quoted in Evans et al., *Exclusion, Exploitation and Extermination: Race Relations in Colonial Queensland*, p. 118.

28 Harrison, "Missions, Fisheries and Government", pp. 105–12.

29 Hey in address to the Presbyterian Church of Queensland General Assembly, 1912. Quoted in Harrison, "Missions, Fisheries and Government", p. 50.

30 According to the Northern Protector, Walter Roth, 105 men were recruited from Mapoon in 1901. "Annual Report of the Northern Protector of Aboriginals for 1901" *Queensland Parliamentary Papers*, vol. 1 (1902), p. 14.

31 "Report of the Committee on Foreign Missions" (September 1896), p. iv.

32 See for example 14 September 1896. Matilda Ward's diary. MSS 1893/11. BOEMAR Records, Mitchell Library.

33 "Annual Report of the Northern Protector of Aboriginals for 1901", *Queensland Parliamentary Papers* vol. 1 (1902), p. 7.

34 "Annual Report of the Northern Protector of Aboriginals for 1901", *Queensland Parliamentary Papers* vol. 1 (1902), p. 7.

35 "Annual Report of the Northern Protector of Aboriginals for 1901", *Queensland Parliamentary Papers* vol. 1 (1902), p. 9.

36 "Report of Board of Missions", *Minutes of Proceedings of the General Assembly of the Presbyterian Church of Australia* (September 1905). p. 71.

37 "Report of the Committee on Foreign Missions", *Proceedings of the Federal Assembly of the Presbyterian Churches of Australia and Tasmania* (September 1898), p. ii.

38 Matilda Ward to Benjamin La Trobe, 23 August 1905. MF 187. Moravian Mission Papers, AIATSIS.

39 'Report of the Committee on Foreign Missions', *Proceedings of the Federal Assembly of the Presbyterian Churches of Australia and Tasmania* (March 1900), p. v.

40 See "Report of the Board of Missions to the Heathen", *Minutes of Proceedings of the General Assembly of the Presbyterian Church of Australia* (September 1906), p. 83. For discussion of mission villages at Yarrabah and elsewhere, see Broome, *Aboriginal Australians*, p. 111.

41 Nicholas Hey, Draft annual report for 1909. MSS 1893/11. BOEMAR Collection, Mitchell Library.

42 Nicholas Hey, 'Report of Mapoon Reformatory and Industrial Home' *Minutes of Proceedings of the General Assembly of the Presbyterian Church of Australia* (September 1905). p. 72.

43 Nicholas Hey, Draft annual report for 1909. MSS 1893/11, BOEMAR Records, Mitchell Library.

44 'Report of Board of Missions' *Minutes of Proceedings of the General Assembly of the Presbyterian Church of Australia* (September 1907). p. 69; Kaye, *The Torres Strait*, pp. 41–2.

45 *Minutes of Proceedings of the General Assembly of the Presbyterian Church of Australia* (September 1910), p. 59.

46 *Minutes of Proceedings of the General Assembly of the Presbyterian Church of Australia* (September 1910), p. 59.

47 *Minutes of Proceedings of the General Assembly of the Presbyterian Church of Australia* (September 1906), p. 83.

48 *Minutes of Proceedings of the General Assembly of the Presbyterian Church of Australia* (September 1909), p. xxix.

49 See reports of 'Board of Missions' *Minutes of Proceedings of the General Assembly of the Presbyterian Church of Australia* 1907–1914.

50 See for example: 18 October 1897; 13 March 1908; 27 January 1910; 25–28 February 1912.

51 25–28 February 1912. Matilda Ward's diary. MSS 1893/11. BOEMAR, Mitchell Library.

52 Laura Schick to Benjamin La Trobe, 21 March 1903. MF 187. AIATSIS.

53 See the series of letters from Edwin Brown to Benjamin La Trobe, May 1902. MF 187, AIATSIS. This includes copies of the correspondence between Brown, Roth and the Presbyterian Board of Missions on the disputed matter.

54 Richter, 'Aurukun' in 'Report of Board of Missions', p. 69.

55 4 March 1911. Robert Hugh Wilson Diaries. MSS F1682. Fryer Library, University of Queensland.

56 Harrison, "Missions, Fisheries and Government", pp. 78–82.

57 *Brisbane Courier*, 1909, cited in Crow, 'Colonialism's Paradox,' pp. 141–31.

58 Hey, *A Visit to Mapoon*; For the new generation of missionaries in North Queensland, see Wharton, "MacKenzie, William", pp. 245–6; Love, "Love, James", pp. 150–1.

59 Hey, *A Visit to Mapoon*, pp. 18–20.

60 Hey, *A Visit to Mapoon*, p. 28.

61 Hey, *A Visit to Mapoon*, p. 29.

62 Hey, *A Visit to Mapoon*, p. 29.

63 Rhyda to Matilda Ward, 23 October 1917. MS 1893/11. BOEMAR Collection, Mitchell Library.

64 See Roberts, *The Mapoon Story*.

CHAPTER THIRTEEN

Mission Dormitories

Intergenerational Implications for Kalumburu and Balgo, Kimberley, Western Australia

CHRISTINE CHOO AND BRIAN F. MCCOY

From the earliest days in the establishment of the Catholic Church in Western Australia, not long after the Swan River Colony was settled by Anglo-Europeans in 1829, the Church hierarchy had the evangelisation of the Indigenous inhabitants of the new colony on its agenda. In January 1846, Bishop Brady of the new Catholic Diocese of Perth and twenty-seven missionaries arrived in the Swan River Colony from Europe. Among them were Spanish Benedictines Dom Jose Maria Benedict Serra and Dom Rosendo Salvado, Irish Sisters of Mercy, Austrian, English, French and Italian priests and catechists. The Benedictines established the first Catholic mission to Aboriginal people at New Norcia in 1846. Attempts by another group of missionaries to set up a Catholic mission in the south-east failed.[1] It was not until 1890 that the Church established its first permanent mission in the Kimberley in the north-west of Western Australia at Beagle Bay. Other Catholic missions that were subsequently established in the Kimberley were directly or indirectly linked to the missions at New Norcia and Beagle Bay. It was not English-speaking missionaries who made these moves of missionary outreach to Aboriginal people in Australia; the predominantly Irish Catholic Church was more concerned about its own life and survival in the context of strong sectarianism.[2] The early Catholic missionaries to the Aboriginal people in Western Australia were from Continental Europe.

The two key elements in the work of the Catholic missions with Aboriginal people of Western Australia — bringing them the "fruits of Christianity" and that of western culture — were inseparable for the missionaries at that time. The process through which the missionaries intended to achieve this involved: *evangelization*, that is, becoming a Catholic Christian; *civilization* or inculturation into western ways; the *protection* from abuse by employers, particularly pastoralists, and station employees, and provision of food and health care for women and children, the old and infirm; the *establishment of Christian families* as people were encouraged to marry people of similar age, raise families, settle and work; and the *education* and training of children and young people to prepare them for assimilation into mainstream society by the women becoming domestic servants and men, labourers and station employees. Each of these aspects of mission work is inextricably linked with the others, and it is not possible to speak of any in isolation. The missions encouraged people from a wide hinterland, belonging to a number of different language and tribal groups, to become sedentary and settle close to the mission hub on a more permanent basis. This was the beginning of an artificial mission-focused "community". The dormitory system then gathered children from these families and from families who had settled nearby or on neighbouring pastoral stations. These children later became an integral part of the apparatus of evangelization and colonization.

This chapter examines the role and impacts of the mission dormitory system on Aboriginal people in the Kimberley, with special reference to dormitories for children from the communities where they were located. It does not aim to describe in detail the history of the Catholic Church's missionary activity in the Kimberley, nor the establishment of dormitories within each of those missions.[3] The focus of the chapter is on two missions: Kalumburu (formerly Drysdale River Mission first established at Pago in 1908, and then transferred to Kalumburu in the late 1930s) and Balgo (Rockhole Station in 1934, Old Balgo Mission in 1939–42 and New Balgo Mission in 1965). These missions were very different, hundreds of kilometres from each other, and established by different missionary orders in different periods in the history of the Kimberley. (See the map overleaf for the locations of Kalumburu, Balgo and other places referred to in this chapter.) Kalumburu, on the far north-west coast, was established by Spanish Benedictine monks from New Norcia, while it was German Pallottines (Society of the Catholic Apostolate) based in Beagle Bay who established Balgo in the semi-desert region in the south-west Kimberley. Both Kalumburu and Wirrimanu (Balgo) are no longer missions but remain very remote communities even today. They demonstrate very common early themes stemming from attitudes at that time to mission work, particularly with attention to children as a key ingredient of mission activity. Any consideration of the dormitory system in Balgo and Kalumburu necessarily raises questions about its intergenerational effects, particularly in the contemporary situation of both communities today. It also raises questions about many other Aboriginal people in Australia who also spent a large part of their lives growing up in government and mission dormitories.

Kimberley Catholic Missions

Catholic missions to Aboriginal people in Western Australia were created in areas beyond the fringes of Western 'civilization', first in New Norcia (1846–47), later in Beagle Bay (1890) and Kalumburu (1908), and much later in Rockhole Station (1934) and Balgo (1942). New Norcia was the 'mother house' of Kalumburu, just as Beagle Bay was for Balgo, and monks and other personnel were sent from the mother house to the newer mission on the fringes of their influence.

There were close links between the Benedictine mission at Kalumburu and the Pallottine mission at Beagle Bay throughout the early life of these missions. It was from Beagle Bay that the pioneer Benedictines, Father Nicholas Emo and the Filipino

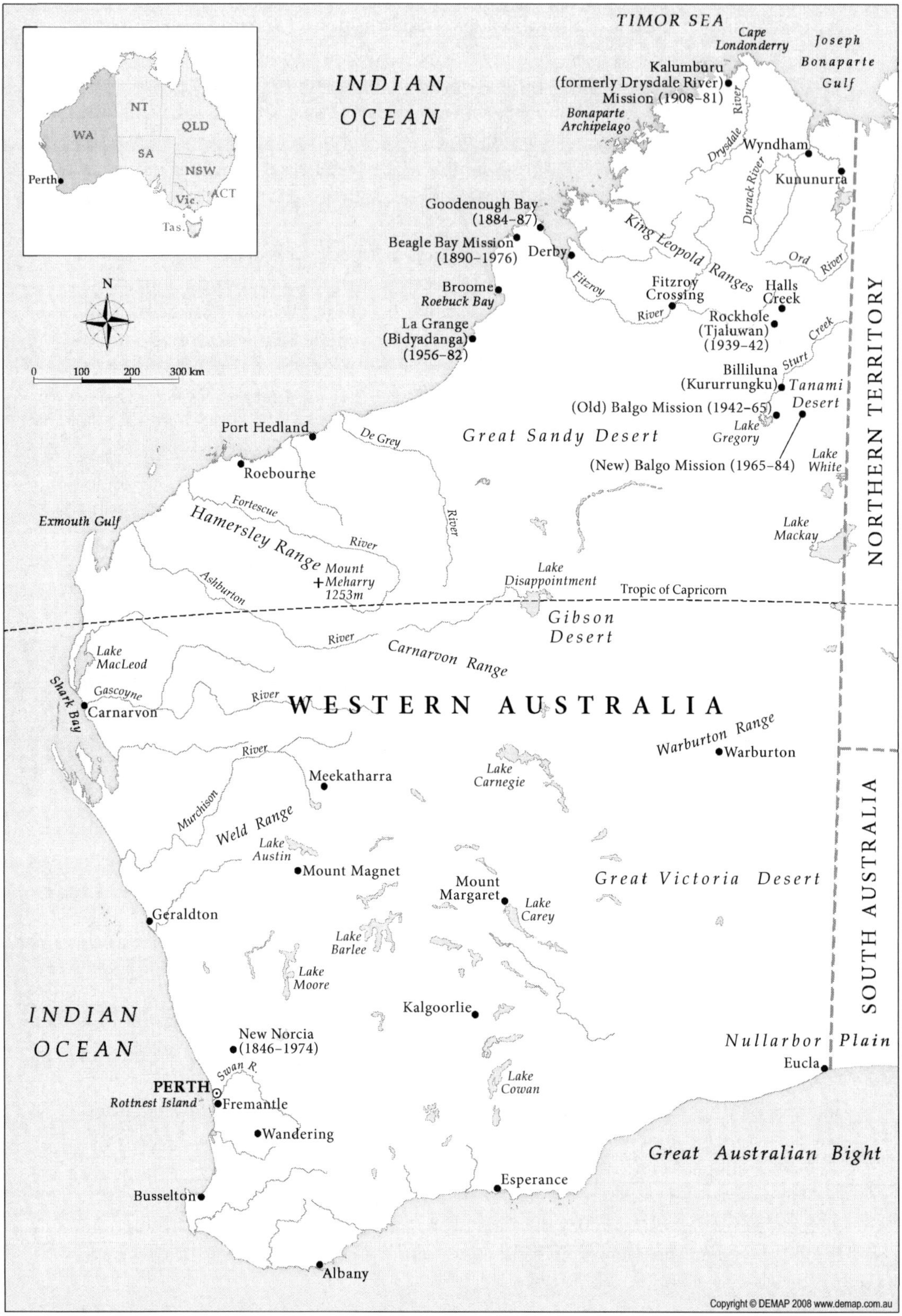
TIMOR SEA
Cape Londonderry
Joseph Bonaparte Gulf
Kalumburu (formerly Drysdale River) Mission (1908–81)
Bonaparte Archipelago
INDIAN OCEAN
NT
QLD
WA
SA
NSW
Perth
Vic.
ACT
Tas.
Drysdale River
Wyndham
Kununurra
Durack River
Goodenough Bay (1884–87)
Beagle Bay Mission (1890–1976)
Derby
King Leopold Ranges
Ord River
Fitzroy River
Fitzroy Crossing
Halls Creek
Broome
Roebuck Bay
La Grange (Bidyadanga) (1956–82)
Rockhole (Tjaluwan) (1939–42)
Sturt Creek
Billiluna (Kururrungku)
Tanami Desert
(Old) Balgo Mission (1942–65)
Lake Gregory
(New) Balgo Mission (1965–84)
Lake White
N
0 100 200 300 km
Port Hedland
De Grey River
Great Sandy Desert
NORTHERN TERRITORY
Roebourne
Fortescue River
Exmouth Gulf
Hamersley Range
Mount Meharry 1253m
Ashburton River
Lake Mackay
Lake Disappointment
Tropic of Capricorn
Gibson Desert
Carnarvon Range
Lake MacLeod
Shark Bay
Gascoyne River
Carnarvon
WESTERN AUSTRALIA
Warburton Range
Warburton
Murchison River
Meekatharra
Lake Carnegie
Weld Range
Lake Austin
Mount Magnet
Mount Margaret
Lake Carey
Great Victoria Desert
SOUTH AUSTRALIA
Geraldton
Lake Barlee
Lake Moore
Kalgoorlie
INDIAN OCEAN
New Norcia (1846–1974)
Nullarbor Plain
Eucla
Swan R.
PERTH
Rottnest Island
Fremantle
Lake Cowan
Wandering
Great Australian Bight
Esperance
Busselton
Albany
Copyright © DEMAP 2008 www.demap.com.au

converts (Manilamen), left to establish the mission at Pago in the far north in 1908. From there luggers, the only form of transport for provisions and personnel, sailed between these missions. In 1909 seven young "half-caste" boys had been sent to Drysdale River Mission from stations in the Liveringa region by the Aborigines Department. When these boys were of marriageable age, they were sent to Beagle Bay by the monks to choose wives from the "mission girls" there.[4] Two girls from Drysdale River were sent to the dormitory at Beagle Bay in 1930 before the sisters arrived at Drysdale River Mission. Girls were sent from Beagle Bay to New Norcia or from Kalumburu to New Norcia for their education.[5]

One common theme in all Catholic missions in the Kimberley was the difficulty that missionaries experienced in living up to their founders' dreams. Both missions required very hard labour and ongoing demands in both establishment and mainte- nance. Most missionaries failed to comprehend or appreciate the complexities of Aboriginal people's values and beliefs. The extreme isolation and distance from "civi- lization" and the utterly unfamiliar climate and natural environment took their toll. On both missions there were examples of Aboriginal resistance. In Kalumburu forms of active resistance included armed attacks on persons and property, burning and stealing. In Balgo, sheep were regularly killed and eaten. Passive resistance included lack of co-operation, abandonment of work and being "cheeky".

There appeared to be a slow acceptance of the "Good News" by the mission resi- dents. Usual measures of successful evangelization, like regular attendance at services and participation in the sacraments, recruitment into the priesthood or religious life, were largely not attained. Nor, at least for some missionaries, was their hope realized that converts would eschew their traditional ways and beliefs. Nevertheless, there has often been a core group of people in both Kalumburu and Balgo who have faithfully followed the Christian way.

It is also important to note that male missionaries always held the authority within the missions. Even when orders of nuns arrived to share the work on the missions they remained under the direction of the local Bishop and the male superiors of the Benedictine or Pallottine orders. A largely male and non-Aboriginal domination of Aboriginal communities continues today and remains one of the legacies of coloniza- tion within these communities.

West Kimberley

In 1878 Bishop Martin Griver, Catholic Bishop of Perth, sent Father Matthew Gibney, Vicar General of Perth, to the north-west to report on possible sites in the Kimberley. In 1884 the Bishop sent Father Duncan McNab to establish a mission at Goodenough Bay, near Derby on the West Kimberley coast. This mission failed and by 1887 was abandoned, destroyed by the traditional owners of the surrounding land.[6] The first permanent mission in the Kimberley, established in 1890 by French Cistercian (Trappist) monks at Beagle Bay, has been called the "birthplace and cradle of Catholic presence in the Kimberleys".[7] In 1899 the Trappists left the mission, unable to cope with the climate and plagued by problems within their order.[8] A Spanish monk, Father Nicholas Emo, who had joined his brother Trappists in the Kimberley in 1895, chose to remain there after the Trappists left. His ministry was primarily to the Catholic Manilamen (Filipinos) who worked in the pearling industry. In Broome he established a small school and mission for the Aboriginal people and in 1897 three boys and eight girls, four of whom were of mixed descent, attended the Broome Orphanage School where Emo was assisted by an Aboriginal woman who was married to a Manilaman.[9] Here the children studied catechism and did specified jobs every day, including washing, ironing, mending, cleaning and kitchen chores. Boys and girls were prepared for work as domestic servants to families of "good repute" in the Broome area.[10] This orphanage was the precursor to the dormitory system in the Kimberley as it was the first time Aboriginal boys and girls were cared for by the missionaries, away from their own families. The Trappists had not previously established such a system in Beagle Bay, where the focus of their mission work had been to reach the families of the traditional owners, and where they were without the presence of nuns.

On 12 January 1901, Beagle Bay Mission was transferred to the Pious Society of Missions (later known as the Society of the Catholic Apostolate or Pallottines) and in April that year Father George Walter and a group of Pallottine priests and lay brothers arrived there.[11] In July 1904 they obtained permission to "collect and train the fatherless half-castes and other aboriginal children who were destitute in Broome", thus building on the work started by Father Emo.[12] However, it was not until 1907 when the St John of God Sisters arrived at Beagle Bay that the dormitories for girls and boys could be finally established. Until the sisters arrived, Beagle Bay Mission supported between 50 and 90 local people. From 1907 the number of people maintained at Beagle Bay Mission increased to between 150 and 250, particularly after the removal of "half-caste" children from pastoral stations in the district to the mission under government legislation enshrined in the *Aborigines Act* of 1905.

Drysdale River Mission (Kalumburu)

The Benedictine mission at Pago on the Drysdale River in the far north of Western Australia was established on 15 August 1908 when Bishop Fulgentius Torres and a small band of Benedictine monks, Father Emo and Manilamen from Broome and Beagle Bay set up camp there. They ventured to these parts of Western Australia in response to the wish, expressed by the ecclesiastical hierarchy at the Third Plenary Council in Sydney in 1905, for the evangelization of the Aboriginal inhabitants of the north-west by the Benedictines.[13] Even though the mission faced resistance from the traditional owners, including hostile attacks in 1910 and 1914, the Benedictines remained at Pago until the late 1930s when they moved the mission to a new location at Kalumburu, near a more reliable source of water. Following the pattern of contact with traditional owners of country on which they intended to start their missions, which had been established by Bishop Salvado in New Norcia, the Benedictines at Pago lived alongside the local traditional owners. Their vision was to preserve and increase the local Aboriginal population, and to offer a safe haven to those under threat from pastoralists and other European settlers. From the earliest days the monks envisaged a place for nuns in their mission but superiors at New Norcia considered it was then too early for non-Aboriginal women at Drysdale for three main reasons: the remoteness of the mission, the threat of attack and the hostility of the local groups.

Balgo Mission

Balgo Mission arose largely from a frustrated vision by the Pallottines of Beagle Bay to provide medical care to the Indigenous inhabitants of the semi-desert region, but it also represented the missionaries' opportunistic risk-taking. The intention to buy Rockhole Station, a sheep station close to Halls Creek, arose from a particular interest of Bishop Otto Raible, Catholic Bishop of the Kimberley, in Aboriginal health, especially leprosy (Hansen's Disease). His intention was to set up a medical centre, a home for the old and infirm and a school. Without warning the government of his intentions, Raible negotiated with Francis Castles to buy Rockhole Station for £1400. On 13 October 1934 Father Francis Huegel, Brother Henry Krallmann and Brother Joseph Schuengel left Broome to take ownership of Rockhole. Accompanying them were Aboriginal men from Beagle Bay: Paddy Meranjian, Willie, George Kelly and Phillip Cox.[14] Although Aboriginal people from Beagle Bay, including a short-lived order of Aboriginal nuns, helped establish Balgo Mission, their contribution has often been minimized and is largely invisible in missionary hagiography.[15]

Bishop Raible wrote to the Western Australian Minister for Aboriginal Affairs in January 1935 to formally request permission to establish a medical service at Rockhole, noting that the Pallottines would erect the hospital buildings and provide trained staff, including nurses (Sisters of St John of God). He then left for Germany to recruit staff for the mission. The Chief Protector of Aborigines declined the Bishop's offer, informing him that other arrangements had been made. Following the recommendations of the 1934 Moseley Royal Commission into Aboriginal Affairs in Western Australia, the Chief Protector had appointed a Medical Inspector of Aborigines to travel throughout the north and had planned to establish a medical clinic at Moola Bulla, the government station in the East Kimberley created in 1910.[16] Greatly disappointed, and after persevering with Rockhole Station for a few more years, Raible sold the station to Ernie Bridge in 1939.[17]

While the Bishop had been planning his new venture at Rockhole, the Pallottine linguist and anthropologist Father Ernest Worms had been making yearly expeditions into the East and West Kimberley from 1933. In October 1938 and May 1939 Worms and Raible travelled south-east of Halls Creek into the more remote areas where they met desert people. The Bishop's intention was to evangelize the people who still lived a nomadic existence in the sand ridges along the Canning Stock Route and further east in the desert region around Lake White.[18] While Worms exhibited interest in the various expressions of Aboriginal culture, his attitudes and behaviour clearly supported the process of assimilation and the superiority of Christian beliefs over others.

Worms believed that assimilation was as inevitable for Aboriginal people as were the dangers of urban life and the benefits of Christianity. His conviction was that the best approach was for "gradual assimilation in contrast to the more hurrying method suggested by certain governmental bodies".[19] He, like other missionaries of that time, rarely distinguished between the values of Christianity and those of western "civilization". The missionaries saw themselves as different from and "kinder" than station people whose interest in Aboriginal people they believed was largely based in economics. In this the Benedictines at Kalumburu in 1908 and the Pallottines at Balgo thirty years later, were in accord.

Establishing a mission south of Halls Creek offered the Catholic church a rare opportunity to work with those who were perceived to be still strong in their culture but also able to receive the benefits of Christianity. Bishop Raible acted on Worms' advice and applied to the Western Australian Government for a lease of 1,000,000 acres further into the desert and adjacent to the Canning Stock Route. In 1939, after their departure from Rockhole Station, the Pallottines' search for an appropriate site took them on a desert sojourn lasting three years, "like the wanderings of nomad shepherds".[20] Brother Frank Nissl, Paddy Meranjian, Bertha Paddy, Phillip Cox and Dick Smith left Rockhole on 8 September 1939, with a large herd of sheep, goats, horses, donkey and camels.[21] They travelled south-east and four weeks later came to Billiluna Station from where they moved to the end of the Billiluna station run, away from the Canning Stock Route, arriving at a place called Comet. Then at Christmas they came to Tjaluwan, a large waterhole where they met a large group of about sixty Aboriginal people, who had anticipated their arrival. They wandered in this semi-desert region in two groups with little water for a further six months until they found suitable waterholes with some good pasture. From here the group finally found a place where they could establish a mission and three years later, in 1942, they settled at old Balgo.[22] There they remained until relocating the mission to the present site now called Wirrimanu in 1965.

Mission Dormitories

Even though two different religious orders operated the Catholic missions in the Kimberley, their model of mission endeavour was practically identical. New Norcia set the model for mission work among the Aborigines in Western Australia. Dom Salvado and the Benedictines at first lived among the traditional owners to the north-east of the Swan River Colony in 1846 before settling permanently in one location — New Norcia. Dom Salvado described this process in his memoir:

> Thus the practical study of the language, laws, traditions and customs of the natives made us realise, among other things, that the very demanding wanderer's life which we had first adopted was only of doubtful use. It called for the sacrifice of health and life on the part of the missionaries, with little to show for it at the end. On the other hand, the method of stability, that is, the founding of a mission where hospitality

could be given to all the natives who wanted to learn a trade and receive religious instruction, would yield good results, without exposing us to all the hardships of the nomadic life . . . But, suppose he is given some food and decides to settle down and become a Christian, who is going to support and clothe him? . . .

The only answer is to provide them with work and subsistence. But before this, one must teach these work-shy nomads to settle down to a community life in one spot. From this arises the necessity of an establishment directed by religious persons, in other words by missionaries who are not concerned for their own interests, but devote themselves entirely to the moral and civil education of their neighbours and the glory of God.

Convinced of this truth, we made some small beginnings, and had the pleasure of seeing good results.[23]

For people who had hunted and gathered for food on a daily basis, the availability of mission rations and a regular supply of cattle and sheep for meat provided a strong attraction to mission life. Here, people were expected to work in order to receive food. Rations were used as a form of control when "troublemakers" were denied access to them or when they were expelled from the mission. People would drift away when rations became scarce (both missions struggled at times for supplies due to their remoteness) or when enticed elsewhere.

At New Norcia, the Benedictines established "orphanages" or "dormitories" for the children who were brought to the mission by parents who went there to work for rations, and for protection from exploitation by other Europeans. Children were sometimes left at the mission by parents due to their mobility as farm labourers. The first College of New Norcia opened in December 1847 when three young boys were admitted there by their parents.[24] Girls were sent away to be cared for by Sisters of Mercy in Perth; the first was sent in 1848.[25] In 1921 Abbot Anselm Catalan founded an order of nuns to assist the Benedictines at New Norcia to care for Aboriginal girls.[26] The children stayed in the dormitories, the girls cared for by nuns and the boys by the monks, while their parents lived in small houses in the mission compound between the monastery, the church and the "orphanage".[27] Although their parents and relatives lived very close by, all school-aged children were institutionalized.

The model of mission settlement used at New Norcia was later repeated at Beagle Bay where the church was the centre of focus, surrounded by the missionaries' living quarters, set apart from housing for those who had come into the mission in an area the missionaries referred to as the "Colony". The adults on the "Colony" worked closely with the missionaries and regularly participated in religious services. At Beagle Bay children from families in the "Colony" were taken into the dormitories from the age of about five or six. They were allowed to see their parents only on weekends and special holidays including special feast days. They were encouraged to speak English and prevented from speaking their own languages. Girls were locked in the dormitories at night. Raised by nuns, brothers and priests, the children soon identified with these adults as parental figures. Boys and girls had to work alongside the nuns and brothers in the gardens, kitchen, bakery, dairy, slaughter house and church sacristy. Besides attending school for a rudimentary education, they assisted in all kinds of work on the mission including building, cleaning, cooking and gardening.

Following the model set at New Norcia in the mid 1800s and later at Beagle Bay from 1901, the missionaries at Drysdale River Mission used rations of tea, flour and tobacco, as well as fruits and vegetables they grew in the mission gardens, to attract the local groups to the mission from the time they landed in Pago in 1908. The missions at Drysdale River and Balgo also kept sheep, goats and later cattle for local consumption. After the initial hostility subsided, the missions were considered by local groups to be a good place for a brief period of rest and refreshment, where people were assured of food rations and tobacco in exchange for a little work, before they moved on. Ready access to a reliable source of food made the mission a valuable meeting place for traditional business, where people belonging to different groups gathered in separate camping grounds. However, once the groups grew accustomed to a sedentary lifestyle closer to the mission, it became increasingly difficult for them to live off the land as they formerly did. Dependence on the mission for supplies and rations was probably greater among the desert people than those who lived closer to the coast at Kalumburu where fish, oysters, turtles and other foods were plentiful in the nearby sea and waterholes. In a relatively short time people became dependent on the rations offered by both missions.

At Beagle Bay the identification with the nuns and the missionaries reached its zenith when the Bishop of Broome, Otto Raible, created the first order of Aboriginal nuns in Australia. These, the Daughters of Our Lady, Queen of the Apostles, comprised girls brought up in the Beagle Bay dormitory by the St John of God sisters, to facilitate the evangelization of Aboriginal people in the Kimberley. Training for six girls commenced in 1938 but by 1951 only one sister remained and the order had to be abandoned. These West Kimberley "native sisters" were sent to assist the Pallottines in Balgo in the 1940s, an endeavour that placed considerable stresses on the young women. Balgo Mission had been considered too physically isolated and demanding for the St John of God sisters whose presence in the Kimberley dated from 1907. However, these "native sisters", born and raised on the coast, were ill-prepared for the isolation and harsh conditions at Balgo. Nor were they prepared for contact with desert people who had recently come to the mission. The Bishop's dream of a new style of evangelization failed.

In Kalumburu there was no similar attempt to develop a local order of religious women or men. The Benedictines' earlier hopes that the boys sent to Pago by government authorities in 1909 would marry mission girls from Beagle Bay, return to Drysdale River Mission and together help to evangelize the tribal people who visited the mission, were thwarted when the young men and their new wives did not return. The girls were fearful of venturing outside their own familiar territory to live among people whom they considered "wild".[28]

The Benedictines followed the New Norcia mission method at Pago and then in the new location of the mission at Kalumburu in the late 1930s. The monks noted that there seemed to be few children among the families who visited the mission for rations; their puzzlement turned into concern. Unlike at Balgo Mission where the number of children does not appear to have been a concern of the missionaries, at Drysdale River Mission the monks sought to encourage families to have more children. Various opinions and theories, too numerous to discuss here, have been offered by the monks and others to account for the low fertility. These included views about the impacts of traditional and ceremonial activities, the demands placed on women in daily life, the risks of childbirth, infanticide, the scarcity of food and perils of a nomadic existence. The monks encouraged family units to camp near the mission where the children could be cared for, and in the 1960s Father Seraphim Sanz, the Mission superintendent, closed the dormitories and built new houses for these families.

There were two distinct phases in the use of dormitories for the care of children at Drysdale River Mission. The first phase was from 1909 to 1931, where a building, although not officially described as a "dormitory", in fact functioned as such for seven young "half-caste" boys. These boys were sent there from Kimberley pastoral stations in 1909 under the *Aborigines Act* of 1905 which formally implemented the removal of mixed race children from their families. The second phase lasted from 1932 until 1962 when the dormitories finally closed. From early 1932 families who came to the mission were encouraged to leave their children at the new St Placid's Orphanage for boys and girls. The arrival of Benedictine Oblate Sisters on 18 August 1931 to commence their work in the community as teachers, nurses and carers, was a significant watershed in the development of the mission and its dormitories.[29]

The children, and some women whose husbands had left the mission for medical treatment or other reasons, remained in the dormitories which were locked at night and supervised by the Benedictine Oblate Sisters. The girls' dormitory functioned like a "woman's camp" under the protection of the mission. While they were physically separated from their families and the community at night, the dormitory children and women continued to have limited contact for some part of the day when they worked in the gardens and orchards, when they attended church services and during the weekends when they went on outings and picnics. However, these contact situations were usually under missionary supervision; the children were discouraged from engaging in traditional activities with their families who camped nearby. Mission "boys" and "girls" entered into Christian marriage, sometimes contrary to the traditional practices of betrothal.[30] The monks encouraged Christian couples to have large families; they were given houses near the mission compound and incentives at the birth of their children. Their children were sent to the mission dormitories when they reached school age.

Unlike the dormitories on missions closer to centres of population and enterprise where mission-trained Aboriginal labour was in demand, Kalumburu was isolated and therefore the dormitory played a different role. To the monks and nuns the dormitory not only functioned as a training and education centre to prepare future generations for contact with the wider world, but also a place where women and girls could be actively protected from what the missionaries considered were the worst aspects of traditional life — sexual promiscuity, child marriage, sexual and physical abuse of women and girls. The monks believed that it was these practices that contributed to the infertility of the people. By "rescuing" the young girls, caring for them and "growing them up" to marry young men who had also grown up in the mission dormitory, the missionaries believed the future of the local people would be ensured.

The separation between children and their parents that was introduced at Beagle Bay was repeated at Balgo Mission. As the desert people moved in and out of the mission from 1942 they sometimes found it convenient to leave their children there while they went hunting, attended ceremonies and performed other traditional activities. The missionaries believed that as children became unsettled when they returned to the care of their parents, it was better for them to remain in the mission dormitories. Here their education and socialization into more "civilized" ways could continue uninterrupted.[31] Plans to establish a girls' dormitory in Balgo were instigated in 1949.[32] In 1950 Father Alphonse Bleischwitz at Old Balgo, described the aims of the mission:

> The principal aim of the Mission, as of all religious missions to the primitive people, is to help these people become ideal Christians. The secondary, but important, aim is to endeavour to give them any positive good which our modern civilization is able to give them, and they on their side are able to absorb to the benefit of their general wellbeing . . . We hope in the near future to have a school for the children, where they will be educated, both in religious and secular matters. Further, we intend to build dormitories for the girls and the boys.[33]

Anthropologists Ronald and Catherine Berndt, who had contact with Balgo Mission from as early as 1957, noted that early in the history of Aboriginal-European contact two tropes were common: *you can't do much with the adults, you just have to concentrate on the children* and, *the only way to do anything with the children is to get them away from the adults.* In Balgo, these views were implemented in a variety of ways: in some situations the children were removed without parental consent or consultation; in other cases parents were happy to leave their children in the "care" of the missionaries.[34]

By 1951, a girls' dormitory had been established at old Balgo, and a boys' dormitory by 1960. Initially, neither was locked at night. There were no rigid restrictions between children and their families and children were not prevented from speaking their languages. However, when it became clear to the missionaries that promised husbands and other young males were interested in contact with the girls, they decided to fence the girls' dormitory and locked both at night. This situation remained until the dormitories closed.

Parents had some opportunities, although quite limited, for regular contact with their children. When Balgo moved to its present site in 1965 a large basketball court and playground lay between the girls' and boys' dormitories. Parents could meet their children here, particularly in the evenings, during film nights, at church and other social occasions. However, this playground remained geographically quite separate from the "camp" where the rest of the children's community, parents, grandparents and younger siblings lived further to the west. As in the other mission dormitories, the children were not fed, nurtured or taught by their parents and older relatives on an ongoing or regular basis. The dormitories in Balgo were closed by Father Ray Hevern (superintendent 1969–84) who believed the children rightly belonged with their parents. In

April 1973 parents were told to resume responsibility for the care of their children and arrangements were made for a gradual transition into their care. Children who were sent to the Balgo dormitories from neighbouring cattle stations remained there until 1979 when the communities of Malarn (Lake Gregory) and Kururrungku (Billiluna) were established.

Impact of Dormitories

Dormitories have intergenerational impacts that are deep and lasting. However this does not presuppose that those who grew up in the dormitories shared a uniform experience, as people describe both positive and negative personal experiences of dormitory life. One of the most important impacts of the dormitories — and something that would affect later generations — was their effect on significant relationships and values that lay at the heart of Aboriginal people's lives. These were relationships that connected people with family, land and the spiritual world. They were relationships that provided a person with a personal sense of meaning within a social and religious world, and with the identification of those who cared, nurtured and protected them. These relationships provided a social and ethical framework that revealed how an Aboriginal person existed in the world and cared for others.

Kanyirninpa is a linguistic metaphor. It is a *Kukatja* word used by some desert people to describe a relationship that links generations; it provides a reciprocity of care with respect that keeps old and young people together. Translated as "looking after", "nurturance" or "holding", it can be understood as a primary and highly significant way to describe how desert and other Aboriginal people understand key relationships, and how those relationships are reproduced across generations. In other words, cultural values and social expressions of *kanyirninpa* lie at the heart of identity, family and social reproduction. *Kanyirninpa* also keeps important value dualities in tension: authority with nurturance, and relatedness with autonomy.[35]

One of the elements that lay the heart of this "holding" was an identification of the mother with child, shortly after the child was born. She was considered as holding her child, not simply to feed and look after her, but to teach, nurture and protect. The husband was also thought to have holding responsibilities. For young men, this holding by the mother would continue until he entered into the adult and sacred space of "men's ceremonies". The rituals around this separation are public and gendered. The boy leaves his mother to follow the men and be held by them. This happens in most cultures, particularly Indigenous ones, where rites of initiation lie at the heart of social and community life and social reproduction.

At Kalumburu during the period when the dormitories were in operation and into the 1970s, upon the birth of a child, the child's mother was expected to bring the placenta to the mission clinic before she could receive the incentives or "Baby Bonus" promised by the mission. In the 1950s the "Baby Bonus" comprising additional flour, tea, sugar (above their normal allocation), soap, baby powder, a tin of jam and other knick-knacks, was publicly presented to new parents.[36] This action required by the mission, keen to encourage the birth of children, constituted a symbolic handing over of the child to the care of the mission. By the 1950s and 60s Christian sacraments, particularly baptism, confirmation and marriage were emphasized by the missionaries at the expense of traditional rites of passage. There was strong encouragement for those who grew up on the mission to transfer their loyalty from their family and community to this new and other "family". As a result, a new Christian community emerged, forged by bonds cemented through dormitory living and through decades of relationships with the missionaries. Nevertheless, as mentioned earlier, there were indications in Kalumburu mission records that community members, including those who grew up in the dormitories, continually engaged in acts of active and passive resistance against the missionaries and their efforts.[37]

What the dormitories effected was the separation of children from their parents and families from a very young age. While it provided the children with greater access to learning English and the ways of the western and Christian worlds, it removed them from those who had the primary responsibility to grow them into adulthood. Even though the dormitories were physically close to the families on the missions, and some social contact between children and their families did occur, this process of assimilation wounded family relationships very deeply.

Dislocation from family and community, particularly in terms of key personal and social relationships, can now be understood to have created a particular form of inter-generational trauma. For young people already struggling to cope with a rapidly changing world, separation brought its own train of hurt. For some of the families in the communities at Kalumburu and Balgo, missionaries may have been among the first non-Aboriginal people they had encountered outside their own. For these, and for the younger generations of their families, while dormitory living opened up new relationships it also constituted a serious and critical breach in cultural continuity as values, beliefs and knowledge could not be passed onto future generations.

Concluding Comments

The 1997 *Bringing Them Home: The Report of the National Inquiry into the Separation of Aboriginal and Torres Strait Islander Children from their Families*,[38] and subsequent focus on the 'Stolen Generations', has tended to overlook the impacts of the removal of Aboriginal children from their families into mission dormitories. Suggesting that there is some similarity of "separation" between those who grew up in mission dormitories and those taken away to other families, institutions and communities, is not to suggest that both can be considered equivalent. In both the Kalumburu and Balgo Missions parents and their children were always visible to each other: they had opportunities to meet as they participated in mission life and Christian ceremonies. While children learned to speak English they also, on the whole, kept their own language, stayed on or near their traditional country and had some contact with older generations. However, they were also confined and controlled by social, cultural and physical "fences" that separated them from being "grown up" by their parents and wider family relations.

There would now seem to be a growing body of empirical evidence that reveals serious intergenerational health implications for those Aboriginal people who were separated from their families. Not only did the experience of separation harm them but also their children, over a range of social and emotional health indicators (including drug use). As the second volume of the Western Australian Aboriginal Child Health Survey, *The Social and Emotional Wellbeing of Aboriginal Children and Young People*, shows, Aboriginal children who experienced separation from their families in Western Australia are now subject as adults to higher rates of social and emotional ill-health than those Aboriginal children who were not separated.[39] Similar ill-health effects have now extended to their children. Separation from immediate and extended family members not only harmed those children at the time of separation, but such harm was then passed on to later generations.

While the groups of older people in Balgo and Kalumburu were not separated from their families, they were prevented from "growing up" their children and grandchildren according to the values that had sustained them and their families for many generations. It is likely that the return of children to their care when the dormitories closed heightened more than a sense of loss. It reinforced what had been denied. For a number of decades the parents and older community members had been unable to provide what was culturally important for their families, and to ensure the life and wellbeing of the children. They had received a very clear message from both mission and government that they were incapable of doing so. Clearly the missionaries believed they were acting "for the good" of the Aboriginal people. However, this was a "good" without relationship, a provision of care without reciprocity, a control over people's lives without mutual respect.

In his apology of 13 February 2008 Prime Minister Rudd stated:

> We reflect in particular on the mistreatment of those who were Stolen Generations — this blemished chapter in our nation's history . . . We apologise especially for the removal of Aboriginal and Torres Strait Islander children from their families, their communities and their country.[40]

The apology has been largely interpreted as directed at those who were removed physically and geographically from their families to be assimilated into the wider white community. The children of Kalumburu and Balgo Missions were also separated, but in a very different way. While they lived in the same community as their parents and family relations, they were separated from significant people and key relationships that were critically important for providing meaning and value within their Aboriginal cultural world. They were separated from obtaining that knowledge and those skills necessary to transmit cultural values to future generations.

The ability of Aboriginal culture to continue into future generations was premised on such practices as including the sharing of meals, oral traditions, ceremonies and hunting across the land. Children and young people were not simply brought up by a mother and a father. They were brought up by uncles, aunties and grandparents and by participation in social and religious occasions when they learned by watching,

Christine Choo and Brian F. McCoy

listening and participating. Once these social occasions were denied, prevented or frustrated, the beginnings of intergenerational "wounding" were introduced. The ability of a culture to socially reproduce became seriously compromised.

Notes

1 Salvado, *The Salvado Memoirs*, pp. 22, 29–34.
2 In 1848 the Catholics of the Swan River Colony numbered 337, about 1.2 percent of the population (Salvado, *The Salvado Memoirs*, p. 7).
3 For an overview of the history of the Catholic Church in the Kimberley refer to Zucker, *From Patrons to Partners*; Nailon and Huegel, *This is your Place*; Durack, *The Rock and the Sand*; Bourke, *The History of the Catholic Church in Western Australia*.
4 The terms 'mission boy' and 'mission girl' were used by missionaries to refer to Aboriginal men and women who lived on the mission under the influence of the missionaries. These included workers and those who had grown up on mission dormitories.
5 Choo, "Dormitories at Kalumburu Mission", p. 25; Choo, *Mission Girls*, pp. 83–4.
6 Zucker, *From Patrons to Partners*, pp. 16–22; Bourke, *The History of the Catholic Church*, pp. 143–5.
7 Nailon and Huegel, *This is your Place*. See also, Nailon, *Emo and San Salvador*, Vol. 1, Chapters 1–7, pp. 17–137.
8 Bourke, *The History of the Catholic Church*, pp. 146–51; Durack, *The Rock and the Sand*, Chapters 7–14, pp. 59–134; Zucker, *From Patrons to Partners*, Chapters 2 and 3, pp. 27–48.
9 According to Brigida Nailon, this woman was reported by H. V. Howe in communication with Mary Durack to have been Madam Anabia Caprio. However no further details of Nailon's source are recorded. Nailon, *Emo and San Salvador*, Vol. 1, p. 40. Durack, mentions Anabia Caprio (Filipino) and his half-caste Aboriginal wife in *The Rock and the Sand*, p. 91.
10 Father Nicholas Emo, parish priest, Broome, evidence (677–712) in *Report of the Royal Commission*, pp. 61–3.
11 For a more detailed history of the work of the Pallottines refer to Nailon, *Nothing is Wasted*; Walter, *Australia*.
12 Choo, *Mission Girls*, Chapter 5, pp. 142–71.
13 Perez, *Kalumburu*, pp. 7–12. See Choo, *Mission Girls*, pp. 64–79 & n. 31, pp 91–2, for an overview and sources on the establishment of Kalumburu.
14 McCoy, *Holding Men*, p. 50.
15 Choo, *Mission Girls*, Chapter 6, pp. 172–85.
16 Kimberley Language Resource Centre, *Moola Bulla*, p. xvi.
17 Byrne, *A Hard Road*, p. 64.
18 Alphonse Bleischwitz and Franz Huegel, "The Start of a Mission at Halls Creek in the Year 1934", compiled by W. H. van Veen, 27 November, 1995. Perth, Pallottine Archives, p. 11.
19 Worms, *Observations on the Mission Field*, p. 378.
20 Durack, *Missions in a Bypassed Land*, p. 102.
21 McCoy, *Holding Men*, p. 53.
22 Byrne, *A Hard Road*, Chapter 16, pp. 70–5.
23 Salvado, *Memoirs*, pp. 54–5.
24 Salvado, *Memoirs*, p. 69.
25 Salvado, *Memoirs*, p. 63.
26 Massam, "To Know How", pp. 44–52.

27 Esmond, "Bush to Building", pp. 14–33.

28 Choo, "Dormitories at Kalumburu Mission", p. 24; Choo, *Mission* Girls, p. 83.

29 Choo, "Dormitories at Kalumburu Mission", pp. 24–8.

30 Choo, "Conflict Between Value Systems", pp. 59–66.

31 McCoy, "They Weren't Separated", pp. 48–69.

32 G. E. Cornish, "Report", 26 August 1949 in Balgo Mission: Reports by Field Officers, Acc 1667, file no. 282/1965, State Records Office of Western Australia, p. 27.

33 Bleischwitz, "Pallottine Mission", p. 62.

34 Berndt and Berndt, "Aborigines", p. 132.

35 McCoy, *Holding Men*, p. 21.

36 *Kalumburu Diary 1953–1955.*

37 Choo, "Dormitories at Kalumburu Mission", pp. 30–2.

38 Human Rights & Equal Opportunity Commission, *Bringing Them Home.*

39 Zubrick et al., "The West Australian Aboriginal Child Health Survey", pp. 463–545.

40 Rudd, *Prime Minister's Apology.*

The Contributors

Peggy Brock is Professor of Colonial and Indigenous History at Edith Cowan University in Perth, Western Australia. She is currently completing a book about Arthur Wellington Clah. She has published extensively on Christian missions and religious change, and the intersections between colonialism and missions, including *Indigenous Peoples and Religious Change* (Brill, 2005).

Christine Choo is a historian and social worker who has published widely on race and gender issues. Her publications include *Aboriginal Child Poverty* (1990), *Mission Girls* (2001), and *History and Native Title* (2003), a co-edited volume of Studies in Western Australian History. She is an Honorary Research Fellow at the University of Western Australia.

Joanna Cruickshank is a lecturer in History at Deakin University. She has published on eighteenth-century evangelicalism in Britain and Aboriginal missions in Australia. Her book, *Passion, Pain and Faith: Revisiting the Place of Charles Wesley in Early Methodism*, is forthcoming in 2009.

Elizabeth Elbourne is an Associate Professor in the Department of History, McGill University, Canada. Past publications include: *Blood Ground: Colonialism, Missions and the Contest for Christianity in Britain and the Eastern Cape, 1799–1853* (2002). More recent work has included articles stemming from her current project on humanitarian networks and debates over the status of indigenous peoples in the white settler empire between the late eighteenth and early nineteenth centuries.

Emeritus Professor Norman Etherington was educated at Yale University and appointed to the Chair of History at the University of Western Australia in 1989. He holds an honorary appointment to the History Department at the University of South Africa. The author of nine books and more than fifty articles and book chapters, he is a Fellow of the Academy of the Social Sciences in Australia, a past President of the Australian Historical Association, a Fellow of the Royal Geographical and Royal Historical Societies of the UK, and member of the Council of the Heritage Council of Western Australia. His most recent, *Mapping Colonial Conquest: Australia and Southern Africa*, was published by the University of Western Australia Press in 2007.

Helen Gardner is a senior lecturer at Deakin University, Melbourne, Australia. Her recent book, *Gathering for God: George Brown in Oceania*, explored the expansion and reception of Methodist missions in the Pacific in the nineteenth century. She has published on the Pacific Islander engagement with Christianity and anthropology in nineteenth-century Oceania and is now embarking on a project on the relationship between church and state in post-independence Melanesia.

Patricia Grimshaw is a Professorial Fellow in the School of Historical Studies at the University of Melbourne, Australia. Her teaching and research interests have focussed on colonialism, women and gender in Australian and the Pacific. She is author of *Paths of Duty: American Missionary Wives in Nineteenth Century Hawai'i* (1989). Recent books include the co-*authored Equal Subjects, Unequal Rights: Indigenous Peoples in British Settler Colonies 1830–1910* (2003), and the co-edited, *Collisions of Cultures and Identities: Settlers and Indigenous Peoples* (2006); *Britishness Abroad: Transnational Movements and Imperial Culture*s (2007); and *Evangelists of Empire? Missionaries in Colonial History* (2008).

Felicity Jensz is a Post-doctoral Fellow at the Cluster of Excellence for Religion and Politics at the Westfälische Wilhelms-Universität Münster, Germany. She is currently working on a transnational study of German missionaries in nineteenth century colonial environments. She has a forthcoming book on Moravian Missionaries in Australia to be published by Brill.

Brian McCoy is a Jesuit priest and medical anthropologist and has lived and worked in a number of Aboriginal and Torres Strait Islander communities within Australia over more than three decades. He witnessed the end of the dormitory system in the Northern Territory and the Kimberley in the 1970s. He returned to complete a PhD at the University of Melbourne in 2003 based on the health and lives of desert men he had known for many years. This research work was published as *Holding Men: Kanyirninpa and the Health of Aboriginal Men* (2008).

Andrew May is Associate Professor in Australian History in the School of Historical Studies at The University of Melbourne. He is the author of a number of volumes of urban history including *Melbourne Street Life* (Australian Scholarly Publishing, 1998), and he was co-editor of *The Encyclopedia of Melbourne* (Cambridge University Press, 2005) and *Evangelists of Empire? Missionaries in Colonial History* (2008). His contribution to this volume anticipates a book-length study of Welsh missionaries and British imperialism in north-east India, forthcoming with Manchester University Press.

Elizabeth E. Prevost is Assistant Professor of History at Grinnell College, Iowa, United States. Her chapter in this volume is drawn from a full-length study of women's missionary encounters in colonial Africa and the impact of foreign missions on British feminism, forthcoming with Oxford University Press. She has also published articles with the *Journal of British Studies* and *History Compass*.

Myra Rutherdale is a member of the Department of History at York University in

The Contributors

Toronto, Canada. She is the author of *Women and the White Man's God: Gender and Race in the Canadian Mission Field* (2002), and co-editor of *Contact Zones: Aboriginal and Settler Women In Canada's Colonial Past* (2005).

Jane Samson is Professor and Associate Chair of the Department of History and Classics at the University of Alberta in Canada. Her research interests include British missionary ethnography and linguistics, naval encounters with Pacific peoples, and Victorian collectors of Pacific material culture. Her latest book, *Race and Redemption: Missionary Anthropology in the South Pacific*, is forthcoming with Eerdmans.

Angela Wanhalla is a lecturer in the Department of History and Art History at the University of Otago, New Zealand. Her research focuses on gender, race and colonialism in nineteenth-century New Zealand, the indigenous history of the North American West, and the history of intimacy, focusing on interracial relationships and hybridity. Her first book, *In/Visible Sight: the Mixed Descent Families of Southern New Zealand*, will be published by Bridget Williams Books in 2009.

Consolidated Bibliography

Abel, Kerry, *Drum Songs: Glimpses of Dene History*, Montreal and Kingston: McGill–Queen's University Press, 1993.

Anderson, Atholl, *Race Against Time*, Dunedin: Hocken Library, 1991.

Anderson, Warwick, *The Cultivation of Whiteness: Science, Health, and Racial Destiny in Australia*, Melbourne: Melbourne University Press, 2006.

Austen, Alvyn, and Jamie Scott, eds, *Canadian Missions, Indigenous Peoples: Representing Religion at Home and Abroad*, Toronto: University of Toronto Press, 2005.

Backhouse, Constance, *Colour-Coded: A Legal History of Racism in Canada, 1900–1950*, Toronto: University of Toronto Press, 1999.

Bagster, Samuel, *The Bible of Every Land*, London: Samuel Bagster and Sons, 1851.

Ballantyne, A. J., "The Reform of the Heathen Body: CMS Missionaries, Maori and Sexuality", In *When the Waves Rolled in Upon Us: Essays in Nineteenth-Century Maori History*, edited by Michael Reilly and Jane Thomson, Dunedin: Otago University Press, 1999.

Ballantyne, Tony, *Orientalism and Race: Aryanism in the British Empire*, New York: Palgrave Macmillan, 2002.

Ballhatchet, Kenneth, *Race, Sex and Class Under the Raj: Imperial Attitudes and Policies and their Critics, 1793–1905*, London: Weidenfield and Nicolson, 1980.

Bareh, Hamlet, *The History and Culture of the Khasi People*, Guwahati: Spectrum Publications, 1985.

Barry, Amanda, Joanna Cruickshank, Andrew Brown-May, and Patricia Grimshaw, eds, *Evangelists of Empire? Missionaries in Colonial History*, Melbourne: eScholarship Resource Centre, 2008.

Bayly, C. A., *Empire and Information: Intelligence Gathering and Social Communication in India, 1780–1870*, Cambridge: Cambridge University Press, 1996.

Bebbington, D. W., *Evangelicalism in Modern Britain: A History from the 1730s to the 1980s* London: Unwin Hyman, 1989.

Beidelman, T. O., "Altruism and Domesticity: Images of Missionizing Women Among the CMS in Nineteenth Century East Africa", In *Gendered Missions: Women and Men in Missionary Discourse and Practice*, edited by Mary Taylor Huber and Nancy C. Lutkehaus, Ann Arbor: University of Michigan Press, 1999, pp. 113–43.

Belcher, Joseph, *The First Hindoo Convert: A Memoir of Krishna Pal, a Preacher of the Gospel to his Countrymen more than Twenty Years*, Philadelphia: American Baptist Publication Society, 1852.

Bell, Diane, *Ngarrindjeri Wurruwarrin: A World that Is, Was, and Will Be*, Melbourne: Spinifex, 1998.

Bennett, John and Susan Rowley, *Uqalurait: An Oral History of Nunavut*, Kingston: McGill–Queen's University Press, 2004.

Berndt, Catherine H., and Ronald M. Berndt, "Aborigines", In *Socialisation in Australia*, edited by F. J. Hunt, Sydney: Angus and Robertson, 1972.

Consolidated Bibliography

Berndt, Catherine H., and Ronald M. Berndt, *A World that Was: The Yaruldi of the Murray River and the Lakes, South Australia*, Melbourne: Melbourne University Press at the Miegunyah Press, 1987.

Biggs, Bruce, *Maori Marriage: An Essay in Reconstruction*, Wellington: Polynesian Society, 1960.

Binney, Judith, *The Legacy of Guilt: a Life of Thomas Kendall*, Auckland: Oxford University Press, 1968.

Binney, Judith, "Whatever Happened to Poor Mr Yate?", *New Zealand Journal of History*, vol. 9, no. 2, 1975, pp. 111–25.

Binney, Judith, *The Legacy of Guilt: A Life of Thomas Kendall*, Second ed., Wellington: Bridget Williams Books, 2005.

Binney, Judith, "'In-Between' Lives: Studies from within a Colonial Society", In *Disputed Histories: Imagining New Zealand's Pasts*, edited by T. Ballantyne and B. Moloughney, Dunedin: Otago University Press, 2006, pp. 93–118.

Bhattacharjee, Jayanta Bhusan, "Social and Religious Reform Movements in Meghalaya in Nineteenth and Twentieth Centuries: Khasi and Jaintia Hills", In *Social and Religious Reform Movements in the Nineteenth and Twentieth Centuries*, edited by S. P. Sen, Calcutta: Institute of Historical Studies, 1979, pp. 448–83.

Birtwhistle, Allen, *In His Armour: The Life of John Hunt of Fiji*, London: Cargate Press, 1954.

Bloemen, Shantha, "The Impact of the American Zulu Mission in Natal from 1890 to 1910", Unpublished Honours Thesis, University of Western Australia, Perth, 1992.

Bolt, Clarence, *Thomas Crosby and the Tsimshian: Small Shoes for Feet Too Large*, Vancouver: University of British Columbia Press, 1992.

Bourke, D. F., *The History of the Catholic Church in Western Australia*, Perth: Archdiocese of Perth [Vanguard Press], 1979.

Bowes, John P., "The Gnadenhutten Effect: Moravian Converts and the Search for Safety in the Canadian Borderlands", *Michigan Historical Review*, vol. 34, no. 1, 2008, 101–17.

Bowie, Fiona and Deborah Kirkwood, eds, *Women and Missions: Past and Present: Anthropological and Historical Perceptions*, Oxford: Berg Publishers, 1993.

Brain, J. B., *Catholics in Natal*, Durban: Archdiocese of Durban, 1982.

Brickell, Chris, *Mates and Lovers: A History of Gay New Zealand*, Auckland: Random House, 2008.

Bringing Them Home: Report of the National Inquiry into the Separation of Aboriginal and Torres Strait Islander Children from their Families, Canberra: Human Rights and Equal Opportunity Commission, 1997.

Brock, Peggy, "Building Bridges, Politics and Religion in a First Nations Community", *Canadian Historical Review*, vol. 24, no. 2 (June), 2000, pp. 159–79.

Brock, Peggy, ed., *Indigenous Peoples and Religious Change*, Leiden: Brill, 2005.

Broome, Richard, *Aboriginal Australians: Black Responses to White Dominance, 1788–2001* Sydney: Allen & Unwin, 2002.

Broome, Richard, *Aboriginal Victorians: A History Since 1800*, Crows Nest: Allen & Unwin, 2005.

Brouwer, Ruth Compton, *New Women for God: Canadian Presbyterian Women and India Missions, 1876–1914*, Toronto: University of Toronto Press, 1990.

Brown, George, "Notes on the Duke of York Group, New Britain and New Ireland", *Journal of the Royal Geographical Society*, vol. 47, 1877, pp, 137–50.

Brown, George, *George Brown, D. D. Pioneer Missionary and Explorer*, London: Hodder and Stoughton, 1908.

Brown, G., *Melanesians and Polynesians, Their Life Histories Described and Compared*, First published 1910 ed, New York: Benjamin Blom, 1972.

Brown, Judith M. and William Roger Louis, eds, *The Twentieth Century*, Vol. IV, The Oxford History of the British Empire, Oxford: Oxford University Press, 1999.

Brown-May, Andrew, "Collision and Reintegration in a Missionary Landscape: The View from the Khasi Hills, India", In *Collisions of Cultures and Identities: Settlers and Indigenous Peoples* edited by Patricia Grimshaw and Russell McGregor, Melbourne: History Department, University of Melbourne, 2006, p. 141–61.

Burton, J. W., *A Hundred Years in Fiji*, London: Epworth Press, 1936.

Byrne, Francis, *A Hard Road: Brother Frank Nissl, 1888–1980: A Life of Service to the Aborigines of the Kimberleys*, Nedlands: Tara House Publishing, 1989.

Carey, Hilary M., "Companions in the Wilderness? Missionary Wives in Colonial Australia, 1788–1900", *Journal of Religious History*, vol. 19, no. 2, 1995, pp. 227–48.

Carey, Hilary, ed, *Empires of Religion*, London: Palgrave, 2008.

Carey, S. Pearce, *William Carey D. D., Fellow of the Linnaean Society*, London: Hodder and Stoughton Limited, 1924.

Carey, William, *An Enquiry into the Obligations of Christians, to use Means for the Conversion of the Heathens*, Leicester: Ann Ireland, 1792.

Carter, David J., *Where The Wind Blows . . . A History of the Anglican Diocese of Calgary, 1888–1968*, Calgary: Anglican Dioscese of Calgary, 1968.

Chesterman, John and Brian Galligan, *Citizens Without Rights: Aborigines and Australian Citizenship*, Cambridge: Cambridge University Press, 1997.

Choo, Christine, "Conflict Between Value Systems: Marriage Laws and the Drysdale River Mission in the 1940s", *New Norcia Studies*, vol. 2, 1994, pp. 59–66.

Choo, Christine, *Mission Girls: Aboriginal Women on Catholic Missions in the Kimberley, Western Australia, 1900–1950*, Crawley: University of Western Australia Press, 2001.

Choo, Christine, "Dormitories at Kalumburu Mission, 1908–1962," *New Norcia Studies*, vol. 16, 2008, pp. 23–34.

Christophers, Brett, *Positioning the Missionary: John Booth Good and the Confluence of Cultures in Nineteenth-Century British Columbia*, Vancouver: University of British Columbia Press, 1998.

Chuchiak IV, John F., "The Sins of the Fathers: Franciscan Friars, Parish Priests, and the Sexual Conquest of the Yucatec Maya, 1545–1808", *Ethnohistory*, vol. 54, no. 1, 2007, pp. 69–127.

Coates, Ken S., *Best Left as Indians: Native-White Relations in the Yukon Territory, 1840–1973*, Montreal & Kingston: McGill–Queen's University Press, 1991.

Codrington, R, *A Sermon Preached at St Paul's Cathedral Church Auckland NZ, on the Occasion of the Ordination of George Sarawia*, Auckland: Upton and Co, 1873.

Codrington, Robert, "Religious Beliefs and Practices in Melanesia", *The Journal of the Anthropological Institute of Great Britain and Ireland*, vol. 10, 1881, pp. 261–316.

Codrington, Robert, *The Melanesians. Studies in their Anthropology and Folk-Lore*, Oxford: Clarendon Press, 1891.

Codrington, Robert and J. Palmer, *A Dictionary of the Language of Mota*, London: Society for Promoting Christian Knowledge, 1896.

Cody, H. A., *An Apostle of the North: Memoirs of the Right Reverend William Carpenter Bompas*, Reprint of 1908 ed., Edmonton: University of Alberta Press, 2002.

Colenso, J. W., *Church Missions Among the Heathen in the Diocese of Natal*, London, n.d.

Colenso, William, "Contributions towards a Better Knowledge of the Maori Race", *Transactions and Proceedings of the Royal Society of New Zealand*, vol. 11, 1878, pp. 77–106.

Colley, Linda, *Captives: Britain, Empire and the World, 1600–1850*, London: Jonathan Cape, 2002.

Consolidated Bibliography

Collison, Henry William, *In the Wake of the War Canoe: A Stirring Record of Forty Years' Successful Labour, Peril and Adventure Amongst the Savage Tribes of the Pacific Coast, and the Piratical Head-Hunting Haida of the Queen Charlotte Islands, British Columbia*, edited by Charles Lilliard, Victoria, BC: Sono Nis Press, 1981.

Comaroff, Jean, and John Comaroff, *Of Revelation and Revolution: Christianity, Colonialism and Consciousness in South Africa*, Vol. 1 and 2, Chicago: University of Chicago Press, 1991, 1999.

Coombes, Annie, *Reinventing Africa. Museums, Material Culture and Popular Imagination in Late Victorian and Edwardian England*, New Haven: Yale University Press, 1994.

Cottier, Jeanette, "Elizabeth Fairburn/Colenso: Her Times", Masters Thesis, Victoria University of Wellington, Wellington, 2000.

Cox, Jeffrey, *The British Missionary Enterprise Since 1700*, London: Routledge, 2008.

Crais, Clifton, *White Supremacy and Black Resistance in Pre-industrial South Africa* Cambridge: Cambridge University Press, 1992.

Cruickshank, Joanna, "'To exercise a beneficial influence over a man': Marriage, Gender and the Native Institutions in Early Colonial Australia", In *Evangelists of Empire? Missionaries in Colonial History*, edited by Amanda Barry, Joanna Cruickshank, Andrew Brown-May and Patricia Grimshaw, Melbourne: eScholarship Resource Centre, 2008.

Dawson, Graham, *Soldier Heroes: British Adventure, Empire and the Imagining of Masculinities*, London: Routledge, 1994.

de Gruchy, Steve, "The Alleged Political Conservatism of Robert Moffat", In *The London Missionary Society in Southern Africa: Historical Essays in Celebration of the Bicentenary of the London Missionary Society in Southern Africa, 1799–1999*, edited by John de Gruchy, Cape Town: David Philip, 1999, pp. 17–36.

de Kock, Leon, *Civilizing Barbarians: Missionary Narrative and African Textual Response in Nineteenth-Century South Africa*, Johannesburg: Witwatersrand University Press, 1996.

de Santis, Solange, "Team Translates Bible Into Inukitut, Anglican Journal", <http://www.anglicanjournal.com/issues/2002/128/jun/06/article/team-translates-bible-into-inukitut/>, access date: 20 November.

Dening, Greg, *Islands and Beaches. Discourse on a Silent Land. Marquesas 1774–1880*, Honolulu: University of Hawai'i Press, 1980.

Dieffenbach, Ernst, *Travels in New Zealand*, Christchurch: Capper Press, 1974.

Dkhar, E. Weston, *Primary Education in the Khasi and Jaintia Hills*, Shillong: Sevenhut Enterprise, 1993.

Dunae, Patrick A., "Boys' Literature and the Idea of Empire, 1870–1914", *Victorian Studies*, vol. 24, Autumn 1980.

Duncan, William, *Metlakatlah: Ten Years' Work Among the Tsimshean Indians*, London: Church Missionary Society, 1869.

Durack, Mary, *Missions in a Bypassed Land*, Wirrimanu, Kutjungka Catholic Parish Archives Balgo, 1960.

Durack, Mary, *The Rock and the Sand*, London: Constable, 1969.

Durrad, W. J., *The Attitude of the Church to the Suqe*, Melanesian Mission Occasional Papers No. 1, Norfolk Island: Melanesian Mission Society, 1920.

Dutta, Promatha Nath, *Impact of the West on the Khasis and Jaintias: A Survey of Political, Economic and Social Changes*, New Delhi: Cosmo Publications, 1982.

DuVernet, Bishop Frederick, "News From the Front: Diocese of Caledonia", *Across the Rockies*, October 1911, p. 51.

Edmond, Rod, *Representing the South Pacific: Colonial Discourse from Cook to Gauguin*, Cambridge: Cambridge University Press, 1997.

Elbourne, Elizabeth, *Blood Ground: Colonialism, Missions and the Contest for Christianity in the Cape Colony and Britain, 1799–1853*, Montreal: McGill–Queen's University Press, 2002.

Elbourne, Elizabeth, "Word Made Flesh: Christianity, Modernity and Cultural Colonialism in the Work of Jean and John Comaroff", *American Historical Review*, vol. 108, 2003.

Elbourne, Elizabeth, "Robert Moffat", In *Dictionary of National Biography*, Oxford: Oxford University Press, 2004.

Elbourne, Elizabeth, "African Missionary Wives in the London Missionary Society in Nineteenth-Century Southern Africa: Negotiating Race and Gender", In *Groupe d'étude sur l'histoire de l'Amérique symposium; Les Rencontres Coloniales / Colonial Encounters*, University of Montreal: Unpublished paper, May 2006.

Encyclopedia of Wales, "Jones, Thomas (1810–1849) Missionary", In *The Welsh Academy Encyclopedia of Wales*, edited by John Davies, Nigel Jenkins, Menna Baines and Peredur I. Lynch, Cardiff: University of Wales Press, 2008, p. 433.

Erlank, Natasha, "'Raising up the Degraded Daughters of Africa': The Provision of Education for Xhosa Women in the Mid-Nineteenth Century", *South African Historical Journal*, vol. 43, 2000, pp. 24–38.

Erlank, Natasha, "Sexual Misconduct and Church Power on Scottish Mission Stations in Xhosaland, South Africa, in the 1840s", *Gender & History*, vol. 15, no. 1, 2003, 69–84.

Errington, F. and D. Gewertz, *Articulating Change in the "Last Unknown"*, Boulder: Westview Press, 1995.

Esmond, Ian, "Bush to Building: The First Aboriginal Cottages at New Norcia", *New Norcia Studies*, vol. 15, 2007, pp. 14–33.

Etherington, Norman, *Preachers, Peasants and Politics in Southeast Africa, 1835–1880* London: Royal Historical Society, 1978.

Etherington, Norman, "Natal and Zululand from Earliest Times to 1910, A New History", In *Christianity and African Society*, edited by A. Duminy and B. Guest, Pietermaritzburg: University of Natal Press, 1989, pp. 294–5.

Etherington, Norman, "Missions and Empire", In *Historiography*, edited by Robin W. Winks, Oxford: Oxford University Press, 1999.

Etherington, Norman, *Great Treks: The Transformation of South Africa, 1815–1854*, London: Longmans, 2001.

Etherington, Norman, "The Missionary Writing Machine in Nineteenth-Century Kwazulu-Natal", in *Mixed Messages. Materiality, Textuality, Missions*, edited by Jamie S. Scott and Gareth Griffiths, New York: Palgrave Macmillan, 2005, pp. 37–50.

Etherington, Norman, ed., *Missions and Empire*, Oxford: Oxford University Press, 2005.

Evans, Julie, Patricia Grimshaw, David Philips, and Shurlee Swain, *Equal Subjects, Unequal Rights: Indigenous Peoples in British Settler Colonies, 1830–1910*, Manchester, New York: Manchester University Press, 2003.

Fanon, Frantz, *The Wretched of the Earth*, Harmondsworth, Middlesex: Penguin Books, 1967.

Fitzgerald, Tanya, "Jumping the Fences: Maori Women's Resistance to Missionary Schooling in Northern New Zealand, 1823–1835", *Paedagogica Historica*, vol. 37, no. 1, 2001, pp. 175–92.

Fleming, Archibald Lang, *Archibald the Arctic*, New York: Appleton, 1956.

Frankenberg, Ruth, *White Women/Race Matters: The Social Construction of Whiteness*, Minneapolis, Minnesota: University of Minnesota Press, 1993.

Frankenberg, Ruth, ed., *Displacing Whiteness: Essays in Social and Cultural Criticism*, Durham and London: Duke University Press, 1997.

Consolidated Bibliography

Frykenberg, R. E., "Christian Missions and the Raj", In *Missions and Empire*, edited by Norman Etherington, Oxford: Oxford University Press, 2005, pp. 126–8.

Galois, R. M., "Colonial Encounters: The Worlds of Arthur Wellington Clah", *BC Studies*, vol. 115 and 116, 1997/1998.

Gardner, Helen Bethea, *Gathering for God: George Brown in Oceania*, Dunedin: University of Otago Press, 2006.

Gardner, Helen Bethea, "'The Origin of Kinship in the Pacific': Lewis Henry Morgan and Lorimer Fison", *Oceania*, vol. 78, 2008, pp. 137–51.

Gardner, Helen Bethea, "The Faculty of Faith: Evangelical Missionaries Social Anthropology and the Claim for Human Unity", In *Foreign Bodies: Oceania and the Science of Race, 1750–1940*, edited by B. Douglas and C. Ballard, Canberra: ANU E-Press, 2008, pp. 259–82.

Ghosh-Schellhorn, Martina, "Flocking to the Colonised Mission: Welsh Encounters of the Khasi Kind", In *Colonies, Missions, Cultures*, edited by Gerhard Stiltz, Tübingen: Stauffenberg, 2001, p. 141.

Gifford, Paul, *The Christian Churches and the Democratization of Africa*, Leiden: Brill, 1995.

Graham, Elizabeth, *Medicine Man to Missionary: Missionaries as Agents of Change among the Indians of Southern Ontario, 1784–1867*, Toronto: Peter Martin, 1975.

Grant, John Webster, *Moon of Wintertime: Missionaries and Indians of Canada in Encounter since 1534*, Toronto: University of Toronto Press, 1984.

Grimshaw, Patricia, *Paths of Duty: American Missionary Wives in Nineteenth-Century Hawaii*, Honolulu: University of Hawaii Press, 1989.

Grimshaw, Patricia, "Faith, Missionary Life, and the Family", In *Gender and Empire*, edited by Philippa Levine, Oxford: Oxford University Press, 2004.

Grimshaw, Patricia, and Russell McGregor, eds, *Collisions of Cultures and Identities: Settlers and Indigenous Peoples*, Melbourne: RMIT Publishing, 2006.

Grimshaw, Patricia, and Peter Sherlock, "Women and Cultural Exchanges", In *Missions and Empire*, edited by Norman Etherington, Oxford: Oxford University Press, 2005, pp. 173–93.

Gunn, Mary, and L. E. Codd, *Botanical Exploration of Southern Africa*, Cape Town: A.A. Balkema for the Botanical Research Institute, 1981.

Gunson, Niel, *Messengers of Grace: Evangelical Missionaries in the South Seas, 1797–1860*, Melbourne: Oxford University Press, 1978.

Gunson, Niel, "British Missionaries and their Contribution to Science in the Pacific Islands", In *Darwin's Laboratory: Evolutionary Theory and Natural History in the Pacific*, edited by R. and P. F. Rehbock MacLeod, Honolulu: University of Hawaii Press, 1994, pp. 283–317.

Haebich, Anna, *For Their Own Good: Aborigines and Government in the Southwest of Western Australia, 1900–1940*, Perth: University of Western Australia Press, 1988.

Haggis, Jane, and Margaret Allen, "Imperial Emotions: Affective Communities of Mission in British Protestant Women's Missionary Publications c. 1880–1920", *Journal of Social History*, vol. 41, no. 3, 2008, pp. 691–716.

Hall, Catherine, *Civilising Subjects: Colony and Metropole in the English Imagination*, Chicago: University of Chicago Press, 2002.

Hamilton, Carolyn, ed., *The Mfecane Aftermath: Reconstructive Debates in Southern African History*, Johannesburg: Witwatersrand Press, 1995.

Hansen, Holger Bernt, *Mission, Church and State in a Colonial Setting: Uganda 1890–1925*, London: Heinemann, 1984.

Hanson, Holly, "Queen Mothers and Good Government in Buganda: The Loss of Women's Political Power in Nineteenth-Century East Africa", in *Women in African Colonial Histories*, edited by Jean Allman et al., Bloomington, IN: Indiana University Press, 2002, pp. 219–36.

Harrison, John, "Missions, Fisheries and Government in Far North Queensland, 1891–1919", Honours Thesis, University of Queensland, 1974.

Hassé, E. R., *Women's Work in the Foreign Missions of the Moravian Church: Paper Read at the Free Church Council March 9th, 1879*, Ashton-under-Lyne: Griffin & Sheard, 1897.

Haweis, Thomas, "The Very Probable Success of a Proper Mission to the South Sea Islands", *The Evangelical Magazine*, vol. 3, July 1795, pp. 262–70.

Herbert, Christopher, *Culture and Anomie. Ethnographic Imagination in the Nineteenth Century*, Chicago: Chicago University Press, 1991.

Heuer, Berys, "Maori Women in Traditional Family and Tribal Life, 1769–1840", *Journal of the Polynesian Society*, vol. 78, no. 4, 1969, pp. 448–94.

Hilliard, David, *God's Gentlemen: A History of the Melanesian Mission 1849–1942*, St Lucia: University of Queensland Press, 1978.

Hodgson, Dorothy L., *The Church of Women: Gendered Encounters Between Maasai and Missionaries*, Bloomington: Indiana University Press, 2005.

Howard, Basil, *Rakiura: A History of Stewart Island, New Zealand*, Dunedin: Reed, 1940.

Huber, Mary Taylor, and Nancy Lutkehaus, "Introduction: Gendered Missions at Home and Abroad", in *Gendered Missions: Women and Men in Missionary Discourse and Practice*, edited by Mary Taylor and Nancy Lutkehaus, Ann Arbor: University of Michigan Press, 1999.

Huber, Mary Taylor, and Nancy Lutkehaus, eds, *Gendered Missions: Women and Men in Missionary Discourse and Practice*, Ann Arbor: University of Michigan Press, 1999.

Hunt, Nancy Rose, *A Colonial Lexicon of Birth Ritual, Medicalization and Mobility in the Congo*, Durham: Duke University Press, 1999.

Hunter, Jane, *The Gospel of Gentility: American Women Missionaries in Turn-of-the-Century China*, New Haven: Yale University Press, 1984.

Hyslop, Jonathan, "Making Scotland in South Africa: Charles Murray, the Transvaal's Aberdeenshire Poet", in *Colonial Lives Across the British Empire: Imperial Careering in the Long Nineteenth Century*, edited by David Lambert and Alan Lester, Cambridge: Cambridge University Press, 2006.

Jackson, Eleanor, "From Krishna Pal to Lal Behari Dey: Indian Builders of the Church in Bengal, 1800–1894", In *Converting Colonialism: Visions and Realities in Mission History, 1706–1914* edited by Dana L. Robert, Grand Rapids, Cambridge: William B. Eerdmans Publishing Company, 2007, pp. 166–205.

James, Louis, "Tom Brown's Imperialist Sons", *Victorian Studies*, vol. 17, September 1973, pp. 89–99.

Jenkins, G., *Conquest of the Ngarrindjeri: The Story of the Lower Lakes Tribes*, Adelaide: Rigby, 1979.

Jensz, Felicity, "Writing the Lake Boga failure", *Traffic*, vol. 3, 2003, 147–61.

Jensz, Felicity, *Influential Strangers: German Moravian Missionaries in the British Colony of Victoria, 1848–1908*, Leiden: Brill, forthcoming.

John Hughes Morris, *The History of the Welsh Calvinistic Methodists' Foreign Mission to the End of the Year 1904*, Vol. first published 1910, New Delhi: Indus Publishing Company, 1996.

Johnson, M. E., *Dayspring in the Far West: Sketches of Mission-work in North-west America*, London: Seeley, Jackson and Halliday, 1875.

Johnston, Anna, *Missionary Writing and Empire, 1800–1860*, Cambridge: Cambridge University Press, 2003.

Consolidated Bibliography

Jones, P., "Unaipon, James (c. 1835–1907)", In *Australian Dictionary of Biography*, Melbourne: Melbourne University Press, 2005, p. 389.

Jyrwa, J. Fortis, *The Wondrous Works of God: a Study on the Growth and Development of the Khasi-Jaintia Presbyterian Church in the 20th Century*, Shillong: M. B. Jyrwa, 1980.

Keegan, Timothy, ed., *Moravians in the Eastern Cape, 1828–1928: Four Accounts of Moravian Mission Work on the Eastern Cape Frontier* Paarl: Paarl Print, 2004.

Kelm, Mary-Ellen, *Colonizing Bodies: Aboriginal Health and Healing in British Columbia, 1900–50*, Vancouver: University of British Columbia Press, 1998.

Kendall, Thomas, *A Grammar and Vocabulary of the Language of New Zealand*, London: Church Missionary Society, 1820.

Kharakor, Philomena, *Biblical Influence on Pre-Independence Khasi Literature*, New Delhi: Scholar Publishing House, 1998.

Kimberley Language Resource Centre, *Moola Bulla: In the Shadow of the Mountain*, Broome: Mugabula Books, 1996.

Krige, Sue, "Segregation, Science and Commissions of Enquiry: The Contestation over Native Education Policy in South Africa, 1930–36", *Journal of Southern African Studies*, vol. 23, no. 3, 1997, pp. 491–506.

Krige, Sue, "'Trustees and Agents of the State'? Missions and the Formation of Policy towards African Education, 1910–1920", *South African Historical Journal*, vol. 40, 1999, pp. 74–94.

Kuper, Adam, "The Death of Piet Retief", *Social Anthropology*, vol. 4, no. 2, 1996, pp. 133–43.

Landau, Paul Stuart, *The Realm of the Word: Language, Gender, and Christianity in a Southern African Kingdom*, London: Heinemann, 1995.

Langmore, Diane, *Missionary Lives: Papua 1874–1914*, Honolulu: University of Hawaii Press, 1989.

LaTrobe, B., *The Moravian Missions. A Glance at 164 Years of Unbroken Missionary Labours* London: Norman and Sons, 1896.

Latukefu, Sione and Ruta Sinclair, "Pacific Islanders as International Missionaries: Papua New Guinea and Solomon Islands", in *Polynesian Missions in Melanesia from Samoa, Cook Islands and Tonga to Papua New Guinea and New Caledonia*, edited by Ron and Marjorie Crocombe, Suva: University of the South Pacific, 1982.

Laugrand, Frederick et. al., eds, *Apostle To The Inuit: The Journals and Ethnographic Notes of Edmund James Peck The Baffin Years, 1894–1905*, Toronto: University of Toronto Press, 2006.

Lester, Alan, and David Lambert, "Missionary Politics and the Captive Audience: William Shewsbury in the Caribbean and the Cape Colony", in *Colonial Lives Across the British Empire: Imperial Careering in the Long Nineteenth Century*, edited by David Lambert and Alan Lester, Cambridge: Cambridge University Press, 2006, pp. 88–113.

Libbey, John, *The Missionary Character and the Foreign Mission Work of the Church of the United Brethren (of Moravians)*, Dubline: Moravian Church Dublin, 1869.

Lillard, Charles, ed., *In the Wake of the War Canoe: William Henry Collison*, Reprint of 1915, ed., Victoria: Sono Nis Press, 1981.

Lillard, Charles, *Warriors of the North Pacific: Missionary Accounts of the Northwest Coast, the Skeena and the Stikine Rivers and the Klondike, 1829–1900*, Victoria: Sono Nis Press, 1984.

Lindstrom, L., "Doctor, Lawyer, Wiseman, Priest: Big-Men and Knowledge in Melanesia", *Man*, vol. 19, 1984, pp. 291–309.

Linn, R., *A Diverse Land: A History of the Lower Murray Lakes and Coorong*, Meningie: Meningie Historical Society, 1988.

Love, J. H., "Love, James Robert Beattie (1889–1947)", in *Australian Dictionary of Biography*, 150–1.

Low, D. A., ed., *The Mind of Buganda: Documents of the Modern History of an African Kingdom*, Berkeley: University of California, 1971.

Lubbock, J., *The Origin of Civilisation*, Chicago: University of Chicago Press, 1978 [1st published 1870].

Macdonald, Charlotte, Merimeri Penfold and Bridget Williams, eds, *The Book of New Zealand Women*, Wellington: Bridget Williams Books, 1993.

Macdonald, Daniel, *The Oceanic Languages: Their Grammatical Structure, Vocabulary and Origin*, London: Henry Frowde, 1907.

MacDonald, George F. and John J. Cove, *Tsimshian Narratives 2*: Trade and Warfare, Ottawa: Canadian Museum of Civilization, 1987.

MacKenzie, John, *The Empire of Nature: Hunting, Conservation and British Imperialism*, Manchester: University of Manchester Press, 1988.

Madeira, Ana Isabel, "Portuguese, French and British Discourse on Colonial Education: Church-State Relations, School Expansion and Missionary Competition in Africa, 1890–1930", *Paedagogica Historica*, vol. 41, no. 1 & 2, 2005, pp. 31–60.

Marks, Shula, *Reluctant Rebellion*, Oxford: Oxford University Press, 1970.

Marsh, Donald, *Echoes from a Frozen Land*, Edited by Winifred Marsh, Edmonton: Hurtig, 1987.

Mason, John and LucyTorode, *Three Generations of the La Trobe Family in the Moravian Church*, Newtownabbey: Moravian History Magazine, 1997.

Mason, J. C. S., *The Moravian Church and the Missionary Awakening in England, 1760–1800*, Suffolk: The Boydell Press for The Royal Historical Society, 2001.

Massam, Katharine, "'To Know How to Be All For All": the Company of St Teresa of Jesus at New Norcia, 1904–1920 ", *New Norcia Studies*, vol. 15, 2007, pp. 44–52.

Mathur, P. R. G., *The Khasi of Meghalaya (Study in Tribalism and Religion)*, New Delhi: Cosmo Publications, 1979.

Maxwell, David, "Writing the History of African Christianity: Reflections of an Editor", *Journal of Religion in Africa*, vol. 36, no. 3–4, 2006, pp. 379–99.

May, Andrew, *Welsh Missionaries and British Imperialism in North-East India*, Manchester: Manchester University Press, forthcoming.

McCoy, Brian, "'They Weren't Separated': Missions, Dormitories and Generational Health", *Health and History, Journal of the Australian and New Zealand Society of the History of Medicine*, vol. 9, no. 2, 2007, pp. 48–69.

McCoy, Brian, *Holding Men: Kanyirninpa and the Health of Aboriginal Men*, Canberra: Aboriginal Studies Press, 2008.

McKenzie, Kirsten, *Scandal in the Colonies: Sydney and Capetown, 1820–1850*, Melbourne: Melbourne University Press, 2004.

McKenzie, Maisie, *The Road to Mowanjum*, Sydney: Angus and Robertson, 1969.

McKeough, Carmel, "Reluctant Defender: the Transformation of a Conservative Mission into a Liberal Political Opposition in the Colony of Natal, 1893–1910", Unpublished Honours Thesis, University of Adelaide, Adelaide, 1982.

McLoughlin, William, "Cherokees and Methodists, 1824–1834", *Church History*, vol. 50, no. 1, 1981, pp. 44–63.

Michaud, Jean, "French Missionary Expansion in Colonial Upper Tonkin", *Journal of Southeast Asian Studies*, vol. 35, no. 2, 2004, pp. 287–310.

Moffat, John Smith, *The Lives of Mary and Robert Moffat*, London: T. Fisher Unwin, 1885.

Moffat, Robert, *Missionary Labours and Scenes in Southern Africa*, London: J. Snow, 1842.

Munro, Doug and Andrew Thornley, eds, *The Covenant Makers: Islander Missionaries in the Pacific*, Suva: University of the South Pacific, 1996.

Consolidated Bibliography

Murray, Peter, *The Devil and Mr Duncan: A History of the Two Metlakatlas*, Victoria: Sono Nis Press, 1985.

Musisi, Nakanyike B., "Women, 'Elite Polygyny,' and Buganda State Formation", *Signs*, vol. 16, 1991, pp. 757–86.

Musisi, Nakanyike B., "Colonial and Missionary Education: Women and Domesticity in Uganda, 1900–1945", in *African Encounters with Domesticity*, edited by Karen Transberg Hansen, New Brunswick: Rutgers University Press, 1992, pp. 172–94.

Musisi, Nakanyike B., "Morality as Identity: the Missionary Moral Agenda in Buganda, 1877–1945", *Journal of Religious History*, vol. 23, 1999, pp. 51–74.

Musisi, Nakanyike B., "The Politics of Perception or Perception as Politics? Colonial and Missionary Representations of Baganda Women, 1900–1945", in *Women in African Colonial Histories*, edited by Jean Allman et al., Bloomington: Indiana University Press, 2002, pp. 95–115.

Nailon, Brigida, *Nothing is Wasted in the Household of God: Vincent Pallotti's Vision in Australia 1901–2001*, Richmond: Spectrum Publications, 2001.

Nailon, Brigida, *Emo and San Salvador*, Vol. 1 and 2, Echuca: Brigidine Sisters, 2004, 2005.

Nailon, Brigida, and Francis Huegel, eds, *This is your Place*, 2nd, ed, Broome: Beagle Bay Community, 2001.

Neill, Stephen, *A History of Christian Missions*, Harmondsworth: Penguin Books, 1964.

Nelson, Elizabeth, Sandra Smith and Patricia Grimshaw, eds, *Letters from Aboriginal Women of Victoria, 1867–1926*, Melbourne: Melbourne University History Monograph Series, 2002.

Newbury, Colin, ed., *The History of the Tahitian Mission, 1799–1830. With Supplementary Papers from the Correspondence of the Missionaries by John Davies*, Cambridge: Hakluyt Society, 1961.

Neylan, Susan, *The Heavens are Changing: Nineteenth-Century Protestant Missions and Tsimshian Christianity*, Montreal and Kingston: McGill–Queen's University Press, 2003.

Neylan, Susan, "Eating the Angel's Food: Arthur Wellington Clash - An Aboriginal Perspective on Being Christian, 1857–1909", in *Canadian Missionaries, Indigenous Peoples: Representing Religion at Home and Abroad*, edited by Alvyn Austin and Jamie S. Scott, Toronto: University of Toronto Press, 2005, 88–108.

Norman, B. M., "Responsible Government in Natal and the American Zulu Mission: 1893–1907", unpublished Honours Thesis, University of Kwazulu-Natal, 1982.

O'Brien, Anne, "Missionary Masculinities, the Homoerotic Gaze and the Politics of Race: Gilbert White in Northern Australia, 1885–1915", *Gender and History*, vol. 20, no. 1 (March), 2008, pp. 68–85.

O'Brien, Anne, "Saving the Empty North: Religion and Empire in Australia", in Carey, Hilary, (ed), *Empires of Religion*, London: Palgrave, 2008.

O'Hanlon, Rosalind, "Masculinity and the Bangash Nawabs of Farrukhabad", In *Bodies In Contact: Rethinking Colonial Encounters In World History*, edited by Tony Ballantyne and Antoinette Burton, Durham and London: Duke University Press, 2005, pp. 19–37.

The Oxford English Dictionary Online, Oxford University Press, <http://dictionary.oed.com/entrance.dtl>, access date: 20 November 2008.

Patterson, E. Palmer, *Mission on the Nass: The Evangelization of the Nishga, 1860–1887*, Waterloo, Ont: Eulachon Press, 1982.

Patterson, E. Palmer, "Nishga Perceptions of Their First Resident Missionary, the Reverend R. R. A. Doolan, 1864-1867", *Anthropologica*, 30, 1988, 119-135.

Patterson, E. Palmer, "Kincolith's First Decade, 1867–1878", *Canadian Journal of Native Studies*, vol. 12, no. 2, 1992, 230–50.

Pelikan, Jaroslav, *Jesus Through the Centuries: His Place in the History of Culture*, New Haven: Yale University Press, 1985.

Perez, Eugene, *Kalumburu : The Benedictine Mission and the Aborigines, 1908–1975*, Wyndham: Kalumburu Benedictine Mission, 1977.

Perry, Adele, *On the Edge of Empire: Gender, Race and the Making of British Columbia*, Toronto: University of Toronto Press, 2001.

Perry, Adele, "The Autocracy of Love and the Legitimacy of Empire: Intimacy, Power and Scandal in Nineteenth-Century Metlakahtlah", *Gender and History*, vol. 16, no. 2, 2004, pp. 261–88.

Pirouet, M. Louise, *Black Evangelists: The Spread of Christianity in Uganda, 1891–1914*, London: Collings, 1978.

Porter, Andrew, *Religion Versus Empire?: British Protestant Missionaries and Overseas Expansion, 1700–1914*, Manchester: Manchester University Press, 2004.

Porter, Frances, and Charlotte Macdonald, eds, *'My Hand Will Write What My Heart Dictates': The Unsettled Lives of Women in Nineteenth-century New Zealand as Revealed to Sisters, Family and Friends*, Auckland: Auckland University Press/Bridget Williams Books, 1996.

Porterfield, Amanda, "The Impact of Early New England Missionaries on Women's Role in Zulu Culture", *Church History*, vol. 66, no. 2, 1997, pp. 72–5.

Predelli, Line Nyhagen, "Sexual Control and the Remaking of Gender: The Attempt of Nineteenth-Century Protestant Norwegian Women to Export Western Domesticity to Madagascar", *Journal of Women's History*, vol. 12, 2000, pp. 81–103.

Prevost, Elizabeth E., *Feminizing Missions: Women's Evangelism in Colonial Africa and the British Metropole, 1865–1930*, Oxford: Oxford University Press, forthcoming.

Rafael, Vicente *Contracting Colonialism: Translation and Christian Conversion in Tagalog Society under Early Spanish Rule*, Durham: Duke University Press, 1988.

Ray, Sidney, "The Study of Melanesian Languages", *The Southern Cross Log*, vol., May 1908, pp. 176–8.

Rees, D. Ben, "Jones, Thomas (1810–1849)", in *Vehicles of Grace & Hope: Welsh Missionaries in India 1800–1970*, edited by D. Ben Rees, Pasadena: William Carey Library, 2002, pp. 100–3.

Renison, Robert John, *One Day at a Time: The Autobiography of Robert John Renison*, edited by Margaret Blackstock, Toronto: Kingswood House, 1957.

"Report from the Select Committee of the House of Lords, appointed to Inquire into the Present State of the Islands of New Zealand, and the Expediency of Regulating the Settlement of British Subjects Therein", in *Great Britain Parliamentary Papers*, 1837–40.

Report of the Royal Commission on the Condition of the Natives {Roth Report}, Perth: Government Printer, 1905.

Richling, Barnett, "'Very Serious Reflections': Inuit Dreams about Salvation and Loss in Eighteenth-Century Labrador", *Ethnohistory*, vol. 36, no. 2, 1989, 148–69.

Richter, D. Julius, *Geschichte der Berliner Missionsgesellschaft, 1824–1924*, Berlin: Verlag der Buchhandlung der Berliner ev. Missionsgesellschaft, 1924.

Riddell, Kate, "A 'Marriage of the Races'? Aspects of Intermarriage, Ideology and Reproduction on the New Zealand Frontier", Masters Thesis, Victoria University of Wellington, Wellington, 1996.

Robert, Dana L., ed., *Gospel Bearers, Gender Barriers: Missionary Women in the Twentieth Century*, Maryknoll, New York: Orbis, 2002.

Robert, Dana L., "Introduction", In *Converting Colonialism: Visions and Realities in Mission History,*

1706–1914, edited by Dana L. Robert, Grand Rapids, Michigan: William B. Eerdmans Publishing Company, 2008, 2008, pp. 1–20.

Robert, Dana L., ed., *Converting Colonialism: Visions and Realities in Mission History, 1706–1914*, Grand Rapids, Michigan: William B. Eerdmans Publishing Company, 2008.

Robert, Dana L., "The 'Christian Home' as a Cornerstone of Anglo-American Missionary Thought and Practice", In *Converting Colonialism: Visions and Realities in Mission History, 1706–1914*, edited by Dana L. Robert, Michigan, Grand Rapids:William B. Eerdmans, 2008, pp. 134–65.

Roberts, J. P., ed., *The Mapoon Story by the Mapoon People*, Fitzroy: International Development Action, 1975.

Rodman, Margaret Critchlow, "The Heart in the Archives: Colonial Contestation of Desire and Fear in the New Hebrides, 1933", *Journal of Pacific History*, vol. 38, no. 3, 2003, pp. 291–312.

Römer, H., *Die Indianer und ihr Freund David Zeisberger*, Gütersloh: C. Bertelsman, 1890.

Ropmay, Dohory, *Ka Centenary History Ka Balang Presbyterian*, Shillong, 1940.

Ross, Cathy, *Women with a Mission: Rediscovering Missionary Wives in Early New Zealand*, Auckland: Penguin, 2006.

Rudd, Kevin, "Prime Minister's Apology to Australia's Indigenous Peoples, 13 February 2008. House of Representatives, Parliament of Australia.", <http://www.pm.gov.au/media/Speech/2008/speech_0073.cfm>, access date: 16 June.

Rutherdale, Myra, *Women and the White Man's God: Gender and Race In Canada's Mission Field*, Vancouver: University of British Columbia, 2002.

Salesa, Damon, "Race Mixing: A Victorian Problem in Britain and New Zealand", PhD Thesis, Oxford University, 2000.

Salvado, Dom Rosendo (translated and edited by E. J. Storman SJ), *The Salvado Memoirs: Historical Memoirs of Australia and particularly of the Benedictine Mission of New Norcia and of the Habits and Customs of the Australian Natives*, Nedlands: University of Western Australia Press, 1977.

Samson, Jane, "Ethnology and Theology: Nineteenth-Century Mission Dilemmas in the South Pacific", In *Christian Missions and the Enlightenment*, edited by Brian Stanley, London: Curzon Press, 2001.

Samson, Jane, "Landscapes of Faith: British Missionary Tourism in the South Pacific", In *Mixed Messages: Materiality, Textuality, Mission*, edited by Jamie S. Scott and Gareth Griffiths, New York: Palgrave Macmillan, 2005, pp. 89–109.

Samson, Jane, *Race and Redemption: British Missionary Ethnography in the South Pacific*, Grand Rapids: Eerdmans, Forthcoming.

Sarawia, George, *They Came to My Island*, Siota: St. Peter's College, 1968.

Sarawia, George, *They Came to My Island*, Honiara: Church of Melanesia, Provincial Press, 1973.

Savage, David W., "Missionaries and the Development of a Colonial Ideology of Female Education in India", *Gender and History*, vol. 9, no. 2, 1997, pp. 201–21.

Schiller, Lawrence D., "The Royal Women of Buganda", *International Journal of African Historical Studies*, vol. 23, 1990, pp. 455–73.

Schneider, H. G., *Missionsarbeit der Brüdergemeine in Australien*, Gnadau: Verlag der Unitäts-Buchhandlung, 1882.

Schoeman, Karel, *A Thorn Bush that Grows in the Path: the Missionary Career of Ann Hamilton, 1817–1823*, Cape Town: South African Library, 1995.

Schultz, E., *Proverbial Expressions of the Samoans*, Wellington: The Polynesian Society, 1953.

Schulze, Adolf, *200 Jahre Brüdermission: Das zweite Missionsjahrhundert*, Vol. II, Herrnhut: Verlag der Missionsbuchhandlung, 1932.

Schütte, H., "To Pulu and his Brothers: Aspects of Societal Transition in the Bismarck Archipelago of Papua New Guinea During the 1870s and 1880s", *Journal de la Société des Océanistes*, vol. 1, no. 2, 1989, pp. 53–68.

Scott, Jamie, "Doctors Divine: Medicine, and Muscular Christianity in the Canadian Frontier Adventure Tale", In *Colonies, Missions, Cultures in the English-Speaking World: General and Comparative Studies*, edited by Gerhardt Stilz, Tübingen: Stauffenburg Verlag, 2001, pp. 13–26.

Semple, Rhonda, *Missionary Women: Gender, Professionalism and the Victorian Idea of Christian Mission*, Woodbridge: Boydell Press, 2003.

Semple, Rhonda A., "Missionary Manhood: Professionalism, Belief and Masculinity in the Nineteenth-Century Imperial Field", *Journal of Imperial and Commonwealth History*, vol. 36, no. 3, September 2008, pp. 397–415.

Singh, Maina Chawla, *Gender, Religion and 'Heathen Lands'*, New York: Garland Publishing, 2000.

Sinha, Mrinalini, *Colonial Masculinity: The 'Manly' Englishman and the 'Effeminate Bengali' in the Late Nineteenth Century*, Manchester: Manchester University Press, 1995.

Smith, George, *The Life of William Carey, D. D. Shoemaker and Missionary. Professor of Sanskrit, Bengali and Marathi in the College of Fort William, Calcutta*, London: John Murray, 1885.

Smith, Vanessa, *Literary Culture and the Pacific: Nineteenth-century Textual Encounters*, Cambridge: Cambridge University Press, 1998.

Snaitang, O. L., *Christianity and Social Change in Northeast India*, Shillong: Vendrame Institute, 1993.

Spangenberg, August Gottlieb, *Unterricht für die Brüder und Schwestern welche unter den Heiden am Evangelio dienen, Zweiter durchgesehene und vermehrte Ausgabe*, Gnadau: Verlag der Buchhandlung der Evangelischen Brüder-Unität, 1837.

Spangenberg, August Gottlieb, *Instructions for Missionaries of the Church of the Unitas Fratrum, or United Brethren. Translated from the German, 2nd (Revised and Enlarged) edn*, London: Brethren's Society for the Furtherance of the Gospel among the Heathens, 1840.

Stanley, Brian, *The Bible and the Flag: Protestant Missions and British Imperialism in the Nineteenth and Twentieth Centuries*, Leicester: Apollos, 1990.

Stanley, Brian, *Christian Missions and the Enlightenment*, Grand Rapids, Michigan: William. B. Eerdmans Publishing Company, 2001.

Stanley, Brian, "Carey, William (1761–1834)", Oxford University Press, <http://www.oxforddnb.com/view/article/4657>, access date: 9 June 2008.

Sten, H. W., *Khasi Poetry (Origin and Development)*, New Delhi: Mittal Publications, 1990.

Stevens, Kate, "Gathering Places: The Mixed Descent Families of Foveaux Strait and Rakiura/Stewart Island, 1824–1864", Honours Research Essay, University of Otago, 2008.

Stock, Eugene, *History of the Church Missionary Society, its Environment, its Men and its Work*, 4 vols, London: Church Missionary Society, 1899–1916.

Stock, Eugene, *Metlakahtla and the North Pacific Mission of the Church Missionary Society*, London: Church Missionary Society House, 1881 (2nd ed).

Stock, Eugene, "Women Missionaries in C. M. S. Fields", *Church Missionary Intelligencer and Record*, May 1894.

Stock, Harry Thomas, "A Resume of Christian Missions among the American Indians", *American Journal of Theology*, vol. 24, no. 3, 1920, pp. 368–85.

Stock, Sarah G., ed., *Story of the Year: Being the CMS Short Popular Report*, London: Church Missionary Society, 1895–1901.

Stocking, G., *Victorian Anthropology*, New York: Macmillan, 1987.

Strayer, Robert W., *The Making of Mission Communities in East Africa: Anglicans and Africans in Colonial Kenya, 1875–1935*, London: Heinemann, 1978.

Stuart, Doug, "'Of Savages and Heroes': Discourses of Race, Gender and Nation in the Evangelical Mission to Southern Africa in the Early Nineteenth Century", PhD thesis, University of London, London, 1994.

Sugirtharajah, R. S., *The Bible and Empire: Postcolonial Explorations*, Cambridge: Cambridge University Press, 2005.

Summers, Carol, "Intimate Colonialism: The Imperial Production of Reproduction in Uganda, 1907–1925", *Signs*, vol. 16, 1991, pp. 787–807.

Summers, Carol, "'If You Can Educate the Native Woman . . . ': Debates over the Schooling and Education of Girls and Women in Southern Rhodesia, 1900–1934", *History of Education Quarterly*, vol. 36, no. 4, 1996, p. 452.

Swain, Tony and Deborah Bird Rose, eds, *Aboriginal Australians and Christian Missions: Ethnographic and Historical Studies*, Bedford Park, SA: Australian Association for the Study of Religions, 1988.

Talukdar, Sharmila Das, *Khasi Cultural Resistance to Colonialism*, Guwahati, Delhi: Spectrum Publications, 2004.

Taplin, G., "Notes on a Comparative Table of Australian Languages", *Journal of the Anthropological Institute of Great Britain and Ireland*, vol. 1, 1872, pp. 84–8.

Taplin, G., *The Narrinyeri*, Adelaide: J. T. Shawyer, 1873.

Taplin, G., "The Narrinyeri", In *The Native Tribes of South Australia*, edited by J. D. Woods, Adelaide: E. S. Wigg and Son, 1879, pp. 1–156.

Taplin, G., *The Folklore, Manners, Customs and Languages of the South Australian Aborigines*, Adelaide: Government Printer, 1879.

Thorne, Susan, *Congregational Missions and the Making of an Imperial Culture in Nineteenth-Century England*, Stanford, California: Stanford University Press, 1999.

Thornley, Andrew, *Inheritance of Hope: John Hunt, Apostle of Fiji*, Suva: University of the South Pacific, 2000.

Timm, Uwe, *Deutsche Kolonien*, Köln: Kiepenheuer & Witsch, 2001.

Timoteo, Pastor. Translated by the Rev. J. E. Newell, "Notes on the Kabadi Dialect of New Guinea", *Journal of the Polynesian Society*, vol. 24, no. 6, 1897, pp. 201–8.

Tomlin, J., *Missionary Journals and Letters Written During Eleven Years' Residence and Travels Amongst the Chinese, Siamese, Javanese, Khassias, and Other Eastern Nations*, London: James Nisbet and Co., 1844.

Tosh, John, *Manliness and Masculinities in Nineteenth-Century Britain*, Harlow: Pearson, 2005.

Tremewan, Peter, "French Tupuna: French-Maori Families", in *The French and the Maori*, edited by John Dunmore, Waikanae: The Heritage Press, 1992, pp. 122–31.

Twaddle, Michael, "The Emergence of Politico-Religious Groupings in Late-19th Century Buganda", *Journal of African History*, vol. 29, 1988, pp. 81–92.

Twells, Alison, "Missionary 'Fathers' and Wayward 'Sons' in the South Pacific, 1797–1825", in *Gender and Fatherhood in the Nineteenth Century*, edited by Trev Lynn Broughton and Helen Rogers, Hampshire: Palgrave Macmillan, 2007.

Usher, Jean, *William Duncan of Metlakatla: A Victorian Missionary in British Columbia*, Publications in History no. 5, Ottawa: National Museums of Canada.

Venuti, Lawrence, *The Scandals of Translation: Towards an Ethics of Difference*, London: Routledge, 1998.

Vibert, Elizabeth, *Traders' Tales: Narratives of Cultural Encounters in the Columbian Plateau*, Norman: University of Oklahoma Press, 1997.

Vibert, Elizabeth, "Writing 'Home': Sibling Intimacy and Mobility in a Scottish Colonial Memoir", In *Moving Subjects: Gender, Mobility and Intimacy in an Age of Global Empire*, edited by Tony Ballantyne and Antoinette Burton, Chicago: University of Illinois Press, 2009.

Voisey, Paul, ed., *A Preacher's Frontier: The Castor, Alberta Letters of Rev. Martin Holdom, 1909–1912*, Calgary: Historical Society of Alberta, 1996.

Wallace, Lee, *Sexual Encounters: Pacific Texts, Modern Sexualities*, Ithaca: Cornell University Press, 2003.

Wallace, Paul A. W., "They Knew the Indian: The Men Who Wrote the Moravian Records", *Proceedings of the American Philosophical Society*, vol. 95, no. 3, 1951, 290–5.

Walls, Andrew, "British Missions", In *Missionary Ideologies in the Imperialist Era*, edited by T. Christensen and W. R. Hutchison, Copenhagen: Aros, 1982.

Walter, George, *Australia: Land, People, Mission*, Broome: Bishop of Broome, 1982.

Wanhalla, Angela, "'One White Man I Like Very Much': Intermarriage and the Cultural Encounter in Southern New Zealand, 1829–1850", *Journal of Women's History*, vol. 20, no. 2, 2008, pp. 34–56.

Wanhalla, Angela *In/Visible Sight: the Mixed Descent Families of Southern New Zealand*, Wellington: Bridget Williams Books, Forthcoming 2009.

Wassmann, J., "The Politics of Religious Secrecy", In *Emplaced Myth, Space, Narrative, and Knowledge in Aboriginal Australia and Papua New Guinea*, edited by A. Rumsey and J. Weiner, Honolulu: University of Hawaii Press, 2001, pp. 43–71.

Waugh, Earle, ed., *Alberta Elders' Cree Dictionary by Nancy LeClaire and George Cardinal*, Edmonton: University of Alberta Press, 1998.

Wellcome, Henry S., *The Story of Metlakahtla*, London and New York: Saxon, 1887.

Wellenreuther, Hermann and Carola Wessel, eds, *The Moravian Mission Diaries of David Zeisberger, 1772–1781*, University Park, Pennsylvania: Pennsylvania State University Press, 2005.

Westmeier, Karl-Wilhelm, "Becoming All Things to All People: Early Moravian Missions to Native North Americans", *International Bulletin of Missionary Research*, vol. 21, no. 4, 1997, pp. 172–6.

Wharton, Geoff, "MacKenzie, William Frederick (Bill) (1897–1972)", In *Australian Dictionary of Biography*, Melbourne: Melbourne University Press, 2000.

White, Luise, *Speaking with Vampires: Rumour and History in Colonial Africa*, Berkeley: University of California Press, 2000.

Whitehead, Margaret, "Women Were Made For Such Things: Women Missionaries in British Columbia 1850s to 1940s", *Atlantis*, vol. 14, Fall 1988, pp. 141–50.

Whitehead, Margaret, "'A Useful Christian Woman': First Nations Women and Protestant Missionary Work in British Columbia", *Atlantis*, vol. 18, Fall–Summer 1992–93, pp. 142–66.

Whiteley, William H., "The Moravian Missionaries and the Labrador Eskimos in the Eighteenth Century", *Church History*, vol. 35, no. 1, 1966, pp. 76–92.

Wilkinson, Linda, "Fractured Families, Squatting and Poverty: The Impact of the 1886 "Half-Caste" Act on the Framlingham Aboriginal Community", in *Law and History in Australia*, edited by Ian Duncanson and Diane Kirkby, Bundoora: La Trobe University, 1986, 1–25.

Consolidated Bibliography

Woollacott, Angela, *Gender and Empire*, Hampshire: Palgrave Macmillian, 2006.

Worms, Ernest A., "Observations on the Mission Field of the Pallottine Fathers in North-west Australia", In *Diprotodon to Detribalization: Studies of Change among Australian Aborigines*, edited by A. R. Pilling and R. A. Waterman, East Lansing: Michigan State University Press, 1970.

Yahya, Eliasu, "The Christian Missions and Western Education in Ilorin, Nigeria: A Century of Resistance and Challenge, 1847–1957", *Journal of Muslim Minority Affairs*, vol. 21, no. 1, 2001, pp. 149–54.

Zubrick, S. R., S. R. Silburn, D. M. Lawrence, F. G. Mitrou, R. B. Dalby, E. M. Blair, J. Griffin, H. Milroy, J. A. De Maio, A. Cox, and J. Li, *The Western Australian Aboriginal Child Health Survey: Forced Separation from Natural Family, Forced Relocation from Traditional Country or Homeland, and Social and Emotional Wellbeing of Aboriginal Children and Young People: Additional Notes*, Perth: Curtin University of Technology and Telethon Institute for Child Health Research, 2005.

Zucker, Margaret, *From Patrons to Partners: A History of the Catholic Church in the Kimberley, 1884–1984*, second ed., Fremantle: University of Notre Dame Australia Press, 2005.

Index

Index

Index

Index